DISABLED JUSTICE?

Disabled Justice?: Access to Justice and the UN Convention on the Rights of Persons with Disabilities *presents a well-crafted conceptual framework through which the author provides an intelligent and instructive critique of access to justice for people with disabilities identifying key areas for reform that go to the heart of building an inclusive justice system.*
Rosemary Kayess, University of New South Wales, Australia

The CRPD, for the first time in the history of international human rights law, recognizes access to justice as a distinct human right. Drawing upon the intersectionality inherent to disability, Eilionóir Flynn in this path breaking study competently constitutes the symbolic, procedural, substantive and participatory components of this right.
Amita Dhanda, Centre for Disability Studies, Nalsar University of Law, India

Disabled Justice?
Access to Justice and the UN Convention on the Rights of Persons with Disabilities

EILIONÓIR FLYNN
National University of Ireland, Galway

LONDON AND NEW YORK

First published 2015 by Ashgate Publishing

Published 2016 by Routledge
2 Park Square, Milton Park, Abingdon, Oxon OX14 4RN
711 Third Avenue, New York, NY 10017, USA

Routledge is an imprint of the Taylor & Francis Group, an informa business

Copyright © 2015 Eilionóir Flynn

Eilionóir Flynn has asserted her right under the Copyright, Designs and Patents Act, 1988, to be identified as the author of this work.

All rights reserved. No part of this book may be reprinted or reproduced or utilised in any form or by any electronic, mechanical, or other means, now known or hereafter invented, including photocopying and recording, or in any information storage or retrieval system, without permission in writing from the publishers.

Notice:
Product or corporate names may be trademarks or registered trademarks, and are used only for identification and explanation without intent to infringe.

British Library Cataloguing in Publication Data
A catalogue record for this book is available from the British Library

The Library of Congress has cataloged the printed edition as follows:
Flynn, Eilionóir, 1986- author.
  Disabled justice? : access to justice and the UN Convention on the Rights of Persons with Disabilities / by Eilionóir Flynn.
      pages cm
  Includes bibliographical references and index.
  ISBN 978-1-4724-1859-3 (hardback)
  1. People with disabilities – Civil rights. 2. Justice, Administration of. 3. Convention on the Rights of Persons with Disabilities and Optional Protocol (2007 March 30) I. Title.
  K637.F57 2015
  342.08'7 – dc23

2014030032

ISBN 9781472418593 (hbk)

Printed in the United Kingdom
by Henry Ling Limited

Contents

Acknowledgements vii
Foreword ix

Introduction 1

1 Access to Justice and its Relevance for People with Disabilities 5

2 Access to Justice and its Intellectual Antecedents in International Human Rights Law 21

3 Accessing the Law: Information, Advice and Representation 49

4 Access and Participation in Court: Structures, Evidence and Procedures 83

5 Incorporating Disability in Legal Education and Practice: A Call for Consciousness-Raising 117

6 Participatory Justice, Deliberation and Representation in Public and Political Life 141

Conclusion and Recommendations for Reform 171

Index 175

Options

Acknowledgements

So many people contributed to the writing of this book. I would first like to thank Anna Lawson, with whom I first wrote about this topic, for working with me to develop my ideas about 'justice' and 'access' in more depth – much of the framework I build in Chapter 1 and the analysis of existing human rights law in Chapter 2 draws on our article on this topic.

I also want to thank Theresia Degener for kindly agreeing to write the foreword for this book, and for continuing to produce powerful intersectional scholarship on feminism and disability, while combining her work on the UN Committee on the Rights of Persons with Disabilities with educating the next generation of students in disability rights. My profound gratitude also goes to Sara Ryan, who knows all too well how difficult it is to achieve justice for disabled people, for generously allowing me to use the artwork of her amazing son, Connor Sparrowhawk, also known as 'LB', short for Laughing Boy, for the cover of this book.

I am incredibly grateful to my students on the LLM in International and Comparative Disability Law, in particular Elizabeth Kamundia, Charlotte May-Simera, Innocentia Mgijima, Kiran Wagle and Alberto Vasquez, for lively discussions in class on access to justice from a global perspective – and for inviting me to confront the lived reality of people with disabilities in very different parts of the world.

Special thanks also go to the staff and student volunteers in the Disability Legal Information Clinic at the National University of Ireland, Galway who actively work to ensure that people with disabilities have the practical means to access justice. I would like to particularly acknowledge Clíona de Bhailís, who in addition to being the student co-ordinator of the Clinic, wrote an excellent minor thesis on litigation capacity which I cite in Chapter 4.

I owe a huge debt of thanks to Gerard Quinn for reminding me that I should write this book (since I kept talking about it) – and to all of my colleagues at the Centre for Disability Law and Policy for accommodating me when I kept disappearing to do so. A very special thanks goes to Anna Arstein-Kerslake and Lucy Series – my legal capacity gurus – for many long and fruitful discussions about the nature of justice, and what access to it might mean in the context of disability, as well as for their scholarship on legal capacity and litigation respectively, which I cite throughout Chapters 2 and 3.

Finally, as always, I want to thank Eoin Daly, for encouraging me to think about the political dimensions of justice, as well as for his love and support throughout the entire writing process.

Foreword

Access to justice is one of the many human rights which have been denied to disabled people throughout the world and throughout history. It is sad knowledge that access to justice in most countries is usually available to those who have financial, political or cultural power, whereas minorities or other groups experiencing discrimination and subordination are excluded from it. The paradox that those most in need for access to justice are the least likely to receive it remains one of the most compelling human rights issues of the 21st century. People with disabilities, just like women, the LGBTQI community, children or people of colour, belong to these foreclosed groups.

The Convention on the Rights of Persons with Disabilities of 2006 (CRPD) enshrines the human right to access to justice in its Article 13. The CRPD is a treaty of many firsts: for example, the first international human rights treaty of the 21st century, the first human rights treaty with a mandatory national monitoring body (Article 33), the first human rights treaty to acknowledge multiple discrimination (Article 6). Another first can be found in Article 13, which is the first stand-alone provision in UN human rights treaties on the right to access to justice. As with other provisions of the CRPD, we can expect Article 13 CRPD to lead to further development and improvement of international human rights law in general, once implementation, jurisprudence and legal commentaries have been developed.

The present book of Eilionóir Flynn is a highly valuable contribution in this regard. The book touches upon a long neglected subject in disability law and policy. Despite accessibility being the key topic of the disability movement, access to justice for people with disability has not been the target of many campaigns nor has it been theoretically explored.

The present book meets the high standard Eilionóir Flynn has set with her first publication on the CRPD, 'From Rhetoric to Action', and in all research and advocacy activities we have undertaken together. This new book offers a brilliant account and further development of theories of justice and how they can be applied to persons with disabilities. Her comprehensive and holistic concept of access to justice contributes to mainstream legal and political theory with a disability and intersectional perspective. It also offers palpable solutions on how to achieve reform: recognition, inclusion and awareness raising are the three main tracks for a roadmap to reform in access to justice.

I congratulate Eilionóir Flynn for producing another outstanding contribution to academic knowledge and research in international disability rights studies. No doubt this book will prove to be a useful tool for our work in the UN Committee on the Rights of Persons with Disabilities and for other human rights bodies as well as for governments and civil society.

Theresia Degener

Introduction

I came to the topic of access to justice through my PhD research on disability advocacy, where I focused on a human rights framework for advocacy practice, which would link advocacy theory to the concepts of access to justice and equal citizenship. I subsequently developed this theory further in a paper on the right to advocacy,[1] and started to broaden my focus to explore access to justice for people with disabilities through collaborative research with Anna Lawson.[2] At the same time, I was thinking through ideas about equal recognition before the law and the right to support in the exercise of legal capacity in a paper with Anna Arstein-Kerslake,[3] which led to interesting discussions on the barriers to making 'justice' claims which stem from denials of legal capacity – and how the experience of people with disabilities echoed those of other marginalised groups, especially women, in seeking substantive equality.

I was also having lively debates with students in my Advocacy and Access to Justice class about the challenges in securing access to justice for people with disabilities in the global context – especially given the differences in value systems and beliefs about disability and equality in different parts of the world. My students also raised issues about the difficulties in accessing justice in jurisdictions where democracy and the rule of law were not political priorities – or where informal justice systems operated at community level in a way which sometimes further stigmatised and marginalised the experience of people with disabilities.

These ideas led me to write a book on this subject – to go beyond the general acknowledgment that people with disabilities face barriers in accessing justice, and to provide a contextual analysis of how these barriers operate in different parts of our justice system, as well as some tentative suggestions for how they could be removed. I particularly wanted to focus on how to provide people with disabilities with a space in which their claims can be heard, and ensure that their voices are heard in the wide variety of fora in which justice is done. Given that

---

1 E Flynn, 'Making Human Rights Meaningful for People with Disabilities: Advocacy, Access to Justice and Equality before the Law' (2013) 17(4) *International Journal of Human Rights* 491.

2 A Lawson and E Flynn, 'Disability and Access to Justice in the European Union: Implications of the UN Convention on the Rights of Persons with Disabilities' (2013) 4 *European Yearbook of Disability Law* 7.

3 E Flynn and A Arstein-Kerslake, 'Legislating Personhood: Realising the Right to Support in Exercising Legal Capacity' (2014) 10(1) *International Journal of Law in Context* 81.

people with disabilities are not a homogeneous group, and include people with many different identities, genders, cultures, value systems and beliefs – I wanted to draw on theories of justice from an intersectional standpoint – to fully capture the challenges and opportunities for reform in the sphere of access to justice.

In the following chapters I explore access to justice for people with disabilities – first from a theoretical standpoint in Chapter 1, and subsequently in Chapter 2 setting out the access to justice framework within international human rights law, focusing specifically on the UN Convention on the Rights of Persons with Disabilities, which addresses this topic. In Chapters 3–6 I apply the conceptual and human rights framework for access to justice in a number of discrete areas – Chapter 3 focuses on access to the law (including legal advice and representation), Chapter 4 on participation in the justice system (especially in courts and tribunals), Chapter 5 on legal education and training and Chapter 6 on participation in public and political life (particularly in the legislative sphere where deliberative processes are used to debate the 'justice' claims of people with disabilities).

While this research is relatively broad-ranging, I need to acknowledge some of its limitations. I draw on Fraser's theory of justice as recognition and redistribution;[4] and Crenshaw's understanding of intersectional discrimination in Chapter 1[5] as a framework for this book, and try to incorporate the experiences of other marginalised groups in the fields I explore in Chapters 3–6 (accessing the law, participating in the justice system, legal education and training and political participation), I most frequently focus on gender equality as a comparative example. However, I also try to incorporate examples from 'race' and ethnicity, class, and cultural minorities wherever possible. Therefore, this book is not a comprehensive analysis of the efforts of all marginalised groups to access justice – although I think it presents a useful starting point for others who wish to explore the synergies between the disability movement and other social movements in this field even further.

The focus of this book is both international and comparative, so throughout the substantive chapters, I provide illustrative examples of the operation of access to justice in various legal systems around the world. Since my goal was to examine concrete examples of barriers and also seek out good practices, this research does not attempt to draw conclusions about access to justice in a general sense for people with disabilities in any of the countries where examples are provided, but rather to provide a contextual analysis of how access to justice operates for people with disabilities. My research was in part limited by language barriers, and in general I have only included examples for which I could find some literature in the English language, and primarily drew from the experience in the countries with which I am most familiar: Ireland, the United Kingdom, the United States

---

4   N Fraser, 'From Redistribution to Recognition? Dilemmas of Justice in a "Post-Socialist" Age' (1995) *New Left Review* 68.
5   K Crenshaw, 'Mapping the Margins: Intersectionality, Identity Politics, and Violence against Women of Color' (1991) *Stanford Law Review* 1241.

and the European Union, as well as Commonwealth countries such as India, South Africa, Canada, Australia and New Zealand. The book does not purport to provide a comprehensive overview of the justice system in each of these countries, but simply highlights aspects of the various systems which pose barriers to people with disabilities, and examines some examples of how attempts to overcome these barriers have been made in various different contexts.

Finally, I chose to focus on specific aspects of what I perceive as the broad justice system which exist in most domestic jurisdictions, i.e. access to the law; participation in the justice system; legal education and training and political participation, within which to examine the experiences of people with disabilities. I have not addressed in detail issues such as the post-trial experiences of people with disabilities – particularly in the criminal context including the penal system, or the alternatives to detention in the prison system, such as diversion programmes for offenders with disabilities and/or involuntary detention in the mental health context. Similarly, due to time and space constraints I have not considered in any great detail how informal justice systems and alternative dispute resolution mechanisms (including religious and cultural dispute resolution forums) accommodate people with disabilities or how these might be reconfigured in the context of disability – although I believe this is an extremely important topic and one deserving of further research and analysis.

A final note on terminology is also important here – as throughout the text I tend to use the terms 'people/persons with disabilities' and 'disabled people' interchangeably to write about those who are the subject of my enquiry. While there are many different schools of thought about the labels which we ascribe to individuals, I use these specific terms interchangeably to reflect my adherence to both a contextualised social understanding of impairment and disabling barriers[6] and a human-rights based approach which acknowledges the diversity of humanity and the universal personhood we all share.[7]

In essence, I view this book as a conversation-starter – to expose some key ways in which our justice system has failed people with disabilities in the past, and to prompt further research into the ways in which people with disabilities might be better accommodated in their attempts to frame their concerns as claims for justice, and to recognise where the justice system has failed to accommodate their

---

6   M Oliver, 'The Social Model in Action: If I had a Hammer' in C Barnes and G Mercer (eds), *Implementing the Social Model of Disability: Theory and Research* (The Disability Press, 2004), 18; J Bickenbach, 'Minority Rights or Universal Participation: The Politics of Disablement' in M Jones and L A Marks (eds), *Disability, Divers-Ability and Legal Change* (Martinus Nijhoff, 1999), 101.

7   G Quinn and T Degener (eds), *Human Rights and Disability: The Current Use and Future Potential of United Nations Human Rights Instruments in the Context of Disability* (Office of the United Nations High Commissioner for Human Rights, 2002); R Kayess and P French, 'Out of Darkness Into Light? Introducing the Convention on the Rights of Persons with Disabilities' (2008) 8(1) *Human Rights Law Review* 1.

perspectives. In proposing solutions to these challenges, I aim as much as possible to illustrate universal design approaches which can help to make the justice system more accessible to all citizens – while acknowledging the need to continue to provide specific forms of reasonable accommodation to people with disabilities based on the unique forms of intersectional discrimination they experience.

Chapter 1
Access to Justice and its Relevance for People with Disabilities

1. Introduction

Much scholarship has focused on the notion of 'justice' for people with disabilities – from legal, philosophical and sociological perspectives. However, although there is much academic dispute on what 'justice' requires in the context of disability (including scholars who adhere to social contract theories such as Rawls' Theory of Justice[1] or Sen and Nussbaum's capabilities approach[2]), this chapter will move beyond political theories of justice to explore whether there is any consensus on what 'access to justice' means for people with disabilities. In so doing, I will first consider the uniqueness of people with disabilities as a group with many different identities and experiences, and what the search for justice might mean in this specific context. Drawing on existing scholarship in the field of 'access to justice'[3] I will then consider how 'access to justice' might be interpreted with regard to people with disabilities, and how this might address some of the barriers to accessing justice which people with disabilities experience.

In order to fully understand the various barriers experienced by people with disabilities in accessing justice (undertaken in more detail in Chapters 3–6) this chapter will set an intersectional frame for analysis. Drawing on Fraser's understanding of justice as recognition and redistribution, together with Crenshaw's theory of intersectionality,[4] I will put forward a proposed framework for examining the inclusiveness of the justice system as a whole. While the experiences of people with disabilities will be the primary standpoint from which access to justice is explored, I acknowledge that people with disabilities are not a

---

1   J Rawls, *A Theory of Justice (Revised Edition)* (Oxford University Press, 1999).

2   See e.g. A Sen, *Inequality Reexamined* (Harvard University Press, 1992); A Sen, *The Idea of Justice* (Penguin, 2009); M Nussbaum, *Frontiers of Justice* (Belknap Press, Harvard University Press, 2006); and M Nussbaum, 'The Capabilities of People with Cognitive Disabilities' (2009) 40 *Metaphilosophy* 331.

3   See e.g. Y Ghai and J Cottrell, 'Conclusions and Reflections' in Y Ghai and J Cottrell (eds), *Marginalised Communities and Access to Justice* (Routledge, 2010), 232; D Rhode, 'Access to Justice' (2000–2001) 69 *Fordham Law Review* 1785; H Genn, *Judging Civil Justice* (Cambridge University Press, 2010); J M Jacobs, *Civil Justice in the Age of Human Rights* (Ashgate, 2007).

4   K Crenshaw, 'Mapping the Margins: Intersectionality, Identity Politics, and Violence against Women of Color' (1991) *Stanford Law Review* 1241.

homogeneous group – and that individuals with disabilities have many different languages, cultures, ethnicities, ages and genders, and seek to reflect this multi-faceted experience in my critiques of the justice system and proposals for reform.

Finally, I consider the work of Bahdi – who defines access to justice as comprising substantive, procedural and symbolic components – with reference to the lived experience of people with disabilities. Based on an argument developed with Lawson in a previous article, I suggest that 'participatory' justice must be added to Bahdi's conceptualisation to achieve effective access to justice for people with disabilities, and consider how Bahdi's work interacts with that of Fraser and Crenshaw to provide a framework for intersectional analysis of people with disabilities' experiences in accessing justice before deliberating on how these theories are reflected in the human rights framework addressed in Chapter 2.

2. People with Disabilities and the Search for Justice

In philosophical scholarship on disability, justice has been one of the most prominent topics of discussion. In part, this may be because disability poses such interesting challenges to social contractarian ideas of justice, which rely primarily on deliberative processes, mutual agreement and reciprocity as the basis for determining what justice owes to individuals, and how social and political institutions should operate. Similarly, as an 'identity' for which equal recognition is sought, disability is a complex one – with contested definitions, models and approaches to determining who exactly 'people with disabilities' are – in order to ensure that principles of justice can be applied to them.

Although discourse on the definition or models of disability is often presented as quite polarised, for the purpose of this book I will use an adapted version of the social model of disability, as conceptualised by Oliver,[5] and broadly reflected in human rights law, particularly in the UN Convention on the Rights of Persons with Disabilities (CRPD), which claims that the disadvantages experienced by people with disabilities are the product of social and environmental factors, which in interaction with the individual's impairment, present barriers to full participation and inclusion.[6]

This approach represents a shift away from the medical or individualist conception of 'disability', which labelled people according to their impairment and viewed all the problems experienced by people with disabilities as a direct result of their impairment, rather than problems arising from a society which was structured according to the needs of the majority, who did not experience disability. Within the social model of disability, 'disability' is viewed as separate from 'impairment'. 'Impairment' is the term used to describe the medical condition or functional limitation affecting a particular individual, whereas 'disability' is

---

5   M Oliver, *The Politics of Disablement* (Macmillan, 1990).
6   Article 1, CRPD.

the term given to the societal barriers experienced by people with physical or mental impairments. Although many people suffer societal disadvantage due to gender, race, sexuality or poverty, the term 'disability' applies solely to the type of disadvantage suffered specifically by people with impairments.

Of course, this is not to state that disabled people cannot suffer multiple types of societal disadvantage due to other factors such as those outlined above; it is merely to clarify that a particular type of societal disadvantage affects individuals who have impairments and to recognise that specific redress for this disadvantage must be sought through reform of law and policy.

The approach to disability represented by the social model is one which fits well with thinking about justice and the intersection of disability with other identities, as the social model understands disability in relation to societal, political and environmental factors, just as a broad conception of 'justice' must acknowledge this multiplicity of factors in order to ensure equal treatment. While Oliver and other proponents of the social model, particularly in British disability studies, favour the term 'disabled people', the terminology used by the UN Convention on the Rights of Persons with Disabilities is 'persons with disabilities'. Since I view the human rights model of disability contained within the Convention as one which is inspired by, and draws upon, the social model of disability, I use the terms 'disabled people' and 'people with disabilities' interchangeably throughout this book to describe the broad disability community.

As stated at the outset of this chapter, I do not propose to provide a comprehensive analysis of all theories of justice as applied to disability – but before considering what analytical framework should be applied to access to justice questions, it is important to briefly consider the purpose of seeking justice for people with disabilities. Anita Silvers addresses this core question, by asking us to consider 'whether justice requires only that the presence of people with disabilities be recognized, or whether, in a just society, they must be equalized as well'.[7] She perceives the dilemma of difference posed by people with disabilities as a question of equality, stating that '[f]irst, we must decide whether the disadvantages characteristically associated with those differences we identify as physical, sensory or cognitive impairments are artificial or natural. Second, we must come to terms with whether we are morally or politically obligated to mitigate the specific kind(s) of disadvantage occasioned by those sorts of differences – that is, whether we are required to equalize people because of their disabilities'.[8] In her view, the disadvantages caused to people with disabilities by artificial means – i.e. stigma, discrimination, lack of opportunity to participate in society, are the only kinds that we, as a society, are morally and politically obligated to remedy – as she claims that distributive justice, particularly in the form of income or resource

---

7 A Silvers, 'Formal Justice' in A Silvers, D Wasserman and M B Mahowald (eds), *Disability, Difference, Discrimination: Perspectives on Justice in Bioethics and Public Policy* (Rowman & Littlefield, 1998), 14.

8 Ibid., 15.

transfers via the welfare state, have in general, been counter-productive in terms of the claims to equality made by people with disabilities.

The question of what 'justice' requires for people with disabilities has been addressed by a wide range of scholars including Silvers and others – some from the perspective of social contractarian accounts such as Rawls' Justice as Fairness, and others in the context of Sen and Nussbaum's capabilities approach. However, in the specific context of disability, justice is often defined in relation to its opposite – as injustice seems somehow easier to recognise. Since the focus of this book is on access to justice (although broadly defined), it is not feasible or desirable to comprehensively address all the different accounts of justice, and their relevance or application to people with disabilities. Conversely, it seems inappropriate to consider how access to justice might be achieved for people with disabilities without some regard to what 'justice' means in this context. Therefore, I propose to base my approach to access to justice, defined further below, on a combined approach to Fraser's approach to justice as constituting mutual claims for recognition and redistribution, and Crenshaw's understanding of the intersectional nature of discrimination and disadvantage.

(In)Justice, Discrimination and Intersectionality

Fraser's conception of justice[9] as responding to the desires for recognition and redistribution is particularly relevant here – as disability has been used to critique the way in which existing theories of distributive justice operate (focusing on individual impairment without regard to social and environmental barriers). Although her seminal work on recognition and redistribution was written without reference to disability, I propose to use her frame of reference as a starting point to explore forms of injustice as experienced by people with disabilities. Her approach is particularly relevant for this task, as she acknowledges the intertwined nature of unfair economic distribution with cultural practices that fail to recognise certain groups or individuals as worthy of equal treatment – and yet, by considering cultural and economic injustices as separate, she proposes a framework for addressing both forms of injustice in a holistic and comprehensive manner.

Interestingly, she also does not require the adoption of any particular existing theory of justice as a starting point (an approach which is useful in the context of disability, considering that there are so many competing accounts, and critiques, of the application of such theories to persons with disabilities).[10] Rather, she considers that any of the accounts of distributive and egalitarian justice, along with the work of critical political theorists on cultural injustice, share a common concern for both recognition and redistribution. Since her work is primarily written from the

---

9 N Fraser, 'From Redistribution to Recognition? Dilemmas of Justice in a "Post-Socialist" Age' (1995) *New Left Review* 68.

10 See for example E F Kittay and L Carlson (eds), *Cognitive Disability and its Challenge to Moral Philosophy* (Wiley-Blackwell, 2010).

standpoint of gender and race as identities for which individuals seek recognition and redistribution, it is also particularly suited to an intersectional approach to justice, which I propose to use throughout this book.

Crenshaw also acknowledges that self-identification as a member of a minority group can be viewed both as 'a source of strength, community, and intellectual development' and as a source of tension with concepts of social justice which seek to empty identities such as race, gender or sexual orientation of any social significance.[11] Her main claim is that the shortcomings of identity politics lie in assumptions that identity categories such as gender or race represent a finite, concrete, homogeneous set of experiences, which do not account for the difference of experiences that can occur within these groups, or where individuals claim multiple, and intersecting, identities.

This risk in disability studies discourse was also identified by Morris, who contends that the experiences of women with disabilities were often omitted from both feminist writing and disability studies scholarship.[12] It is clear that people with disabilities, as expressed above, do not constitute a homogeneous group, and differences in impairment type, as well as experiences of other identities (including gender, class and race, for example) impact on individual experience, for example, in the context of the justice system, which is the focus of this work. It is clear that this intersection of experiences must be acknowledged in any critique of the justice system and proposals for reform. However, it is beyond the scope of this work to address all possible ramifications of the various identity combinations which people with disabilities may experience in terms of securing effective access to justice. Therefore, the approach taken in Chapters 3–6 will be to draw on the experiences of other groups which may be relevant in the context of disability, in providing proposals for reform.

Fraser builds on Crenshaw's analysis of identity politics, with the aim of creating 'a critical theory of recognition, one which identifies and defends only those versions of the cultural politics of difference that can be coherently combined with the social politics of equality'.[13] Her work focuses on the identities of gender and race, as she views these as categories for which individuals seek both cultural recognition and social equality. Although Fraser recognises the intertwined dimensions of socio-economic and cultural injustices, her analysis proceeds by separating these two concepts and proposing distinct remedies for socio-economic injustice, on the one hand (mainly involving political economic reforms for redistribution) and cultural injustice on the other. Her proposed remedies for cultural injustices are perhaps most relevant in the context of access to justice for people with disabilities, as she suggests that remedies for this type

---

11 K Crenshaw, 'Mapping the Margins: Intersectionality, Identity Politics, and Violence against Women of Color' (1991) *Stanford Law Review* 1241.
12 J Morris, *Pride Against Prejudice* (The Women's Press, 1991), 4–5.
13 N Fraser, 'From Redistribution to Recognition? Dilemmas of Justice in a "Post-Socialist" Age' (1995) *New Left Review* 68, 69.

of injustice can range from respect for the value of cultural diversity to 'the wholesale transformation of societal patterns of representation, interpretation and communication in ways that would change everybody's sense of self'.[14]

Fraser poses the 'recognition-redistribution dilemma' in which she argues that one set of claims can undermine the other – since recognition claims are generally based on acknowledging and valorising difference, whereas redistribution claims tend to dismantle differences in favour of an equalised, or neutral, approach. She provides hypothetical examples at either end of a spectrum – whereby some groups can achieve justice simply by redistribution (e.g. the Marxist conception of the working class) whereas others might simply seek recognition (e.g. groups defined by sexual orientation) without any corresponding need for economic redistribution. By contrast with these hypothetical collectives (which Fraser acknowledges for the purpose of her analysis may not correspond to the justice claims made by these groups in the real world), she posits that some groups, such as those defined by gender and race, occupy a mid-point on the spectrum. Similarly, people with disabilities can be said to occupy this shared space – where the injustices experienced cannot be traced solely to either cultural or economic factors, but are a product of both simultaneously.

However, since the types of oppression experienced by these 'bivalent collectives' have both cultural and economic roots, Fraser demonstrates that the remedies required may pull in opposite directions – e.g. for gender, requiring simultaneously the recognition of difference between genders (and valorising that difference) for cultural justice to be achieved, but ignoring or devaluing difference in the economic sphere to achieve just redistribution. As possible solutions, she proposes the concepts of affirmation – 'remedies aimed at correcting inequitable outcomes of social arrangements without disturbing the underlying framework that generates them' and transformation 'remedies aimed at correcting inequitable outcomes precisely by restructuring the underlying generative framework'.[15] Pursuing affirmative remedies for cultural and economic injustices leads, she suggests, to the policies of mainstream multiculturalism and the liberal welfare state respectively; whereas transformative remedies suggest approaches such as deconstruction and socialism.

Attempts to remedy cultural and economic injustice which use combinations of affirmative and transformative solutions tend to be unsuccessful, she argues, as these remedies have opposing premises – affirmation acknowledges stable, coherent, identities and structures, whereas transformation seeks to destabilise in order to reform. On the whole, Fraser prefers the use of a transformative approach to cultural and economic injustices, as affirmative remedies for redistribution can undermine claims for recognition. She argues that affirmative economic solutions can validate oft-perceived stereotypes of certain collectives (e.g. those of race, gender or disability, in this context), as weak, constantly requiring the support of

---

14   Ibid., 73.
15   Ibid., 82.

income transfers, incapable of progressing on merit in the open labour market, etc. and can cause resentment as the group which seeks recognition is regarded as being of less moral worth than others by the very nature of its request for redistribution. However, at the same time she acknowledges that the transformative economic solutions may be at odds with the identities and interests of many of the collectives they propose to serve, as these collectives are currently constituted in the real world.

Fraser's approach is of particular interest in the context of both justice and access to justice for people with disabilities. Her recognition of the complex, interlinked nature of identities, sources of injustice and potential remedies is one which bears the closest resemblance to many real-world scenarios in which individuals and groups make claims of justice. While, on the surface, 'access to justice' may seem to be more relevant to cultural injustice, as Fraser describes it, many of the barriers to effectively accessing the various spheres of justice (legal, political, administrative, etc.) also stem from economic structures which are prejudiced towards, or unduly impact upon, persons with disabilities. In recognition of her proposition that most forms of cultural injustices (discrimination, exclusion, segregation, devaluing of specific identities, etc.) are connected to, and have ramifications for, economic systems and processes, her solutions seem to be a valid starting point from which to consider the experiences of persons with disabilities and their efforts to access justice. The notions of 'access' and 'justice' in this context will be considered further in the following section, bearing in mind Fraser's broader approach to advancing the justice claims of marginalised groups, such as persons with disabilities.

3. Access to Justice and Disability: A Holistic Approach to Securing Equality

The term 'access to justice' is generally used to refer to access to the legal system, and immediately brings to mind the rights to due process and legal representation.[16] This, I would suggest, is too narrow an interpretation; and for the purpose of this book I will use a broader definition which goes beyond the formal legal system and questions of 'access' to this, to a more holistic understanding of what justice means for people with disabilities. Bahdi[17] argues that access to justice scholarship reveals an increasing tendency to adopt this broader approach and thus to address issues of justice as well as issues of access. Similarly, Cappelletti and Garth support a wider approach:

---

16 See e.g. D Rhode, 'Access to Justice' (2000–2001) 69 *Fordham Law Review* 1785.

17 R Bahdi, *Background Paper on Women's Access to Justice in the MENA Region* (International Development Research Centre (IDRC), Women's Rights and Citizenship Program (WRC) and the Middle East Regional Office (MERO), Middle East and North African (MENA) Regional Consultation, 9–11 December 2007, Cairo, Egypt).

The words 'access to justice' are admittedly not easily defined, but they serve to focus on two basic purposes of the legal system – the system by which people may vindicate their rights and/or resolve their disputes under the general auspices of the state. First, the system must be equally accessible to all; second, it must lead to results that are individually and socially just.[18]

In the specific context of disability, Lord et al. provide the following definition for access to justice:

'Access to justice' is a broad concept, encompassing people's effective access to the systems, procedures, information, and locations used in the administration of justice. Persons who feel wronged or mistreated in some way usually turn to their country's justice system. In addition, persons may be called upon to participate in the justice system, for example, as witnesses or as jurors in a trial. Unfortunately, persons with disabilities have often been denied fair and equal treatment before courts, tribunals, and other bodies that make up the justice system in their country because they have faced barriers to their access. Such barriers not only limit the ability of persons with disabilities to use the justice system, they also limit their contributions to the administration of justice.

The ability to access justice is of critical importance in the enjoyment of all other human rights. For example, a person with a disability who feels that she or he has been denied the right to work may wish to turn to the justice system to seek a remedy. However, if the justice system fails to accommodate their physical, communication or other disability-related needs, and/or expressly discriminates against her or him, then clearly denial of access to the justice system also results in denial of protection of the right to work. Similarly, a person with a disability who has been the victim of a crime may wish to report the crime to the police and press charges against the offender. However, if he or she is denied physical access to the police station, clear communication with the police, or access to information that is understandable, then that person may not be able to fully exercise her or his rights as a victim. These examples demonstrate that human rights are *indivisible*, *interdependent* and *interrelated*.[19]

This conceptualisation of access to justice gives an indication of the complexity and breadth of issues facing persons with disabilities in their interactions with the systems, procedures and locations where justice is administered. The specific

---

18 M Cappelletti and B Garth, 'Access to Justice: The Newest Wave in the Worldwide Movement to Make Rights Effective' (1978) 27(2) *Buffalo Law Review* 181.

19 J Lord, K N Guernsey, J M Balfe, V L Karr and N Flowers (eds), *Human Rights: Yes! Action and Advocacy on the Rights of Persons with Disabilities* (Human Rights Resource Center, 2009), ch 12, para 12.1.

concerns raised by Lord et al. will be addressed more fully in Chapters 3–6, but are worth noting here to highlight the types of experiences where 'justice' is engaged.

In the context of her analysis of women's access to justice in the Middle East and North Africa, Bahdi identifies three distinct but interlinking components of access to justice – substantive, procedural and symbolic.[20] This framework provides a useful starting point for the analysis of access to justice which is particularly relevant in the context of disability. Lawson and I have drawn on Bahdi's framework in a previous piece of research,[21] which I will use as a starting point for my discussion of her ideas throughout this chapter and the following chapter. As previously argued, however, Bahdi's framework has limitations and, in order to capture disability-related dimensions of access to justice and accommodate the principles of the UN Convention on the Rights of Persons with Disabilities, it requires expansion to accommodate notions of 'participatory' justice.[22] I will now consider the components of 'access to justice' set out by Bahdi with specific reference to disability, and how these components could be strengthened using the human rights framework in the UN Convention.

Substantive Access to Justice

For Bahdi, the substantive element of access to justice 'concerns itself with an assessment of the rights claims that are available to those who seek a remedy'.[23] It focuses on the content of the legal rules and principles which shape the decisions made about those who make a 'justice claim'. As argued elsewhere, this concept 'extends beyond individual tribunal or court rulings into the realms of constitutional and statutory law reform processes and demands the adoption of laws promoting substantive equality which are sensitive to social context'.[24]

Bahdi's notion of substantive access to justice is deeply intertwined with the idea of respect for the equality of all citizens, but she does not claim to provide any overarching theory of justice to guide the distribution of societal resources or

---

20 R Bahdi, *Background Paper on Women's Access to Justice in the MENA Region* (International Development Research Centre (IDRC), Women's Rights and Citizenship Program (WRC) and the Middle East Regional Office (MERO), Middle East and North African (MENA) Regional Consultation, 9–11 December 2007, Cairo, Egypt).

21 A Lawson and E Flynn, 'Disability and Access to Justice in the European Union: Implications of the UN Convention on the Rights of Persons with Disabilities' (2013) 4 *European Yearbook of Disability Law* 7.

22 Ibid., at 17.

23 R Bahdi, *Background Paper on Women's Access to Justice in the MENA Region* (International Development Research Centre (IDRC), Women's Rights and Citizenship Program (WRC) and the Middle East Regional Office (MERO), Middle East and North African (MENA) Regional Consultation, 9–11 December 2007, Cairo, Egypt), at 3.

24 A Lawson and E Flynn, 'Disability and Access to Justice in the European Union: Implications of the UN Convention on the Rights of Persons with Disabilities' (2013) 4 *European Yearbook of Disability Law* 7 at 13.

opportunities. In this respect, she takes a similar approach to Fraser and Crenshaw, as discussed above, who elaborate theories to address exclusion and injustice without premising these on existing theories of justice. While Bahdi does not elaborate a theory of justice, she indicates that the substantive element of access to justice requires the development of laws and policies which promote substantive equality and stresses that this cannot usually be achieved without the involvement of the disadvantaged group. In the context of gender inequality, she explains that:

> Given that substantive equality requires an in-depth understanding of social context, one must make claims about strategies aimed at promoting equality with caution. Such strategies must be devised with the direct input of those whose lives they are designed to protect. This can usually only be attained through direct communication with the women whose lives are under consideration. Such an approach proves respectful of the right to self-determination. It also results in an understanding of the real barriers to equality and the kinds of solutions which must be fashioned to produce such results.[25]

This point clearly resonates with the experience of the disability movement, which sought active involvement in the development of laws, policy and practice affecting people with disabilities using the slogan 'nothing about us without us'.[26] The importance of active participation by previously excluded groups was further highlighted in the negotiation of the Convention on the Rights of Persons with Disabilities,[27] acknowledged by many to be the most inclusive human rights treaty drafting process with an overwhelming number of civil society participants. This involvement can be directly linked to the innovative articulation of equality of opportunity which appears in the Convention.[28] As argued elsewhere, the starting point for determining the content of substantive justice for people with disabilities should be the human rights norms contained in the CRPD – since these were developed with the direct input of people with disabilities themselves:

---

25 R Bahdi, *Background Paper on Women's Access to Justice in the MENA Region* (International Development Research Centre (IDRC), Women's Rights and Citizenship Program (WRC) and the Middle East Regional Office (MERO), Middle East and North African (MENA) Regional Consultation, 9–11 December 2007, Cairo, Egypt), at 28.

26 D Goodley, *Self-Advocacy in the Lives of People with Learning Disabilities* (Open University Press, 2000), 81.

27 This slogan was adopted by the International Disability Caucus, available at: <http://www.un.org/esa/socdev/enable/documents/Stat_Conv/nzam.doc> (accessed 30 April 2010).

28 See further, on the drafting process, S Trömel, 'A Personal Perspective on the Drafting History of the United Nations Convention on the Rights of Persons with Disabilities' in G Quinn and L Waddington (eds), *European Yearbook of Disability Law* (Intersentia, 2009); and, on the innovative nature of the resulting instrument, F Mégret, 'The Disabilities Convention: Human Rights of Persons with Disabilities or Disability Rights?' (2008) 30 *Human Rights Quarterly* 494; and G de Burca, 'The European Union in the Negotiation of the UN Disability Convention' (2010) 35(2) *European Law Review* 174.

Without the active participation of people with disabilities, attempts to design laws and policies which will achieve disability equality and inclusion at domestic level are unlikely to succeed. There is a high risk that particular dimensions of the disadvantage and exclusion experienced by disabled people would go unnoticed or unaddressed. Indeed, the need to avoid such a state of affairs provided the principal rationale for the elaboration of the CRPD. Substantive access to justice for disabled people can be achieved only by facilitating their entry into, and full participation in, the legal professions, the legislature and other public offices; and by involving disabled people's organizations in the design and delivery of laws, policies and services.[29]

Procedural Access to Justice

Bahdi's concept of procedural access to justice is closer to the traditional, or narrow, interpretation of 'access to justice' as the process by which claims are adjudicated, generally in legal or administrative systems. She argues, however, for a wider approach to understanding the procedural component of access to justice as including 'the types of institutions where one might bring a claim, the rules that govern the complaint and conduct of the parties once the complaint is brought within a particular institution, the particular mandate of a given institution and the factors – outside of the substantive law itself – which influence the nature and quality of the encounter for [individuals] within a particular legal institution'.[30] She also stresses that in order to achieve procedural justice one should examine the 'opportunities and barriers to getting one's claim into court (or other dispute resolution forum)'.[31]

With respect to disability, it is clear that procedural access to justice requires the removal of barriers to bringing justice claims and the introduction of supports to enable people to participate effectively in proceedings designed to administer justice. As argued elsewhere, the dismantling of these disabling barriers 'will demand that attention be given to structures which are outside the classic justice system (such as schools, residential establishments, social services and the political sphere) which provide the context in which complaints or claims might first be voiced'.[32]

---

29   A Lawson and E Flynn, 'Disability and Access to Justice in the European Union: Implications of the UN Convention on the Rights of Persons with Disabilities' (2013) 4 *European Yearbook of Disability Law* 7 at 15.
30   R Bahdi, *Background Paper on Women's Access to Justice in the MENA Region* (International Development Research Centre (IDRC), Women's Rights and Citizenship Program (WRC) and the Middle East Regional Office (MERO), Middle East and North African (MENA) Regional Consultation, 9–11 December 2007, Cairo, Egypt), 28.
31   Ibid.
32   A Lawson and E Flynn, 'Disability and Access to Justice in the European Union: Implications of the UN Convention on the Rights of Persons with Disabilities' (2013) 4

Bahdi argues for the removal of procedural barriers to accessing justice for all those seeking to make a claim. She defines the procedural component of access to justice as including 'factors – outside of the substantive law itself – which influence the nature and quality of the encounter' and these presumably would include the level of participation of other people from marginalised groups in the justice system. Therefore, in the context of disability, procedural access to justice would require attention to be given to removing the barriers which prevent people with disabilities from participating in the justice system in a wide variety of roles, for example, as lawyers, witnesses, judges, jurors and observers.

The procedural and substantive components of access to justice as defined by Bahdi are inherently intertwined, as noted by Genn, who argues that: 'If the law is the skeleton that supports liberal democracies, then the machinery of ... justice is some of the muscle and ligaments that make the skeleton work.'[33] A similar sentiment has been expressed by the EU Agency for Fundamental Rights, stating that: '[t]he possibility of enforcing a right is central to making fundamental rights a reality. Access to justice is not just a right in itself but also an enabling and empowering right in so far as it allows individuals to enforce their rights and obtain redress. In this sense, it transforms fundamental rights from theory into practice'.[34]

Symbolic Access to Justice

The final aspect of Bahdi's framework concerns 'symbolic' access to justice, which she defines as an approach which 'steps outside of doctrinal law and asks to what extent a particular legal regime promotes citizens' belonging and empowerment'.[35] Her concept of symbolic access to justice relates to a society in which, due in part at least to its laws and justice system, individuals from marginalised communities are fully included and empowered to participate as equal citizens. She acknowledges the difficulties associated with demonstrating the impact on wider social structures and relations of specific statutes, judicial decisions or the justice system as a whole. However, as argued elsewhere, 'recognition of the importance of the symbolic element of access to justice clearly requires monitoring of the levels of inclusion and participation of the relevant group – a process which, like the identification

---

European Yearbook of Disability Law 7 at 15.

33   H Genn, *Judging Civil Justice* (Cambridge University Press, 2010), 4.

34   EU Agency for Fundamental Rights, *Access to Justice: An Overview of Challenges and Opportunities* (EU Agency for Fundamental Rights, 2011), foreword.

35   R Bahdi, *Background Paper on Women's Access to Justice in the MENA Region* (International Development Research Centre (IDRC), Women's Rights and Citizenship Program (WRC) and the Middle East Regional Office (MERO), Middle East and North African (MENA) Regional Consultation, 9–11 December 2007, Cairo, Egypt), at 3.

of the ingredients of substantive equality, cannot be effectively conducted without the involvement of the group concerned'.[36]

This 'symbolic' component of access to justice is closely linked to what Bahdi terms the 'precursor' access to justice question – the extent to which law can be harnessed to achieve progressive social change. However, as discussed in the context of procedural justice above, it is difficult to determine the impact of legal change on shifting social and cultural norms, and the extent to which these norms in turn influence or lead to subsequent legal reform. Bahdi notes in the context of equality for women that:

> At one end of the spectrum, skeptics maintain that legal reform is the bastion of the naïve and law is merely another instrument of social and economic power. Legal optimists, by contrast, recognize that much work remains to be done before women can claim justice through the legal system. However, they maintain that piece-meal legal reforms can be interpreted as signs of progress and that the legal system can promote women's rights and women's development.[37]

Basser-Marks and Jones similarly acknowledge that law is only part of the solution to redressing the inequality of people with disabilities:

> Lawyers have a tendency to believe that law will provide solutions to complex social and political problems. While there is clearly a place for well thought-out laws, and having appropriate law is, in fact, very important to disadvantaged or vulnerable members of the society, law is at best only part of any strategy required to provide rights for people with disabilities.[38]

Therefore, in the context of disability, this notion reaffirms Bahdi's claim that access to justice involves some consideration of what 'justice' for the particular marginalised group entails. As argued elsewhere, for disabled people this will involve a broader examination of 'justice' outside the narrow confines of the legal system – incorporating political, social and cultural activities which further the participation of disabled people and their recognition as equal citizens.[39]

---

36 A Lawson and E Flynn, 'Disability and Access to Justice in the European Union: Implications of the UN Convention on the Rights of Persons with Disabilities' (2013) 4 *European Yearbook of Disability Law* 7 at 16.

37 R Bahdi, *Background Paper on Women's Access to Justice in the MENA Region* (International Development Research Centre (IDRC), Women's Rights and Citizenship Program (WRC) and the Middle East Regional Office (MERO), Middle East and North African (MENA) Regional Consultation, 9–11 December 2007, Cairo, Egypt).

38 Ibid., at 3.

39 A Lawson and E Flynn, 'Disability and Access to Justice in the European Union: Implications of the UN Convention on the Rights of Persons with Disabilities' (2013) 4 *European Yearbook of Disability Law* 7 at 17.

Introducing a Fourth Element: Participatory Access to Justice?

Bahdi identifies substantive, procedural and symbolic components of access to justice. This categorisation provides a helpful lens through which to view the broad scope of access to justice issues and debates for marginalised groups. It does stress the importance of involving disadvantaged sectors of society in the process of elaborating the content of substantive equality and substantive justice. It also includes, in the procedural component of access to justice, factors other than legal rules which affect the experience of parties to a dispute. Developments in the disability field (which will be discussed in further detail in the following chapter),[40] however, make it clear that issues of citizenship and participation in the justice system in capacities other than those of claimant, victim or defendant are a major component of achieving access to justice. In recognition of this, Lawson and I have argued elsewhere[41] that a participatory element should also be regarded as one of the key components of access to justice and that it should sit alongside Bahdi's substantive, procedural and symbolic components.

A participatory element of access to justice is closely linked to conceptions of equal citizenship, and also deeply rooted in the experience of negotiating the CRPD, and the finally agreed text of that Convention's article on 'access to justice' (Article 13), which will be explored more fully in the following chapter. As argued previously, this notion goes beyond the conventional focus of access to justice instruments on the rights of parties to a dispute. It reflects the importance ascribed by Article 13, and indeed the CRPD as a whole, to the participation of disabled people in all aspects of the life of their communities.[42] This is also evident in the process of negotiating the text in the first place, which Kayess and French describe as involving 'the highest level of participation by representatives of civil society, overwhelmingly that of persons with disability and disabled persons organisations, of any human rights convention in history'.[43]

Equal access to and participation in the justice system as a whole is significant for achieving access to justice in the context of disability. In support of this argument, Solum highlights the important role played by the meaningful participation of parties to a dispute in conferring legitimacy on the judicial process.[44] Similarly,

---

40   See, in addition to the CRPD, literature such as S Ortoleva, 'Inaccessible Justice: Human Rights, Persons with Disabilities and the Legal System' (2011) 17 *ILSA Journal of International and Comparative Law* 281; and V D Amar, 'Jury Service As Political Participation Akin to Voting' (1994–1995) 80 *Cornell Law Review* 203.

41   A Lawson and E Flynn, 'Disability and Access to Justice in the European Union: Implications of the UN Convention on the Rights of Persons with Disabilities' (2013) 4 *European Yearbook of Disability Law* 7 at 43.

42   See, in particular, Articles 4(3), 19, 29 and 33.

43   R Kayess and P French, 'Out of Darkness into Light? Introducing the Convention on the Rights of Persons with Disabilities' (2008) 8 *Human Rights Law Review* 1, 3–4.

44   L B Solum, 'Procedural Justice' (2004) 78 *Southern California Law Review* 181.

Genn has stressed the social value of ensuring that opportunities to participate in the judiciary are not confined to a narrow sector of society, arguing as follows:

> It is simply no longer acceptable for an institution of such power and influence to appear to exclude well-qualified candidates who are neither male nor white ... The shortage of women and minority ethnic judges, in particular in more senior positions, is and should be interpreted as exclusion from power. The diversity issue is about participation in powerful practices. It is about participation in the small and large decisions that shape the society in which we live.[45]

The right to participate on an equal basis with others in the justice system, not simply as litigant or defendant, but also in the roles of witness, judge, juror,[46] lawyer or magistrate is an essential element of citizenship, the significance of which is acknowledged by the articulation of the broad right to access justice in Article 13 of the CRPD. This notion reflects the principle of the justice system as a public good to which citizens should have equal access and opportunity to contribute, which appears in feminist scholarship,[47] and which, as argued elsewhere, is reflected in the way in which access to justice is defined in the CRPD, as will be discussed in further detail in the following chapter. Of course, to achieve true participatory justice, the diversity of the disability community must be recognised, particularly the ways in which disability interacts with other identities and how this can shape the experience of the individual and determine the person's interaction with the justice system as a whole.

4. Conclusion

This four-dimensional understanding of access to justice (as comprising symbolic, procedural, substantive and participatory components) is used as a basic framework to analyse various aspects of the justice system, and the experiences of persons with disabilities in accessing these, which will be considered in the following substantive chapters. These elements of effective access to justice fit well with intersectional understandings of disadvantage posited by Crenshaw – acknowledging that people with disabilities may claim many different identities outside the 'disability' collective: including race, gender, class, sexuality, etc.

---

45 H Genn, *Judging Civil Justice* (Cambridge University Press, 2010), 153. See also S Ortoleva, 'Inaccessible Justice: Human Rights, Persons with Disabilities and the Legal System' (2011) 17 *ILSA Journal of International and Comparative Law* 281.

46 See V D Amar, 'Jury Service As Political Participation Akin to Voting' (1994–1995) 80 *Cornell Law Review* 203.

47 The argument that civil justice should be viewed in this way, rather than simply as a private service provided to the particular disputants, is a key theme of H Genn, *Judging Civil Justice* (Cambridge University Press, 2010).

Similarly, Fraser's approach to remedying cultural and economic injustices through transformative strategies for recognition and redistribution have echoes throughout the four components for access to justice proposed as a general framework for further analysis of these elements as experienced by people with disabilities, in the following substantive chapters. Prior to engaging in this analysis, however, it is important to consider the trajectory of international human rights law up until this point, with a particular focus on the innovations of the CRPD – which will be addressed in detail in the next chapter.

Chapter 2
Access to Justice and its Intellectual Antecedents in International Human Rights Law

1. Introduction

Prior to the entry into force of the UN Convention on the Rights of Persons with Disabilities (CRPD), there was no specific articulation of a general right to 'access justice' in the core text of any UN human rights treaty. Therefore, as argued elsewhere,[1] the precursors to a specific right to 'access justice' were the rights to an effective remedy and a fair trial – first enumerated in the Universal Declaration of Human Rights (UDHR) in 1948, subsequently reiterated in core human rights treaties such as the International Covenant on Civil and Political Rights, and expanded on in General Comments of the Human Rights Committee and Committee on Economic, Social and Cultural Rights.

Traces of these rights, and other rights closely connected to accessing justice (e.g. rights to political participation) are found in all core UN human rights treaties – including the Convention on the Elimination of All Forms of Racial Discrimination (CERD), the Convention on the Elimination of All Forms of Discrimination Against Women (CEDAW), the Convention Against Torture (CAT), the Convention on the Rights of the Child (CRC) the Convention on the Protection of the Rights of All Migrant Workers and the Convention for the Protection of All Persons from Forced Disappearance. These references enforce the notion that without effective access to justice, particularly at the domestic or local level where remedies are most meaningful to the individual, the strength of universal human rights is weakened, and their content devalued.

In this chapter I will analyse the development of a right to access justice in the CRPD from these pre-existing norms, and consider the different ways in which the right is expressed in these core treaties, in light of the varying target groups to which each treaty is addressed, in order to demonstrate the multi-dimensional nature of the right. I will also consider the expression of the right to access justice in regional human rights treaties in Africa, Europe and the Americas to provide a global perspective on the articulation of the right to access justice. Finally, I will

---

1   A Lawson and E Flynn, 'Disability and Access to Justice in the European Union: Implications of the UN Convention on the Rights of Persons with Disabilities' (2013) 4 *European Yearbook of Disability Law* 7.

examine the treatment of the right in the CRPD, the first treaty to specifically enumerate such a right, and its interpretation by the UN Committee on the Rights of Persons with Disabilities in concluding observations delivered to date, as well as in the General Comments on Articles 9 and 12 in so far as these can be applied to the right to access justice in Article 13.

Core Human Rights Norms on Access to Justice: The Right to an Effective Remedy

The first reference to the right to an effective remedy in international law is to be found in the UDHR which, although initially adopted as a document containing common aspirations which were not intended to be legally binding, over the years has come to be recognised as encompassing customary norms of international law.[2] Article 8 states that '[e]veryone has the right to an effective remedy by the competent national tribunals for acts violating the fundamental rights granted him by the constitution or by law'. The reference to rights granted by the constitution or by law is significant here because most other international instruments which recognise the right to a remedy confine that recognition to remedies for violations of rights contained in those instruments, rather than in the domestic legal frameworks of States Parties which sign and ratify the relevant treaties.[3]

Roht-Arriaza contends that this right to an effective remedy requires the remedy to be individualised and adjudicatory.[4] She therefore argues that the payment of compensation to large groups of individuals claiming to have been affected by grave human rights abuses (including killings, torture and inhuman or degrading treatment perpetrated by a previous regime) would not be an 'effective remedy'. This idea of an individualised and adjudicatory remedy is particularly important for people with disabilities, as argued elsewhere, since it 'facilitates the awarding of remedies which require the performance of reasonable accommodation

---

2 M Haleem, '*The Domestic Application of International Human Rights Norms*' in *Developing Human Rights Jurisprudence: Volume 1* (Commonwealth Secretariat, 1988), 91.

3 See for example Article 2(3), International Covenant on Civil and Political Rights (1966). Farrell writes that this Article was added to the Universal Declaration on the recommendation of Mexico, and was based on the Latin-American notion of *amparo* (a concept closely related to *habeas corpus* in the common law tradition), but extending beyond the context of unlawful deprivations of liberty to ensure remedies were available for breaches of a broad range of fundamental rights. See B Farrell, 'Does the Universal Declaration of Human Rights Implicitly Provide for a Right to Habeas Corpus?' (1998) 16(1) *American University Washington College of Law Human Rights Brief* 2.

4 N Roht-Arriaza, 'State Responsibility to Investigate and Prosecute Grave Human Rights Violations in International Law' (1990) 78(2) *California Law Review* 449.

obligations – obligations which cannot be performed or regulated without regard to the specific circumstances of the case and of the disabled person in question'.[5]

Provost similarly argues that access to justice necessarily entails the award of a remedy for breach of a right[6] and that 'a substantive right to a remedy is clearly created by international human rights law'.[7] This argument is supported by the fact that, even where the right to an effective remedy is not explicitly stated in human rights conventions, it is generally recognised in the jurisprudence of the relevant treaty monitoring bodies. For example, the Committee on Economic, Social and Cultural Rights provided guidance in General Comment 9[8] as to what constitutes an effective remedy for breach of economic, social and cultural rights, specifying that it may take the form of a non-judicial, administrative remedy. This General Comment also emphasises that effective remedies should be accessible, affordable and timely.

Core Human Rights Norms on Access to Justice: The Right to a Fair Hearing

As argued elsewhere the right to 'access justice' can also be regarded as having developed from the right to a fair hearing,[9] which, like the right to an effective remedy, has been enshrined in international human rights law since the UDHR. According to Article 10 of that instrument, '[e]veryone is entitled in full equality to a fair and public hearing by an independent and impartial tribunal, in the determination of his rights and obligations and of any criminal charge against him'. The drafters of this article were working in the shadow of the atrocities of Nazi Germany and were thus extremely conscious of how the impact of rights-violations is exacerbated where there is no access to an impartial, independent judiciary.[10]

The International Covenant on Civil and Political Rights (ICCPR) also contains a right to a fair hearing to establish whether individual rights have been violated, which highlights how this right must be respected in particular for criminal proceedings. According to Article 14(1): 'In the determination of any criminal charge against him, or of his rights and obligations in a suit at law, everyone shall

---

5   A Lawson and E Flynn, 'Disability and Access to Justice in the European Union: Implications of the UN Convention on the Rights of Persons with Disabilities' (2013) 4 *European Yearbook of Disability Law* 7 at 18.

6   R Provost, *International Human Rights and Humanitarian Law* (Cambridge University Press, 2002), 44.

7   Ibid., 43.

8   Committee on Economic, Social and Cultural Rights, General Comment No. 9 – The domestic application of the Covenant (1998), E/C.12/1998/24.

9   A Lawson and E Flynn, 'Disability and Access to Justice in the European Union: Implications of the UN Convention on the Rights of Persons with Disabilities' (2013) 4 *European Yearbook of Disability Law* 7 at 19.

10 J Morsink, *The Universal Declaration of Human Rights: Origins, Drafting and Intent* (University of Pennsylvania Press, 1999), 50–52.

be entitled to a fair and public hearing by a competent, independent and impartial tribunal established by law'. Article 14(2) then goes on to list the due process rights of defendants which apply in criminal cases, and much of the jurisprudence on Article 14 has focused on the application of this subsection.

In its first General Comment on Article 14, the Human Rights Committee (HRC) noted that most States Parties were providing information only on due process rights in the context of criminal charges and were failing to report on procedures to determine an individual's rights and obligations in civil cases or constitutional challenges.[11] In keeping with the concerns upon which Article 10 of the UDHR was drafted, the Committee requested States to provide further information on the independence and impartiality of the judiciary, including the criteria used for appointment, terms of office, promotion, transfer and cessation of duties.[12]

In its most recent General Comment on Article 14 (published in 2007), the HRC elaborates on the concept of procedural justice – and demonstrates how the narrow right to a fair and public hearing contains links to the broader notion of access to justice. It states:[13]

> The right to equality before courts and tribunals, in general terms, guarantees, in addition to the principles mentioned in the second sentence of Article 14, paragraph 1, those of equal access and equality of arms, and ensures that the parties to the proceedings in question are treated without any discrimination ... Access to administration of justice must effectively be guaranteed in all such cases to ensure that no individual is deprived, in procedural terms, of his/her right to claim justice.

The HRC went on to note that the 'availability or absence of legal assistance often determines whether or not a person can access the relevant proceedings or participate in them in a meaningful way'.[14] While Article 14 requires States to ensure free legal aid for defendants only in criminal trials, the HRC urged States to provide legal assistance beyond the criminal context – and suggested that, if Article 14 is read in conjunction with Article 2(3) on the right to an effective remedy, the need for State provision of legal assistance in a broad range of cases can be inferred.[15] It also considered the issue of costs – and urged States to reconsider legal duties which require the awarding of costs to a winning party

---

11 Human Rights Committee, General Comment No. 13 – Equality before the courts and the right to a fair and public hearing by an independent court established by law (1984) para 2.

12 Ibid., para 3.

13 Human Rights Committee, General Comment No. 32 – Article 14: Right to equality before courts and tribunals and to a fair trial (2007), CCPR/C/GC/32 at paras 8–9.

14 Ibid., para 10.

15 Ibid.

'without consideration of the implications thereof or without providing legal aid [as to do so] may have a deterrent effect on the ability of persons to pursue the vindication of their rights under the Covenant in proceedings available to them'.[16]

In short, the international human rights norms regarding the right to a fair hearing can be said to contain a number of substantive and procedural safeguards. These have been summarised by the Australian Human Rights Law Resource Centre as follows:

- equal access to, and equality before, the courts;
- the right to legal advice and representation;
- the right to procedural fairness;
- the right to a hearing without undue delay;
- the right to a competent, independent and impartial tribunal established by law;
- the right to a public hearing; and
- the right to have the free assistance of an interpreter where necessary.[17]

These safeguards, outlined in international human rights norms, provide important mechanisms for ensuring procedural justice as discussed in the previous chapter. They have considerable relevance for people with disabilities – in particular, the right to equal access to and equality before the courts (which resonates with the right to equal recognition as a person before the law and rights to accessible court procedures) and the right to the free assistance of an interpreter (which is particularly relevant to people with communication difficulties or people who use sign language). The disability-specific implications of these rights will be discussed in further detail throughout Chapters 3 and 4.

2. Fair Procedures, Effective Remedies and Non-Discrimination in Access to Justice in Specific Minority Human Rights Treaties

Certain aspects of the right to access justice (such as the right to complain to an independent authority and to receive adequate redress for violation of rights) for various minority groups or for specific human rights violations, appear in many of the core UN human rights which followed the ICCPR and the International Covenant on Economic, Social and Cultural Rights (ICESC). While, as discussed further below, no treaty until the CRPD enumerated a broad, stand-alone right to access justice, it is worth considering the contributions of these specific treaties in

---

16   Ibid., para 11.
17   Human Rights Law Resource Centre, 'The Right to a Fair Hearing and Access to Justice: Australia's Obligations' (Human Rights Law Resource Centre, 2009), available at:
   <http://www.hrlrc.org.au/files/hrlrc-submission-access-to-justice-inquiry.pdf> (accessed 4 June 2012), 3.

the development of international human rights jurisprudence on access to justice – especially when considering access to justice from an intersectional perspective.

The UN Convention Against Torture (CAT) sets out in some detail in Articles 13 and 14 the opportunities for complaint which should be available to victims of torture, cruel, inhuman or degrading treatment or punishment, the need for effective and impartial investigative procedures and protection from intimidation, and the right to redress for rights violated under the Convention, specifically mentioning an enforceable right to fair and adequate compensation. These specific requirements relate to key aspects of access to justice – the need for an impartial judiciary, removing disincentives to reporting the violation of human rights, an accessible complaints mechanism for reporting rights violations, and the need for redress to compensate for such violations – including financial compensation and rehabilitation. While these provisions apply specifically to torture, they reflect broader access to justice concerns which are relevant to people with disabilities among other citizens, especially with regard to the accessibility of complaints mechanisms and the types of redress for rights violations which are required.

These requirements to provide redress were expanded on by the Committee Against Torture in General Comment 3 on Article 14,[18] in which the Committee clarified that 'redress' in Article 14 encompasses the concepts of 'effective remedy' and 'reparation',[19] and should include five key elements: restitution, compensation, rehabilitation, satisfaction and guarantees of non-repetition.[20] The Committee also highlighted the importance of victim participation in the redress process, and established that 'the restoration of the dignity of the victim is the ultimate objective in the provision of redress'.[21] The procedural and substantive components of 'redress' were emphasised by the Committee – and this reasoning can be applied beyond the specific context of torture to access to justice as a whole, as will be explored further below.

General Comment 3 also provides a good example of an intersectional approach, acknowledging the centrality of the non-discrimination principle in ensuring effective access to justice:

> States parties shall ensure that access to justice and to mechanisms for seeking and obtaining redress are readily available and that positive measures ensure that redress is equally accessible to all persons regardless of race, colour, ethnicity, age, religious belief or affiliation, political or other opinion, national or social origin, gender, sexual orientation, gender identity, mental or other disability, health status, economic or indigenous status, reason for which the person is detained, including persons accused of political offences or terrorist acts, asylum-seekers, refugees or others under international protection, or

---

18 Committee against Torture, General Comment No. 3 (2012), CAT/C/GC/3.
19 Ibid., para 2.
20 Ibid., para 6.
21 Ibid., para 4.

any other status or adverse distinction, and including those marginalized or made vulnerable on bases such as those above. Culturally sensitive collective reparation measures shall be available for groups with shared identity, such as minority groups, indigenous groups, and others.[22]

The General Comment goes on to specify the need for training of police, prison staff, judicial personnel and others in the justice system to ensure accessibility of complaints and redress systems to those who might be marginalised or experience discrimination, removing obstacles to redress which might disproportionately impact on individuals due to discrimination, and the need for national monitoring and reporting to oversee levels of implementation of the Convention at grassroots level.

The UN Convention on the Elimination of All Forms of Racial Discrimination contains two provisions of relevance to the right to access justice – Article 5(a) and Article 6. Article 5 protects the right to equal treatment – and paragraph (a) specifically ensures equal treatment before 'tribunals and all other organs administering justice'. Here again, we see the application of the non-discrimination principle to proceedings in the justice system. Article 6 is more linked to existing statements of the right to an effective remedy, but links this to the right to protection – which is a more proactive (rather than reactive) approach to combating rights-violations. It states as follows:

> States Parties shall assure to everyone within their jurisdiction effective protection and remedies, through the competent national tribunals and other State institutions, against any acts of racial discrimination which violate his human rights and fundamental freedoms contrary to this Convention, as well as the right to seek from such tribunals just and adequate reparation or satisfaction for any damage suffered as a result of such discrimination.

In the general recommendations issued by the Committee on the Elimination of All Forms of Racial Discrimination on Article 5, the Committee has specified that the right to non-discrimination before tribunals and other organs of the justice system is to 'be enjoyed by all persons living in a given State' and not simply confined to citizens.[23] Further, in its general recommendation on Article 6, the Committee specified that

> [T]he right to seek just and adequate reparation or satisfaction for any damage suffered as a result of such discrimination, which is embodied in article 6 of the Convention, is not necessarily secured solely by the punishment of

---

22 Ibid., para 32.
23 Committee on the Elimination of All Forms of Racial Discrimination, General Recommendation No. 20: Non-discriminatory implementation of rights and freedoms (Art. 5) 03/15/1996, para 3.

the perpetrator of the discrimination; at the same time, the courts and other competent authorities should consider awarding financial compensation for damage, material or moral, suffered by a victim, whenever appropriate.[24]

While the Convention on the Elimination of All Forms of Discrimination Against Women does not contain any explicit references to access to justice, the right to a fair trial or an effective remedy, it does include some important rights which are relevant to access to justice in the broad sense, such as rights to equal participation in public and political life in Articles 7 and 8, and the right to equality before the law which includes equal recognition of legal capacity for women and men, and equal treatment in all stages of procedure in courts and tribunals in Article 15. These issues will be returned to in the consideration of discrete aspects of access to justice in the following chapters.

Similarly, the Convention on the Rights of the Child (CRC) does not address access to justice per se for children, but does emphasise the importance of the child's participation in processes and decisions made concerning them[25] – which include proceedings in the justice system. This has been reinforced by subsequent general comments of the Committee on the Rights of the Child – particularly comments 10 (children's rights in juvenile justice),[26] 12 (the right of the child to be heard)[27] and 14 (the right of the child to have her best interests taken into account as a primary consideration).[28] Further to the entry into force of the Convention, subsequent UN guidelines have been agreed on access to justice for children – the most relevant of which is the UN Common Approach to Justice for Children.[29] In addition, an Optional Protocol to the CRC was adopted in 2011 to allow for a communications procedure to the Committee for individuals from State Parties who wish to report a violation of rights under the Convention – which itself ensures greater access to justice in the sphere of international human rights.

The Convention on the Protection of the Rights of All Migrant Workers adopted in 1990 echoes the guarantees of equal treatment before the law and the right to a fair trial (Article 18), and the right to an effective remedy (Article 83), using the language contained in the UDHR, ICCPR and ICESC, as discussed above. No particular concerns of migrant workers regarding access to justice are enumerated

---

24 Committee on the Elimination of All Forms of Racial Discrimination, General Recommendation No. 26: Article 6 of the Convention 03/24/2000, para 2.

25 Article 12, Convention on the Rights of the Child (1989).

26 Committee on the Rights of the Child, General Comment No. 10 (2007) Children's rights in juvenile justice, CRC/C/GC/10.

27 Committee on the Rights of the Child, General Comment No. 12 (2009) The right of the child to be heard, CRC/C/GC/12.

28 Committee on the Rights of the Child, General Comment No. 14 (2013) The right of the child to have his or her best interests taken into account as a primary consideration CRC/C/GC/14.

29 Office of the High Commissioner for Human Rights, UN Common Approach to Justice for Children (Geneva and New York, 2008).

in the text of the Convention beyond these general guarantees – and as of yet, no General Comments issued by the Committee have addressed these issues.

The International Convention for the Protection of All Persons from Enforced Disappearance also contains some discrete references to mechanisms for accessing justice. Similar to the Convention Against Torture, it requires States Parties to investigate acts of enforced disappearance and to bring those responsible to justice (Article 2), to guarantee the right of victims of enforced disappearance to an effective remedy (Article 8), judicial and due process safeguards for individuals deprived of their liberty (Article 17), and the right to a fair trial for individuals accused of an offence of enforced disappearance before a competent, independent and impartial court or tribunal established by law (Article 11). Since the Convention is a relatively new one, adopted in 2006 (the same year as the CRPD), its Committee has not yet published any general comments or recommendations on these Articles, which could provide further guidance on securing access to justice in these situations.

This overview of UN human rights treaties and their provisions on access to justice provides a useful context for considering the intersectionality of these issues. Some of the Conventions discussed simply echo the specific fair trial and effective remedy guarantees contained in their predecessors, whereas others address broader access to justice concerns – including the need for effective complaints and investigation mechanisms, participation of marginalised communities in political and public life, and equality before the law. While each of the Conventions addressed in this section purport to apply to a specific minority group, their provisions on access to justice potentially have a much broader application and provide a good basis for considering how the access to justice concerns of the disability community may be addressed within the mainstream of international human rights protections.

3. Regional Human Rights Treaty Provisions on Access to Justice

Following the emergence of rights linked with accessing justice (such as the right to an effective remedy and fair trial) in international human rights law, regional human rights treaties have reflected these norms in their own provisions. While some have borrowed directly from the language used in the UN instruments, others have introduced more nuanced conceptions of access to justice in consideration of the relevant regional context. The three regional conventions which I will focus on in this section are the European Convention on Human Rights (ECHR), the African Charter of Human and People's Rights and the American Convention on Human Rights, as these three contain the most relevant references to the rights to an effective remedy, fair trial and access to justice.

Article 13 of the ECHR states as follows: 'Everyone whose rights and freedoms as set forth in this Convention are violated shall have an effective remedy before a national authority notwithstanding that the violation has been committed by persons acting in an official capacity'. This is clearly influenced by the language of the UDHR, which was drafted only two years earlier, and, in turn, seems to have influenced the language subsequently used in Article 2(3) ICCPR, as discussed above. The European context, along with the international human rights context in the wake of the Second World War, was clearly mindful of the violation of rights committed in an official capacity by members of the Nazi regime in Germany, and sought to address this in its newly created human rights instruments.

Similarly, Article 6 of the ECHR reflects the language of Article 10 UDHR and states that: 'In the determination of his civil rights and obligations or of any criminal charge against him, everyone is entitled to a fair and public hearing within a reasonable time by an independent and impartial tribunal established by law.' However, the ECHR goes beyond this basic assertion provided in the UDHR by listing a number of core components to ensure the independence and impartiality of the judiciary, including the public pronouncement of judgments,[30] the presumption of innocence,[31] and specific due process protections for those charged with criminal offences.[32] Again, the backdrop of the Second World War can clearly be seen here in terms of ensuring the independence of the judiciary – and the language of this article may also owe something to the Constitution of the United States of America in its enumeration of the due process rights of criminal defendants.

A different context is presented by Article 7.1 of the African Charter, which states that: 'Every individual shall have the right to have his cause heard.' As a whole, the African Charter is far more cognisant of the relationship between individual rights and corresponding obligations or duties, and also of the need for justice to be done not just at an individual level, but in a manner that reflects societal and community interests, or the common good.[33] Heyns recognises that the African Commission's interpretation of Article 7 has primarily focused on the operation of military tribunals, and a lack of adherence to judgments by national governments and courts.[34] However, in the context of disability, D'Sa notes that Article 7 of the African Charter, much like Article 5 ECHR, does not preclude preventive detention of persons with disabilities (which could include detention in a psychiatric facility) – or provide whether the determination of this cause should be heard by the normal court or tribunal, or a special procedure.[35]

---

30   Article 6(1), ECHR.
31   Article 6(2), ECHR.
32   Article 6(3), ECHR.
33   RM D'Sa, 'Human and People's Rights: Distintive Features of the African Charter' (1985) 29(1) *Journal of African Law* 72.
34   C Heyns, 'Civil and Political Rights in the African Charter' in M Evans and R Murray, *The African Charter of Human and People's Rights: The System in Practice 1986–2000* (Cambridge University Press, 2002).
35   RM D'Sa, 'Human and People's Rights: Distinctive Features of the African Charter' (1985) 29(1) *Journal of African Law* 72 at 75.

Finally, Article 25 of American Convention on Human Rights sets out a right to judicial protection as follows:

> Everyone has the right to simple and prompt recourse, or any other effective recourse, to a competent court or tribunal for protection against acts that violate his fundamental rights recognised by the constitution or laws of the state concerned or by this Convention, even though such violation may have been committed by persons acting in the course of their official duties.

Again, this echoes the language of the ECHR, UDHR and ICCPR, which all preceded the drafting of the American Convention. In addition, Article 25 sets out that States must 'ensure that any person claiming such remedy shall have his rights determined by the competent authority provided for by the legal system of the state; develop the possibilities of judicial remedy; and ensure that the competent authorities shall enforce such remedies when granted'.[36] The additional requirement that remedies must be enforced where granted is a particularly noteworthy addition here, as it reflects the international experience, alluded to by scholars on the African Charter, that judgments which find a violation of rights are not always followed or respected by the relevant national authorities.

Having considered these regional human rights treaties, it is clear that different interpretations and facets of access to justice – primarily the rights to an effective remedy and fair procedures in civil or criminal cases, have been prioritised and acknowledged in both regional and global human rights systems. However, it should be noted that none of these, prior to the entry into force of the UN CRPD, had specifically addressed the barriers to access to justice experienced by persons with disabilities. These issues will be addressed in the following section as I consider the development of this specific right in the Convention on the Rights of Persons with Disabilities.

4. Introducing a 'New' Right? Access to Justice in the CRPD

As argued elsewhere, the articulation of a specific right to access justice in international human rights law did not occur until the adoption of the CRPD.[37] As can be seen from the discussion above regarding the inclusion of elements of the right to access justice in other treaties, no significant attention was paid by pre-existing international human rights law to the disability-specific dimensions of accessing justice. Although Lawson and I have also documented the drafting of

---

36 Article 25(2), American Convention on Human Rights, 1969.
37 A Lawson and E Flynn, 'Disability and Access to Justice in the European Union: Implications of the UN Convention on the Rights of Persons with Disabilities' (2013) 4 *European Yearbook of Disability Law* 7 at 21.

Article 13 CRPD elsewhere,[38] it is so important to this discussion that I will include the key developments for Article 13 the negotiation of the CRPD here again in order to provide context for an analysis of the implications of the text that finally emerged.

In the first draft of the Convention produced in January 2004 by the Working Group of the Ad Hoc Committee,[39] there was no article on access to justice. However, a footnote to the working group's report on Article 4 (on General Obligations), noted that previous versions of that article had included specific provisions on remedies.[40] These had not been incorporated into the Working Group's final draft due to the concern that there was insufficient consensus in international human rights law on the issue to justify including a specific article on remedies or access to justice.[41] This concern was based on the fact that a right to an effective remedy appeared in the UDHR and the ICCPR but not the ICESC, and so was not universally acknowledged in the three core UN human rights treaties.

In the observations made by civil society representatives on the text prepared by the Working Group, the Asia-Pacific Forum of National Human Rights Institutions suggested adding the following paragraphs to the draft of Article 4:

> Each State Party to this Convention undertakes: (a) To ensure that any person or class of persons whose rights or freedoms recognized in the Convention are violated shall have an effective remedy, whether the violation has been committed by persons or entities acting in an official capacity or by private persons or entities; (b) To ensure that any person claiming such a remedy shall have his or her right thereto determined by competent judicial, administrative or legislative authorities, or by any other competent authority provided for by the legal system of the State ... as well as the right to seek from such tribunals just and adequate reparation or satisfaction for any damage suffered as a result of such discrimination; and (c) To ensure that the competent authorities shall enforce such remedies when granted.
>
> States Parties recognize that access to effective remedies may require the provision of free legal assistance to persons with disabilities and the modification or flexible application of existing laws and practice regulating matters of procedure and evidence.[42]

---

38 Ibid.

39 See United Nations Enable, Ad Hoc Committee, Working Group to draft a Comprehensive and Integral International Convention on the Protection and Promotion of the Rights and Dignity of Persons with Disabilities, Report to the Ad Hoc Committee, Annex I (16 January 2004), available at: <http://www.un.org/esa/socdev/enable/rights/ahcwgreporta4.htm> (accessed 5 June 2012).

40 Ibid., at footnote 18.

41 Ibid.

42 See United Nations Enable, NGO Comments on the draft text – Draft Article 4, Proposal by Asia Pacific Forum of National Human Rights Institutions (25 May 2004),

From an initial reading, this wording appears to reflect pre-existing obligations on the right to an effective remedy in international human rights law. This follows the approach of much of the drafting process for the CRPD, given that the mandate of the Ad Hoc Committee was not to create any new rights but merely to restate the application of existing human rights norms to people with disabilities.[43] However, on closer examination, the suggested amendment contains some elements which appear to go beyond pre-existing human rights norms. These 'new' additions include the recognition of the need for legal aid in order to access justice, the need for the flexibility in existing laws of procedure and evidence to accommodate disabled witnesses and defendants, and the reaffirmation of a positive obligation on the State and public bodies to enforce such remedies.

In third session of the Ad Hoc Committee in June 2004,[44] Chile proposed that there should be a separate article on access to justice in the Convention, worded as follows: 'States Parties must guarantee adequate access to law for persons with disabilities to facilitate their ability to address justice in judicial proceedings that could be contentious or not.'[45] Chile suggested that, in order to guarantee this right, courts would have to train judges and judicial staff on the rights of persons with disabilities.

By the end of the fourth session of the Ad Hoc Committee in August 2004,[46] despite the proposals made by Chile and the Asia-Pacific Forum, there had been no movement to draft a separate article on access to justice. Instead, access to justice issues were addressed within what was then draft Article 9 on recognition as a person before the law. The relevant part of that draft article then read as follows:

States Parties shall: ...

ensure that persons with disabilities who experience difficulty in asserting their rights, in understanding information, and in communicating, have access to assistance to understand information presented to them and to express their

---

available at: <http://www.un.org/esa/socdev/enable/rights/ahc3ngoa4.htm> (accessed 5 June 2012).

43 United Nations Press Releases, 'Chairman says draft convention sets out detailed code of implementation and spells out how individual rights should be put into practice' (15 August 2005), SOC/4680, available at: <http://www.un.org/News/Press/docs/2005/soc4680.doc.htm> (accessed 20 April 2012).

44 Landmine Survivors Network, *Daily Summary of Discussion at Third Session of UN Convention on the Rights of Persons with Disabilities, Ad Hoc Committee, 3 June 2004* (Landmine Survivors Network, 2004), Volume 4(8).

45 Ibid.

46 Landmine Survivors Network, *Daily Summary of Discussions on Article 9 at Fourth Session of UN Convention on the Rights of Persons with Disabilities, Ad Hoc Committee, 26 August 2004* (Landmine Survivors Network, 2004), Volume 5(4).

decisions, choices and preferences, as well as to enter into binding agreements or contracts, to sign documents, and act as witnesses.[47]

Although this draft Article eliminated any direct reference to the right to an effective remedy *per se* it did include key elements of what became the right to access to justice in the final text of Article 13 – including the need to have accessible information on rights and entitlements; the need for support with communication to assert rights; the entitlement to be recognised as competent to act as a witness in legal proceedings; and the entitlement to give legal instruction in order to pursue and enforce rights. However, as discussed elswhere 'the issue of the State's obligation to make access to justice a reality outside the narrow confines of the legal system was not addressed in this draft'.[48]

During the fifth session of the Ad Hoc Committee in February 2005, the question of whether a separate article was needed in order to guarantee equal access to justice was discussed. Many delegations supported a proposal to draft a separate article on this issue, including Costa Rica, Mexico, Chile, the EU, Norway and Japan. Several delegations then met informally to draft Article 9 bis, which read as follows: 'States Parties shall ensure effective access to justice for persons with disabilities on an equal basis with others, facilitating their effective role as direct and indirect participants in all legal proceedings, including the investigative and other preliminary stages'.[49]

In the final two sessions this text was removed from its parent article on recognition as a person before the law, and became Article 13 of the CRPD, which now reads as follows:

> 1. States Parties shall ensure effective access to justice for persons with disabilities on an equal basis with others, including through the provision of procedural and age-appropriate accommodations, in order to facilitate their effective role as direct and indirect participants, including as witnesses, in all legal proceedings, including at investigative and other preliminary stages.

---

47 See United Nations Enable, Ad Hoc Committee, Working Group to draft a Comprehensive and Integral International Convention on the Protection and Promotion of the Rights and Dignity of Persons with Disabilities, Report to the Ad Hoc Committee, Annex I Draft Article 9 (16 January 2004), available at: <http://www.un.org/esa/socdev/enable/rights/ahcwgreporta9.htm> (accessed 12 April 2012).

48 A Lawson and E Flynn, 'Disability and Access to Justice in the European Union: Implications of the UN Convention on the Rights of Persons with Disabilities' (2013) 4 *European Yearbook of Disability Law* 7 at 23.

49 United Nations Enable, Article 13, Status of Discussions, Fifth Session, Ad Hoc Committee, Report of the Coordinator (4 February 2005), available at:
<http://www.un.org/esa/socdev/enable/rights/ahcstata13fisrepcoord.htm> (accessed 12 April 2012).

2. In order to help to ensure effective access to justice for persons with disabilities, States Parties shall promote appropriate training for those working in the field of administration of justice, including police and prison staff.

The final text of Article 13 therefore incorporates some elements of earlier drafts, including the obligation to enable disabled people to act as witnesses and participants in legal proceedings (an idea which first appeared in the draft Article 9) as well as the obligation to train justice officials (as suggested by Chile in the fourth session of the Ad Hoc Committee). It also contains some innovative additions, including the 'provision of procedural and age-appropriate accommodations' – a concept which has clear connections with Article 7 of the CRPD on children with disabilities and which also draws on the Asia-Pacific Forum of National Human Rights Institutions' proposal regarding the adaptation of evidence law and judicial procedures to accommodate people with disabilities. In the next two sections, I consider how Article 13 may be interpreted based on its interactions with other provisions of the Convention.

The Interconnectedness of Article 13 with Other Provisions of the CRPD

The indivisibility and interdependence of all human rights was a recurring theme throughout the drafting of the CRPD and is now affirmed in its preamble.[50] As argued elsewhere, this has two key implications for the analysis of access to justice and Article 13.[51] First, regard must be had to other CRPD provisions when interpreting the requirements of Article 13; and, second, access to justice is not dealt with exclusively by Article 13 but is also addressed by other CRPD provisions.

In interpreting the application of Article 13 to specific areas of law, the most obvious CRPD cross-cutting provision, which must be read in conjunction with Article 13, is Article 5 on non-discrimination. Since the purpose of Article 13 is to 'ensure effective access to justice for persons with disabilities on an equal basis with others' this clearly resonates with the principle of non-discrimination.[52] As argued elsewhere, although the obligation to prohibit discrimination is not explicitly mentioned in Article 13, it is clearly implicit in the phrase 'on an equal basis with others' and, in any event, is a general principle and general obligation of the Convention under Articles 3 and 4 respectively.[53]

---

50   Preamble (c), United Nations Convention on the Rights of Persons with Disabilities (2006).

51   A Lawson and E Flynn, 'Disability and Access to Justice in the European Union: Implications of the UN Convention on the Rights of Persons with Disabilities' (2013) 4 *European Yearbook of Disability Law* 7 at 24.

52   Article 13(1), UN CRPD.

53   A Lawson and E Flynn, 'Disability and Access to Justice in the European Union: Implications of the UN Convention on the Rights of Persons with Disabilities' (2013) 4 *European Yearbook of Disability Law* 7 at 24.

Article 5 prescribes that action which is discriminatory in purpose or effect towards persons with disabilities must be prohibited. This reflects the notion that both direct discrimination (measures explicitly targeted at persons with disabilities) as well as indirect discrimination (measures which appear facially neutral but which have a disproportionate impact on disabled people) are prohibited under the CRPD. It also makes it clear that a failure to provide reasonable accommodation will also amount to discrimination[54] within the meaning of the CRPD.

In the context of access to justice, reasonable accommodation requires the adaptation of standard practice or procedure in order to remove a particular disadvantage at which a specific disabled person would otherwise be placed.[55] As argued elsewhere, examples of reasonable accommodation in accessing justice might include: 'the timetabling of a case (for instance by avoiding an early morning start for a person taking certain types of medication); allowing more frequent breaks for a person with a physical impairment which requires this; allowing a sign language interpreter or reader to accompany a person with sensory impairments; or communicating with a deaf person who has visited a police station in writing rather than orally'.[56]

Article 13(1) does not explicitly mention reasonable accommodation but it does require States to ensure that 'procedural and age appropriate accommodations' are carried out. As argued elsewhere, although the relationship between such accommodations and 'reasonable accommodation' is not explained, these procedural and age-related accommodations may be more generic and less individualised in approach than the obligation in Article 5 to provide reasonable accommodation to persons with disabilities.[57] Further, the obligation to provide such accommodations in the context of access to justice 'cannot be mitigated by arguments about reasonableness and the extent of the burden they would place on the duty-bearer'[58] since the providers of such accommodations will inevitably be the State or public officials involved in the administration of justice.

In the absence of a General Comment on Article 13 or further guidance from the Committee on the Rights of Persons with Disabilities, it is difficult to identify concrete examples of procedural accommodations that might be expected of States in the context of access to justice. As previously discussed, one example might be changing the eligibility criteria for legal aid[59] to ensure that it is open to disabled

---

54 See Article 2, UN CRPD, for a definition of 'discrimination' which includes a failure to provide a reasonable accommodation.
55 Article 2, UN CRPD.
56 A Lawson and E Flynn, 'Disability and Access to Justice in the European Union: Implications of the UN Convention on the Rights of Persons with Disabilities' (2013) 4 *European Yearbook of Disability Law* 7 at 25.
57 Ibid.
58 Ibid.
59 Ibid.

people who wish to pursue discrimination claims.[60] As I have argued elsewhere, the provision of an independent statutory advocate could also fall within the obligations to make procedural accommodations for effective access to justice as outlined in Article 13.[61] There are also examples in many countries of reform in the fields of evidence and procedural law to enable people with disabilities to use different forms of communication to testify in court.[62]

As discussed above, the text of what is now Article 13 was originally envisaged as a component of the right to equal recognition before the law in Article 12. Therefore, it is important to read both articles together to understand the scope of the right to access justice in the CRPD. Kayess and French suggest that both Articles 12 and 13 are extensions of the traditional right to equality before the law[63] As Lawson and I suggest:

> The closeness of the connection between the issues dealt with by these two articles, and their mutually supportive character, was acknowledged throughout the drafting process – without the recognition of legal personality, there can be no recourse to justice and, without access to justice, the right to be recognised as equal before the law is meaningless since it cannot be asserted, applied to specific contexts or enforced.[64]

This is further illustrated by Bartlett, Lewis and Thorold, who claim:

> Some people with disabilities face insurmountable obstacles to accessing justice. The authors of this text have visited institutions in countries which have ratified the Convention where there are obvious abuses taking place against people with mental health problems or intellectual disabilities. A benevolent human rights lawyer visiting such institutions may be in the frustrating position of not being able to do anything if the person with disabilities lacks the capacity to instruct a lawyer. In some countries, the director or staff member of the institution is also the guardian, a situation which creates an obvious conflict of interests.[65]

---

60 See for example C Gooding, 'Disability Discrimination Act: From Statute to Practice' (2000) 20 *Critical Social Policy* 533.

61 E Flynn, 'Making Human Rights Meaningful for People with Disabilities: Advocacy, Access to Justice and Equality before the Law' (2013) 17(4) *International Journal of Human Rights* 491.

62 N Ziv, 'Witnesses with Mental Disabilities: Accommodations and the Search for Truth – The Israeli Case' (2007) 27(4) *Disability Studies Quarterly* 51.

63 R Kayess and P French, 'Out of Darkness into Light? Introducing the Convention on the Rights of Persons with Disabilities' (2008) 8 *Human Rights Law Review* 1, 29.

64 A Lawson and E Flynn, 'Disability and Access to Justice in the European Union: Implications of the UN Convention on the Rights of Persons with Disabilities' (2013) 4 *European Yearbook of Disability Law* 7 at 26.

65 P Bartlett, O Lewis and O Thorold, *Mental Disability and the European Convention on Human Rights* (Martinus Nijhoff, 2007) at 209.

This illustrates a common problem whereby the denial of legal capacity to people with disabilities frustrates their efforts to access justice, as demonstrated by a number of high profile cases before the European Court of Human Rights in which applicants who were deprived of their legal capacity were subsequently barred from any meaningful access to the justice system in order to challenge the original deprivation of legal capacity, or assert other violations of their human rights.[66] Article 12(2)'s requirement that 'States Parties shall recognize that persons with disabilities enjoy legal capacity on an equal basis with others in all aspects of life' is therefore a crucial provision in facilitating access to justice. Similarly, Article 12(3) which requires that appropriate support be provided, where needed, to enable people with disabilities to exercise their legal capacity, is a core precondition for ensuring that individuals can access justice on an equal basis with others.

Two CRPD articles on the subject of 'accessibility' are also of direct relevance for Article 13 on access to justice: Article 9 and Article 21. Article 9 contains a broad expression of the accessibility obligations imposed by the CRPD, requiring States to ensure the physical accessibility of buildings and spaces open to the public;[67] the provision of live assistance and intermediaries such as sign-language interpreters;[68] accessible signage, including in Braille and easy-to-read formats;[69] accessible information and communication technologies;[70] and other forms of assistance and support needed to ensure access to information.[71] However, there has been debate among scholars as to whether the obligations outlined in Article 9 establish accessibility as a right in itself, and if so, whether this right is one which accrues to individuals, or one which is based on affiliation to a particular group of disabled people.[72] By contrast, Article 21 is narrower in scope, since it focuses on the accessibility of information and communication as a component of the right to freedom of expression. While these additional articles on accessibility may overlap with the requirement to make the justice system 'accessible' as outlined in Article 13, Lawson and I suggest that this overlap can be viewed positively, as 'the greater the degree of accessibility that can be incorporated into the justice system, the lower will be the likelihood of individual reasonable accommodations being required [by persons with disabilities]'.[73]

---

66 See e.g. *Shtukaturov v Russia*, Application No. 44009/05, judgment 27 March 2008, (2008 54 EHRR 27), *Salontaji-Drobnjak v Serbia*, Application No. 36500/05, judgment 13 October 2009, *Stanev v Bulgaria, Application No. 36760/06*, judgment 17 January 2012 and *DD v Lithuania, No. 13469/06*, judgment 14 February 2012.

67 Article 9(1)(a), CRPD (2006).

68 Article 9(2)(e), CRPD (2006).

69 Article 9(2)(d), CRPD (2006).

70 Article 9(2)(g)–(h), CRPD (2006).

71 Article 9(2)(f), CRPD (2006).

72 F Mégret, 'The Disabilities Convention: Human Rights of Persons with Disabilities or Disability Rights?' (2008) 30 *Human Rights Quarterly* 494.

73 A Lawson and E Flynn, 'Disability and Access to Justice in the European Union: Implications of the UN Convention on the Rights of Persons with Disabilities' (2013) 4

Another important precondition of the right to access is the need for people with disabilities to be made aware of their rights and the ways in which these rights can be asserted and enforced. Awareness-raising obligations on States are included in Articles 8 and 16(2) of the CRPD – with Article 8 taking a broad approach to the need to raise awareness about the rights contained in the Convention in general; while Article 16(2) addresses the specific need to raise awareness in the context of violence, exploitation and abuse of persons with disabilities. These Articles require States Parties to promote awareness amongst disabled people, their families and society more generally, of the rights of persons with disabilities and how they might be enforced. As argued elswhere: '[a]wareness of one's rights and how to enforce them is, in most cases, an essential pre-requisite to exercising them';[74] a concept which will be discussed in further detail in Chapter 3.

Article 29 is the final CRPD article which should be read in tandem with Article 13 on access to justice. Article 29(b) requires States to '[p]romote actively an environment in which persons with disabilities can effectively and fully participate in the conduct of public affairs, without discrimination and on an equal basis with others, and encourage their participation in public affairs'. This demands that attention be given to the participation of disabled people in the justice system in a wide variety of roles – not just those of plaintiff, victim or defendant. As such, it supplements Article 13's reference to the role of persons with disabilities 'as direct and indirect participants, including as witnesses' in legal proceedings. Reading Articles 13 and 29 together suggests, for example, that people with disabilities have a right to participate in jury service, on an equal basis with others, in countries where jury systems operate. This is confirmed by the following request for information from States included in the Reporting Guidelines of the Committee on the Rights of Persons with Disabilities, which asks States to report on '[t]he availability of reasonable accommodations, including procedural accommodations that are made in the legal process to ensure effective participation of all types of persons with disabilities in the justice system, whatever the role in which they find themselves (for example as victims, perpetrators, witnesses or jury members and others)'.[75]

The theme of participation is consistent throughout the text of the CRPD, and this provides an important lens for conceptualising access to justice for people with disabilities. For example, Article 4(3) requires that:

> In the development and implementation of legislation and policies to implement the present Convention, and in other decision-making processes concerning issues relating to persons with disabilities, States Parties shall closely consult

---

European Yearbook of Disability Law 7 at 26.
    74 Ibid., at 27.
    75 United Nations Committee on the Rights of Persons with Disabilities, *Reporting Guidelines on Treaty Specific Document to be Submitted by States Parties under Article 35(1) of the UN Convention on the Rights of Persons with Disabilities* (United Nations, 2009).

with and actively involve persons with disabilities, including children with disabilities, through their representative organizations.

This resonates deeply with the conceptual framework for access to justice discussed in the previous chapter, which requires the involvement of the marginalised group in developing laws and policies to ensure substantive equality. Similarly, Article 29, as just discussed, requires States to support the establishment and operation of a vibrant civil society sphere, with a focus on supporting disabled people's organisations in order to facilitate the participation of persons with disabilities in political and public life. Finally, Article 33 requires States Parties to establish domestic monitoring mechanisms, including an independent element and with the full participation of disabled people and their representative organisations, to monitor progress towards the implementation of the Convention at a grassroots level.[76] All these articles, when read in conjunction with Article 13, demonstrate the interconnectedness of access to justice to all spheres of equality and human rights which apply to persons with disabilities.

The Scope and Interpretation of Article 13

As Article 13 represents the first explicit statement of a right to access justice in international law, it is worth considering further the scope of this new expression of the right and whether it does in fact go beyond the substance of existing international human rights norms. In this section, I will address how the scope of the right has been shaped by the interpretations provided by the UN Committee on the Rights of Persons with Disabilities – both in the dialogues which it has held with the 10 State Parties examined at the time of writing, and in references to Article 13 in its first two General Comments – on Articles 9 and 12.

The innovative nature of the broad scope of the article has been previously explored,[77] as compared, for example, with statements in other human rights treaties on the rights to an effective remedy and a fair hearing.[78] In this context, Article 13(1) refers to the right to participate in legal proceedings as a 'direct or indirect' participant. As explained above, this means that the right to access justice extends beyond the parties to the dispute. In addition, it deals with participation in jury service and procedural accommodations for witnesses. Another innovative aspect is the fact that Article 13 goes beyond expressions of rights to a fair hearing or to an effective remedy by explicitly requiring disability training to be provided

---

76   See further Mental Disability Advocacy Center, *Building the Architecture for Change: Guidelines on Article 33 of the UN Convention on the Rights of Persons with Disabilities* (MDAC, 2011).

77   A Lawson and E Flynn, 'Disability and Access to Justice in the European Union: Implications of the UN Convention on the Rights of Persons with Disabilities' (2013) 4 *European Yearbook of Disability Law* 7.

78   Ibid.

to the judiciary, police and other staff. In addition, and perhaps rather surprisingly for a right to access justice, the training requirement expressly extends to prison staff.[79] The fact that information about the training of police and prison staff had not been provided in the Tunisian State Report was noted with regret by the Committee in its Concluding Observations.[80]

In the Committee's dialogue with Spain, further information on the right to access justice was requested from the State Party.[81] In response, Spain replied that this issue was covered by the Charter of Citizen's Right to Justice, which applied equally to persons with disabilities.[82] Spain also maintained that physical access to the locations where justice was administered was ensured as far as possible and that accessible communication in court proceedings was available to persons with disabilities. Further, the government noted that an exception to the means test for free legal aid was available to persons with disabilities taking cases regarding equality, non-discrimination or accessibility.[83] Similarly, the government informed the Committee that the 5 per cent quota of persons with disabilities to be employed by public bodies extends to the judiciary and prosecutors – although no information was provided on the numbers of disabled judges and prosecutors currently employed.[84]

However, in CERMI's shadow report on Spain, a different picture of access to justice for persons with disabilities was presented.[85] This shadow report highlighted the level of inaccessible justice buildings throughout the country and the lack of legal obligations ensuring the application of general accessibility rights to the justice system (since measures such as the Citizens' Charter appear to have the status of non-binding soft law or policy instruments).[86] Further, the shadow report raised concerns regarding notary regulations which exclude persons with mental disabilities, and persons who are 'blind, deaf or mute' from acting as legal witnesses on official documents.[87] Similarly, where individuals with disabilities

---

79   Ibid., at 30.
80   United Nations Committee on the Rights of Persons with Disabilities, Concluding Observations: Tunisia (2011), CRPD/C/TUN/CO/1, para 18.
81   United Nations Committee on the Rights of Persons with Disabilities, List of issues to be taken up in connection with the consideration of the initial report of Spain (2011), CRPD/C/ESP/Q/1, para 12.
82   Ministry of Foreign Affairs and International Cooperation, Written Responses to Committee on the Rights of Persons with Disabilities List of issues to be taken up in connection with the consideration of the initial report of Spain (2011), CRPD/C/ESP/Q/1, 11.
83   Ibid.
84   Ibid., 12.
85   CERMI, *Human Rights and Disability: An Alternative Report on Spain* (Madrid, 2010).
86   Ibid., 11.
87   *Reglamento de Organización y Funcionamiento del Notariado* (approved by Royal Decree 45/2007).

are denied legal capacity, this subsequently prevents them from filing suit or lodging complaints regarding any other violation of their fundamental rights – since such cases can only be taken by the individual's legal guardian.[88] Despite these concerns, the Committee chose not to deliver any concluding observations on Article 13.

In its dialogue with Argentina, the Committee on the Rights of Persons with Disabilities requested further information on access to justice specifically for women with disabilities, following up on a previous observation from the Committee on the Elimination of All Forms of Discrimination Against Women.[89] The CEDAW Committee's observation noted that women with disabilities were particularly likely to experience violence and discrimination, as well as barriers in accessing justice when they sought redress for the violation of their rights,[90] and the CRPD Committee asked Argentina to report on measures taken to address these issues. Argentina responded by citing the establishment of an 'Office of Women' by the Supreme Court of Justice, and noting the appointment of a prominent female judge of the High Court to this position in 2009, as a direct response to the CEDAW concluding observations.[91] The government also noted that training for justice officials in all provincial supreme courts, on gender and disability-sensitivity, had been carried out in 2011 and 2012.[92]

However, the Shadow Report on Argentina, prepared jointly by a number of mainstream human rights NGOs with the participation of some disabled people's organisations, highlighted further inconsistencies in the government's responses, including the fact that the National Program of Assistance for Persons with Disabilities in Their Relations with the Administration of Justice created in 2011 was established without the involvement of persons with disabilities or broader civil society.[93] Since its establishment, these organisations felt that little had been clarified about its scope, application and operation. This shadow report also acknowledged that some innovations had been made in the provision of free legal representation to persons involuntarily detained in psychiatric hospitals in Buenos Aires but that this needed to be expanded nationally in order to have greater effect in securing access to justice for persons with psycho-social disabilities in particular.[94] While the Committee on the Rights of Persons with Disabilities

---

88 Art. 7.1 Civil Procedure Act 1/2000 (*Ley 1/2000 de Enjuiciamiento Civil*).

89 United Nations Committee on the Rights of Persons with Disabilities, List of issues to be taken up in connection with the consideration of the initial report of Argentina (2012), CRPD/C/ARG/Q/1, para 10.

90 CEDAW/C/ARG/CO/6, para 16.

91 Ministry of Foreign Affairs and Worship, Written Responses to Committee on the Rights of Persons with Disabilities List of issues to be taken up in connection with the consideration of the initial report of Spain (2012), CRPD/C/ARG/Q/1, para 10.

92 Ibid.

93 REDI, CELS, ADC, FAICA, FENDIM, *Status of Disability in Argentina 2008/2012* (Buenos Aires, 2012), 3.

94 Ibid., 4.

did express concern in its Concluding Observations on Article 6 (Women with Disabilities) that insufficient measures had been taken to secure access to justice for women with disabilities,[95] in light of the previous CEDAW observation, it did not make broader concluding observations on access to justice more generally under Article 13.

However, the Committee did make recommendations about reasonable accommodation in the justice system for women and girls with disabilities specifically, in its Concluding Observations on El Salvador, on the basis that such individuals were at higher risk of becoming 'victims of abuse or neglect owing to the low credibility ascribed to their witness statements'.[96] In light of this, the Committee asked the State Party to '[p]ut in place reasonable procedural accommodation with a gender and age focus to ensure access to justice for persons with disabilities and to provide free legal assistance, information on each case – as early as the police investigation – in accessible formats, access to judicial buildings and the services of trained Salvadoran sign-language interpreters' and to '[a]dopt measures to secure access to justice for women and girls with disabilities, with due consideration paid to their role as witnesses and victims during the trial phase'.[97]

For Peru, the issue of access to justice was not included either on the list of issues prepared by the Committee for dialogue with the State Party, nor in the Concluding Observations. However, the Peruvian National Confederation of People with Disabilities highlighted this issue in their shadow report to the Committee, stating that: 'In Peru, pertinent treatment is not given to persons with disabilities with regard to their access to justice, the speediness of the proceedings in which they are involved, or the necessary training of judges and penitentiary personnel in attending to them. Adapted languages are not used in judicial proceedings'.[98] The Committee did however address very similar issues in its Concluding Observations on both El Salvador and Australia, requiring El Salvador to: '[d]esign training programmes for all those involved in the legal system, including the police, judges, legal professionals, social workers and health-care workers, in both urban and rural areas'[99] and to Australia that 'standard and compulsory modules on working with persons with disabilities be

---

95 United Nations Committee on the Rights of Persons with Disabilities, Concluding Observations: Argentina (2012), CRPD/C/ARG/CO/1, paras 13–14.

96 United Nations Committee on the Rights of Persons with Disabilities, Concluding Observations: El Salvador (2013), CRPD/C/SLV/CO/1, para 30.

97 Ibid., paras 30(a) and (d).

98 Peruvian National Confederation of People with Disabilities, *Alternative Report on the Compliance with the Convention on the Rights of Persons with Disabilities* (Lima, 2012), 10.

99 United Nations Committee on the Rights of Persons with Disabilities, Concluding Observations: El Salvador (2013), CRPD/C/SLV/CO/1, para 30(c).

incorporated into training programmes for police officers, prison staff, lawyers, the judiciary and court personnel'.[100]

With respect to China, while access to justice did not feature on the list of issues devised by the Committee for dialogue with the State Party, the Committee did issue a Concluding Observation on Article 13 which demonstrates the interconnection between access to justice and legal capacity. In its State Report, China had highlighted the establishment of legal aid service centres for persons with disabilities, and the designation of specific public defenders for persons with disabilities as important advances in securing equal access to justice.[101] However, the Committee was sceptical about the independence and effectiveness of these measures in promoting access to justice on an equal basis with non-disabled people. The Committee held as follows:

> While appreciating the establishment of legal aid service centres for persons with disabilities, the Committee notes that these service centres often lack the necessary resources and do not operate on an independent basis. The Committee is concerned that neither the criminal nor the civil procedure laws in China are accessible for the use of persons with disabilities on an equal basis with others and, instead, patronizing measures are put into place, such as the designation of public defenders that treat the person concerned as if they lacked legal capacity.[102]

In the same Concluding Observation, the Committee requested the Chinese government to allocate the necessary human and financial resources to the legal aid service centres. Similar comments were made in the Concluding Observations on El Salvador, where the Committee requested that the State '[s]trengthen the mandate of the Office of the Human Rights Advocate regarding legal remedies for the defence of the rights of persons with disabilities'.[103]

The Committee also required China to review 'its procedural civil and criminal laws in order to make mandatory the necessity to establish procedural accommodation for those persons with disabilities who intervene in the judicial system can do it as subject of rights and not as objects of protection'.[104] Similar concerns can be found in the Committee's Concluding Observations on Paraguay. Here, in respect of Article 13, the Committee noted with concern that criminal

---

100 United Nations Committee on the Rights of Persons with Disabilities, Concluding Observations: Australia (2013), CRPD/C/AUS/CO/1, para 28.

101 Committee on the Rights of Persons with Disabilities, Initial reports submitted by States Parties under article 35 of the Convention: China (2011), CRPD/C/CHN/1, para 55.

102 United Nations Committee on the Rights of Persons with Disabilities, Concluding Observations: China (2012), CRPD/C/CHN/CO/1, para 23.

103 United Nations Committee on the Rights of Persons with Disabilities, Concluding Observations: El Salvador (2013), CRPD/C/SLV/CO/1, para 30(b).

104 United Nations Committee on the Rights of Persons with Disabilities, Concluding Observations: China (2012), CRPD/C/CHN/CO/1, para 24.

law in Paraguay provided for special 'care measures' which could be applied to persons with disabilities without the same level of respect for due process as would be available in a normal criminal trial. The Committee therefore recommended 'that the State party review its legislation with a view to ensuring that criminal sanctions applicable to persons with psychosocial or intellectual disabilities are subject to the same degree and have the same conditions as any other person subject to the justice system, providing in such cases that the administration of justice is done in a manner which is reasonable and respects due process'.[105]

Concerns regarding unequal treatment in the criminal justice system are also echoed in the Committee's Concluding Observations on Australia, which recommends 'the State party to ensure that persons with psychosocial disabilities are ensured the same substantive and procedural guarantees as others in the context of criminal proceedings, and in particular to ensure that no diversion programmes to transfer individuals to mental health commitment regimes or requiring an individual to participate in mental health services are implemented'.[106] In addition, the Committee further requires the State to 'ensure that all persons with disabilities who have been accused of crimes and are currently detained in jails and institutions, without trial, are allowed to defend themselves against criminal charges, and are provided with required support and accommodation to facilitate their effective participation'.[107]

From this analysis, a number of interlinking themes can be seen in the Committee's dialogues with the 10 States Parties it has examined to date on the normative content and obligations under Article 13. These include concerns about legal information, advice and representation for persons with disabilities – especially in the context of free legal aid. The links with other CRPD rights to legal capacity and liberty are also made clear – especially in the context of criminal procedures and legal measures affecting people with psycho-social disabilities. The intersections between gender and disability have also been recognised including the additional barriers which may face women and girls in seeking access to justice. Finally, the need for training of those involved in the administration of justice is clarified – and extended beyond the narrow confines of the justice system to health and social care workers as well as judges, lawyers, police and prison staff. In the absence of a specific General Comment from the Committee on Article 13, its concluding observations to date provide a useful starting point to guide States, and these are further complemented by references to accessing justice

---

105 United Nations Committee on the Rights of Persons with Disabilities, Concluding Observations: Paraguay (2013), CRPD/C/PRY/CO/1, para 32.

106 United Nations Committee on the Rights of Persons with Disabilities, Concluding Observations: Australia (2013), CRPD/C/AUS/CO/1, para 29.

107 United Nations Committee on the Rights of Persons with Disabilities, Concluding Observations: Australia (2013), CRPD/C/AUS/CO/1, para 30.

in the Committee's General Comments on Articles 9 and 12, which I discuss in the following section.

*General Comments on Articles 9 and 12 and
their Relevance for Access to Justice*

The General Comments published by the Committee on Articles 9 and 12 are discussed in further detail in Chapters 3 and 4; however, it is worth commenting briefly on them here insofar as they relate directly to the specific issue of access to justice. While the General Comment on Article 9 focuses on accessibility in general, it does make specific reference to access to justice as follows:

> There can be no effective access to justice if buildings of law-enforcement organs and judiciary aren't physically accessible, if the services they provide, information and communication aren't accessible (Article 13). One has to have accessible safe houses, accessible support services and procedures if one wants to provide effective and meaningful protection from violence, abuse and exploitation to persons with disabilities, especially women, girls and boys with disabilities (Article 16). Accessible environment, transportation, information and communication, and services are a pre-condition for inclusion of persons with disabilities in their respective local communities and independent life (Article 19).[108]

Similarly, the General Comment on Article 12 addresses the specific issue of access to justice in a section outlining the interconnection between the right to legal capacity and other core rights in the CRPD:

> State parties must ensure that persons with disabilities have access to justice on an equal basis with others. The recognition of the right to legal capacity is essential for access to justice in many respects. Persons with disabilities must be recognized as persons before the law with equal standing in courts and tribunals, in order to seek enforcement of their rights and obligations on an equal basis with others. States must also ensure that persons with disabilities have access to legal representation on an equal basis with others. This has been identified as a problem in many jurisdictions and must be remedied – including ensuring that individuals who experience interferences with their right to legal capacity have the opportunity to challenge these interferences (on their own behalf or with legal representation) and to defend their rights in court. (Persons with disabilities have often been excluded from key roles in the justice system, such as the ability to be a lawyer, judge, witness, or member of a jury.)

---

108 Committee on the Rights of Persons with Disabilities, *General Comment on Article 9* (CRPD/C/GC/2) para 33.

Police, social workers and other first responders must be trained to recognise persons with disabilities as full persons before the law and to give the same weight to complaints and statements from persons with disabilities as they would give to non-disabled persons. This entails training and awareness raising in these important professions. Persons with disabilities must also be granted legal capacity to testify on an equal basis with others. Article 12 guarantees support for the exercise of legal capacity, including the capacity to testify in judicial, administrative and other adjudicative proceedings. This support could take various forms, including recognising diverse communication methods, allowing video testimony in certain situations, procedural accommodations and other assistive methods. In addition, the judiciary must be trained and made aware of their obligation to respect the legal personhood of persons with disabilities, including legal agency and standing.[109]

While at the time of writing the Committee has not yet prepared a General Comment on Article 13, these existing General Comments represent an important development in illuminating the Committee's standpoint on access to justice, and may also provide context for future Concluding Observations on Article 13 for States Parties who have yet to undergo dialogue with the Committee.

5. Conclusion

In conclusion, I think it is clear that Article 13 does represent a new expression of the right to access justice and is an innovative provision which pushes the boundaries of existing international human rights norms, as well as posing questions about how it might apply in practice to the lived experience of people with disabilities. These issues may, in time, be addressed further by the Committee on the Rights of Persons with Disabilities. The Committee is currently at an early stage in the development of its jurisprudence on Article 13, but has already made some important points about witness credibility, alternative communication and procedural accommodations, including in the context of testifying in court, the need for legal aid to pursue justice claims for people with disabilities and the right to equal treatment in criminal proceedings, including a fair application of due process on a non-discriminatory basis.

It is worth noting that at the time of writing, the Committee has published its concluding observations on only 10 countries (Spain, Tunisia, Peru, Argentina, Hungary, China, Paraguay, Australia, Austria and El Salvador). It is therefore still very early days for the Committee and it may well address more substantive issues relating to the scope of Article 13 in the forthcoming dialogues with other States Parties. Naturally, the scope and interpretation of Article 13 will also be affected

---

109 Committee on the Rights of Persons with Disabilities, *General Comment on Article 12* (CRPD/C/GC/1), paras 34–35.

by the ways in which the Article is understood and applied at domestic level. It is therefore important for States to acknowledge the broad scope of Article 13 as being concerned with substantive, procedural, symbolic and participatory access to justice, as argued elsewhere,[110] and I will continue to use this framework to analyse the approach taken by various countries in the specific domains of access to justice considered in the following chapters.

---

110   A Lawson and E Flynn, 'Disability and Access to Justice in the European Union: Implications of the UN Convention on the Rights of Persons with Disabilities' (2013) 4 *European Yearbook of Disability Law* 7.

Chapter 3
Accessing the Law: Information, Advice and Representation

1. Introduction

As suggested in Chapter 1, people with disabilities experience many different barriers in accessing justice, and specifically accessing information about the law, their rights, and securing legal representation and advice where needed to advance their interests, as will be addressed in this chapter. These include information and communication barriers – such as a lack of materials in accessible formats (e.g. Braille, sign language, easy-to-read or electronic formats). Attitudinal barriers are also a key concern here – particularly where people with intellectual or psycho-social disabilities are refused access to legal representation or advice on the basis that they 'lack litigation capacity' needed to instruct counsel.[1] Many people with disabilities also live in environments where accessing independent legal information, advice and representation is particularly difficult – especially for those living in institutions. These barriers can be compounded by other factors – including low literacy levels among persons with disabilities, lack of specialised knowledge among legal professionals of the issues facing persons with disabilities, prohibitive costs of litigation, restrictive limits on the availability of legal aid, and barriers to using complaints mechanisms – including law enforcement or police, Ombudsmen, and equality infrastructure (such as Equality Authorities, specific Disability Rights Commissions/Ombudsmen, and National Human Rights Institutions).

In this chapter I will address the barriers facing people with disabilities in three key areas of access to law: access to legal information, access to legal advice and representation, and making a complaint about a rights-violation. While many of the substantive issues may overlap and also have relevance for the access to justice concerns discussed in the following two chapters, they are nonetheless important to address at the outset of any discussion of access to justice for people with disabilities, as, in many cases, these are the fundamental requirements for interacting with various aspects of the justice system. Examples of good practice, drawing from intersectional approaches to access to justice as specified in the Introduction, and opportunities for reform in the specific context of disability, will be discussed briefly in each section – and further expanded upon in the following

---

1   See for example G Ashton, 'Mental Challenges' (2012) 162 *New Law Journal* 7540.

2. Access to Legal Information

The inequality of people with disabilities' access to legal information, advice and representation is analogous to that experienced by other marginalised groups, whose situation has featured more prominently in recent literature. Indeed, although specificities in the process by which people with disabilities are disadvantaged by the justice system should not be overlooked, there are respects in which their experience mirrors the marginalisation of other groups. Ghai and Cottrell's understanding of the inequality of access to justice experienced by 'communities marginalized by history, social structure, gender, ethnicity, class or ideology',[2] resonates deeply for many people with disabilities:

> The principal cause is their ignorance of the law and the ways in which it could protect them against exploitation, violations of their rights and expropriations of their property and labor. Even if there is some awareness of the benefits of the legal system, they are too intimidated by its formalism and ... its arcane rules and procedures, that they can never be more than mere spectators, however deeply the matter before the court concerns their welfare, rights or dignity. They are unable to identify lawyers who might help them, and few of them can afford the expenses of legal action and trials. Often neither lawyers nor courts may be within easy reach. There are likely to be few lawyers or judges from their own community, with whom they might have some rapport, who can understand their circumstances and whom they can trust ...

> Even more fundamentally, there is deep mistrust of the state and its legal system ... They have little confidence that judges will hear their side of the story, and they may have in the past sensed hostility from the courts. The kind of evidence they can produce to support their assertions may not satisfy the formal rules of the admissibility of evidence ... They know that litigation is a long-drawn affair. Some of them may have faced threats or reprisals were they to approach state officials or lawyers with complaints against the wealthy ... Encounters with the state in the past resulted in deprivation of property or rights; they may perceive their security now in distance from the formal system.[3]

These experiences and perceptions underpin many people with disabilities' attempts to access justice, which generally commence with the search for accurate

---

2 Y Ghai and J Cottrell, 'Conclusions and Reflections' in Y Ghai and J Cottrell (eds), *Marginalised Communities and Access to Justice* (Routledge, 2010), 232.

3 Ibid., 232–233.

information about legal rights and entitlements. An oft-cited reason for the lack of litigation on issues of disability rights is a lack of awareness on the part of persons with disabilities and their supporters of the relevant legal rights and obligations which apply to their circumstances.[4] There are a number of interlinked factors which can explain this lack of awareness, the most obvious of which are institutionalisation, lack of opportunities to access legal information, and public information on legal rights being presented in inaccessible formats. These will be considered in turn here.

Institutionalisation as a Barrier to Accessing Legal Information

Policies of segregating people with disabilities and providing assistance and support services in institutional settings have been widely criticised since the mid-20th century onwards,[5] and the rise of the independent living movement has been instrumental in progressing community living with support as an alternative to institutionalised care.[6] While deinstitutionalisation policies and programmes for persons with disabilities have been progressed in many developed countries, including Canada, the United States, and the UK, in many countries it is still common for people with disabilities (both adults and children) to live in institutional settings – such as full-time residential services shared with other people with disabilities (with whom the individual has not chosen to live), group homes, or other types of congregated settings (social care homes, nursing homes, etc.).[7] This means that often the only other people with whom a person with disability might have contact could be paid carers or staff, family members, and other people with disabilities. A comprehensive overview of the independent living movement, and the challenges in practice in implementing effective, rights-based and affordable community-based supports for people with disabilities is beyond the scope of this chapter, but some key elements of the right to choose where and with whom to live, as articulated in Article 19 of the UN Convention on the Rights of Persons

---

4   See for example J Lord, K N Guernsey, J M Balfe, V L Karr and N Flowers (eds), *Human Rights: Yes! Action and Advocacy on the Rights of Persons with Disabilities* (Human Rights Resource Center, 2009), ch 12, para 12.1.

5   See for example S Borbasi, V Botroff, R P Williams, J Jones and H Douglas, '"No Going Back" to Institutional Care for People with Severe Disability: Reflections on Practice through an Interpretive Study' (2008) 30 *Disability and Rehabilitation* 837–847.

6   For a history of the independent living movement, see G DeJong, *The Movement for Independent Living: Origins, Ideology, and Implications for Disability Research* (University Centers for International Rehabilitation, Michigan State University, 1979).

7   See generally, P She and D C Stapleton, *A Review of Disability Data for the Institutional Population: Research Brief* (Rehabilitation Research and Training Center on Disability Demographics and Statistics, Cornell University, 2006). In the specific context of mental health in Europe, see Open Society Foundations and Mental Health Europe, *Mapping Exclusion: Institutional and Community-Based Services in the Mental Health Field in Europe* (Mental Health Europe, 2012).

with Disabilities, will be explored here, in terms of their implications for effective access to justice, and access to legal information in particular.

People with disabilities who live in institutional settings, or in places and with people not of their choosing, may face additional barriers in accessing information about the law, their legal rights, and responsibilities. First, even if residential services are subject to inspection by authorities, and required to meet minimum standards in ensuring that residents have access to information about their rights,[8] in practice, many people with disabilities living in these circumstances may not be in a position to use whatever information about rights is provided to them. This may be due to a combination of factors, including, for example, the lack of choice in respect of many aspects of their lives (leading to a corresponding decline in decision-making skills and a lack of confidence that their circumstances could change for the better), the lack of advocacy support to 'speak up' about their rights or request legal information, and the absence of alternative support options to institutionalisation. These factors combined might lead individuals to believe that regardless of their legal rights, their options for support in reality are limited, and any challenge to authority might result in further limitation of their options.

Institutionalisation is also connected with a whole host of other problems which cause barriers to accessing justice for persons with disabilities. These include a lack of access to public services generally available to the community (such as citizens' information or advice centres), and legal barriers which might prevent family members, advocates or legal professionals from accessing the person in order to provide legal information, such as adult guardianship (especially where the appointed guardian is the director of the institution in which the person resides[9]), or other legal orders concerning the person's placement in the institution which restrict what kinds of access to the community or contact with others the individual might have. An example of this dilemma is the recent English case of *Stokes City Council v Maddocks*,[10] where the Court of Protection held a woman in contempt of court for violating an order not to remove her father from a care home, in one instance, in order to bring him to see a solicitor.

The man in question was in the proceedings represented by the Official Solicitor, as it was deemed that he lacked 'litigation capacity' to instruct his own legal representation, and the court in this case made clear that not only was his

---

8   Such standards and inspections are routinely provided for in many developed countries. For example, in the UK, the Care Quality Commission and Mental Health Commission undertakes this work, and in Ireland these inspections are carried out by the Health Information and Quality Authority and the Mental Health Services Inspectorate.

9   This issue is particularly problematic and common in many Central and Eastern European countries, as has been highlighted by recent jurisprudence in the European Court of Human Rights. For more information see Mental Disability Advocacy Center and SHINE, 'Out of Sight: Human Rights in Psychiatric Hospitals and Social Care Institutions in Croatia' (Hungary and Zagreb, 2011).

10   *SCC v LM & Ors* [2013] EWHC 1137 (COP) 12 April 2012.

daughter liable for contempt of court for bringing him to see a different solicitor, but that the solicitor herself risked contempt of court if she had attempted to advise him. It is unclear from the judgment if the solicitor would risk contempt whether or not she was aware that he lacked litigation capacity and was subject to an order from the Court of Protection, but in any case, the risk of contempt of court is a grave deterrent for legal practitioners who might seek to advise people with disabilities – and it is especially concerning if this could apply to a solicitor who had no knowledge that a potential client was subject to such an order.[11] The issue of litigation capacity will be discussed separately in this chapter, although this case also highlights concerns regarding its use as a barrier to accessing legal information, advice and representation.

Therefore, a vital strategy to overcome barriers to accessing justice stemming from institutionalisation would be to pursue greater choice for persons with disabilities in receiving support in the community, in parallel with recognising that, since so many people still live in institutionalised settings, concerted efforts should be made to ensure that residents have as much access as possible to legal information in a format they can understand and use. This could be achieved through a number of mechanisms, including more stringent requirements on residential service providers to raise awareness about rights, to provide people with disabilities with greater access to general legal information services available to the public (including access to, and training in how to use, the vast array of resources on these topics available on the Internet), and greater access for family members, friends, independent advocacy or in-reach systems to provide this kind of information to people with disabilities who are living in institutions.

Even where people with disabilities have access to community-based supports, live independently, or with family members, they may still face barriers to accessing independent legal information. Where people seek legal information on their rights which may involve disputes with family members, carers, or others involved in providing daily support, many of the same barriers facing people with disabilities in institutional settings may also apply – as their access to legal information may be restricted by care-givers, or the individuals themselves may lack the confidence or the skills to request this information, or simply be unaware that this information is available to them in the first place. Even where legal information is freely available (e.g. from citizens' information or advice bureaux) it may not be provided in a form that is accessible to people with disabilities. This brings to the fore a core issue in disability equality which merits further discussion: the interaction between individual requests for reasonable accommodation, and broader accessibility, or universal design, of goods and services (in this case, legal services and legal information).

---

11 For more on this case see L Series, 'Human Rights will be in Touch', available at: <http://thesmallplaces.wordpress.com/2013/04/24/human-rights-will-be-in-touch/comment-page-1/> (accessed 13 March 2014).

Reasonable Accommodation Obligations for Legal Information

The term 'reasonable accommodation' (also in some domestic contexts referred to as reasonable adjustment)[12] refers to the obligation to modify existing structures, systems or processes, to accommodate the particular requirements of an individual with disability. Lawson defines reasonable accommodation duties as 'requir[ing] duty-bearers to recognise that individuals with certain characteristics (such as physical, sensory, intellectual or psychosocial impairment or a particular religious belief) might be placed at a disadvantage by the application to them of conventional requirements or systems'.[13] Waddington states further that

> [t]he obligation to make a reasonable accommodation is based on the recognition that, on occasions, the interaction between an individual's inherent characteristics, such as impairment, sex, religion, or belief, and the physical or social environment can result in the inability to perform a particular function or job in the conventional manner. The characteristic is therefore relevant in that it can lead to an individual being faced with a barrier that prevents him or her from benefiting from an ... opportunity that is open to others who do not share that characteristic. The resulting disadvantage is exclusion from the job market, or a restricted set of ... opportunities.[14]

In the context of legal services or information for people with disabilities, for example, this might mean providing information in different formats, such as Braille, electronic formats, sign language, or easy-to-read. The 'reasonableness' component of the obligation to accommodate people with disabilities refers to a proportionality test, i.e. the accommodation provided should generally not pose an undue burden (financial or otherwise) on the person providing it.[15] The CRPD, and many domestic disability discrimination laws, recognise that failure to provide reasonable accommodation constitutes discrimination on the basis of disability. Therefore, reasonable accommodation is considered part of the right to equality and non-discrimination owed to an individual. As a result, the 'accommodation' should be tailored and adjusted to the individual's specific requirements, as long

---

12 See Disability Discrimination Act 1995 England and Wales.

13 A Lawson, *Disability and Equality Law in Britain: The Role of Reasonable Adjustment* (Hart Publishing, 2008), 1.

14 L Waddington, 'Reasonable Accommodation' in D Schiek, L Waddington and M Bell (eds), *Cases, Materials and Text on National, Supranational and International Non-Discrimination Law* (Hart Publishing, 2007), 631.

15 The terminology used in legislation varies across different jurisdictions. In the CRPD, the term used for proportionality is 'not imposing a disproportionate or undue burden'. Some jurisdictions impose a lower threshold for certain areas, e.g. the Equal Status Act 2000 in Ireland uses not exceeding 'a nominal cost' as the threshold for reasonable accommodation in respect of provision of goods and services, section 4(2).

as this can be done without placing an undue burden on the body providing the accommodation.

Legal services and information are generally provided either directly by lawyers in private firms, or by public or non-profit bodies which have a specific remit to provide such information and advice. These bodies include equality and human rights bodies, Ombudsman offices, legal clinics (both general legal advice services and disability-specific clinics), citizens'/public information services, and others. For people with disabilities to access these services and obtain the relevant legal information and advice, certain forms of reasonable accommodation may be required. A deaf person visiting a drop-in legal information centre may need the assistance of a sign-language interpreter, and yet the cost of providing this may pose a disproportionate burden on a local community organisation. Public bodies may have greater resources and, as a result, greater duties to accommodate, but may still not be able to meet the specific requirements of some individuals with disabilities. Nevertheless, these constraints and requirements impact on people with disabilities' opportunities to access effective legal information and advice.

Accessibility of Legal Information and Advice

Given the diversity in requirements of individuals, and since corresponding needs to be accommodated will vary, it is also worth considering whether legal information and services can be provided in a way that is more generally accessible to people with disabilities as a whole, or, at a minimum, to specific groups of people with disabilities. This, in short, would be to take a 'universal design' approach to enhance the accessibility of legal services and information to people with disabilities.

Much debate has been generated about accessibility in recent years – and its inclusion as a stand-alone article in the UN CRPD has prompted discussions about whether it is a value, a principle or an individual right.[16] Unlike reasonable accommodation, accessibility does not seem, at least in the CRPD, to form part of the individual right to equality and non-discrimination, but perhaps stems instead from the right to participate in decision-making processes which affect the person, and the right to live independently and be included in the community.[17] Another crucial difference between reasonable accommodation and accessibility is that while reasonable accommodation is an individualised response, accessibility measures are designed to accommodate groups of persons with certain types of disabilities (e.g. making information available electronically for people with visual impairments).

---

16 See generally J Lord, 'Accessibility and Human Rights Fusion in the CRPD: Assessing the Scope and Content of the Accessibility Principle and Duty under the CRPD' delivered at the General Day of Discussion on Accessibility, Committee on the Rights of Persons with Disabilities, Geneva, 7 October 2010.
17 See Articles 4(3) and 19, CRPD.

The two concepts are often confused because, in many cases, they require the same action and result in the same outcome. However, the process of negotiating what the requirements are is very different for accessibility measures to what it should be for reasonable accommodation. Since reasonable accommodation is particular to the individual, only that individual can determine what type of adjustment is required. By contrast, in terms of accessibility, where a service provider wishes to make its services accessible, the legal obligation may simply require them to consult with representative organisations of persons with disabilities, or to adhere to some established industry standard (e.g. building codes) as to what accessibility requirements (e.g. ramps, accessible bathrooms, etc.) are needed.

The Committee's General Comment on Article 9 sets out the distinction between reasonable accommodation duties and legal obligations to provide accessibility as follows:

> Accessibility is group related, whereas reasonable accommodation is individual related. This means that the duty to provide accessibility is an *ex ante* duty. That means the State party has the duty to provide accessibility before individual request to enter or use a place or service. State parties need to set accessibility standards which have to be negotiated with organizations of persons with disabilities, and these standards need to be prescribed to service providers, builders, and other relevant stakeholders.[18]

One of the key arguments in favour of accessibility or universal design approaches has been that these benefit the public more generally, as the purpose of universal design is to make goods and services available and usable by the greatest number of individuals possible. A commonly used example regarding physical accessibility is the fact that ramps, kerb-cuts and low-floor buses lead to greater access for parents with buggies as well as people using wheelchairs. In the context of access to legal information and advice, increasing accessibility for people with disabilities could also lead to greater access for others in a variety of ways. The availability of legal information in a range of formats (e.g. plain English and easy-to-read) could benefit more than just people with disabilities (e.g. those whose first language is not English and people with low literacy skills).

Indeed, many campaigns for legal information to be made available in 'plain English' have stemmed from outside the disability community. One of the most prominent examples is the Plain English Campaign in the UK, spearheaded by Chrissie Maher, concerned that people who had little or no literacy, due to a lack of educational opportunities, were being denied access to information about their basic rights and entitlements – including to social benefits and supports. Maher started her campaign by publishing plain English community newspapers – the

---

18 Committee on the Rights of Persons with Disabilities, *General Comment on Article 9* (CRPD/C/GC/2) at para 22.

Tuebrook Bugle and the *Liverpool News*.[19] These newspapers were designed to be easy to read for adults with poor literacy, and also provided easy-to-understand guides to social welfare benefits and other basic entitlements.

The campaign grew from a local initiative to a nationwide effort when in 1979, Maher and supporters protested in Parliament Square by shredding hundreds of official government forms (including benefit forms) which they felt were inaccessible to those who needed them most.[20] In the two decades that followed, Maher developed a number of initiatives to incentivise government and business actors to produce information that was easy to understand – including the 'Inside Write Awards' for civil servants, the 'Crystal Mark' standard for accessible documents, and the 'Golden Bull Awards' to highlight examples of bad practice or inaccessible public information.[21] Ultimately the campaign spread internationally, hosting workshops and developing links with the United States, India, Canada, Australia, New Zealand, Brazil and Sweden, among others.[22] Maher's words on the importance of easily-understood legal information still resonate in today's context:

> Lawyers will always be needed to explain when everyday language can be used and which words have a specific legal meaning. In the past, lawyers have been accused of using convoluted language merely to baffle and overcharge their clients. But if lawyers adopted our principles when writing to clients and when they drafted law text, I believe that the public's perception of the legal profession would improve. Many lawyers still believe that plain-language documents are 'unsafe' but, unlike traditionally drafted legal documents, none of those that we have worked on have ever had to be presented in court for interpretation. Many lawyers also failed to realize that a plain-language approach to producing law texts involved much more than simply getting rid of archaic legal language.[23]

It should, however, be noted that while producing legal information in plain English can be useful for people with disabilities, as well as others, for many this step is still not sufficient to ensure full accessibility. The term 'plain English' should be distinguished from the term 'easy to read' which is often used to describe documents made accessible to people with intellectual or learning disabilities,

---

19 Plain English Campaign, *Born to Crusade: One Woman's Battle to Wipe Out Gobbledygook and Legalese* (Plain English Campaign, 2009).

20 Martin Cutts and Chrissie Maher, *The Plain English Story* (Plain English Campaign, 1986).

21 Plain English Campaign, *Born to Crusade: One Woman's Battle to Wipe Out Gobbledygook and Legalese* (Plain English Campaign, 2009), 10.

22 Joseph Kimble, 'Plain English: A Charter for Clear Writing' (1992) 9 *TM Cooley L. Rev.* 1.

23 Plain English Campaign, *Born to Crusade: One Woman's Battle to Wipe Out Gobbledygook and Legalese* (Plain English Campaign, 2009), 8.

using pictures or images to accompany simplified language.[24] In recent years, easy-to-read documents have become more widely produced alongside official publications relating to people with disabilities – for example, there are several different easy-to-read versions of the UN Convention on the Rights of Persons with Disabilities,[25] and Ireland's Housing Strategy for People with Disabilities has been published in an easy-to-read version.[26] These developments may be in part attributed to increasing requests for accessible documents made as part of reasonable accommodation requirements or increasing awareness of accessibility standards.

Equally, the provision of legal information in physically accessible locations could benefit others beyond people with disabilities. Nevertheless, some measures which increase access for persons with disabilities (e.g. sign-language interpretation) do not incur benefits for non-disabled people, but may still fall within the obligations to provide accessible legal services, or may be necessary to reasonable accommodate clients with disabilities within the requirements of anti-discrimination legislation.

3. Legal Aid and Legal Representation for People with Disabilities

One topical issue in this context is the availability of legal aid. In many countries worldwide, access to legal aid is increasingly restricted – especially beyond criminal legal aid (which most liberal democracies recognise as a fundamental right). For many people with disabilities, access to civil legal aid is problematic, as further to the means test which all individuals generally need to undergo in order to establish eligibility for such aid, people with disabilities experience additional barriers, including, and perhaps especially, finding a lawyer who is familiar with disability issues and understands the application of the law in a disability context. A report by the Norah Fry Research Centre in the UK confirms these barriers, and highlights the following experiences of people with learning disabilities seeking to access legal services:

> Very few of the people with learning disabilities who took part in the study had initiated contact with a legal service themselves. Most of those who had done so

---

24 See for example, British Institute of Learning Disabilities, Easy Read Information (2013), available at: <http://www.bild.org.uk/easy-read/easy-read-information/> (accessed 31 October 2013).

25 See UN Convention on the Rights of Persons with Disabilities, Easy Read Versions, available at: <http://www.un.org/disabilities/default.asp?navid=14&pid=150> (accessed 31 October 2013).

26 Department of the Environment, Community and Local Government, *National Housing Strategy for People with a Disability – Easy to Read* (Dublin, 2013), available at: <http://environ.ie/en/Publications/DevelopmentandHousing/Housing/FileDownLoad,34362,en.pdf> (accessed 31 October 2013).

had used Citizens Advice Bureaux or a solicitor known to their family ... Most people with learning disabilities were unclear about the role of legal services and did not understand when recourse to legal advice might be considered. They relied upon people they trust to know what to do when confronted with a problem. However, these supporters were not always equipped to recognize the need for legal assistance or how to access a service.[27]

The issues of legal education and disability awareness are addressed more fully in Chapter 5, but it is worth considering here how issues of access affect people with disabilities seeking legal advice.

Partly as a response to barriers in obtaining legal advice, a number of free legal advice clinics have emerged in recent decades, focusing solely on disability rights issues. Some prominent examples include the Disability Law Service in the UK,[28] ARCH Disability Law Centre in Canada,[29] the Disability Discrimination Legal Service in Australia[30] and the National Disability Rights Network in the United States.[31] This is in addition to a number of more impairment-specific legal advice services, which are sometimes provided directly by support organisations for people with specific types of disabilities, such as the Deaf Law Centre in the UK, a service provided by the Royal Association for Deaf People.[32]

While these clinics and centres all provide an important service which is badly needed, their existence suggests that general legal aid services are not really accessible to people with disabilities, and therefore, while these specialised services continue to operate, there may be less pressure on governments to increase the accessibility of publicly available legal advice services to people with disabilities.

---

27 Norah Fry Research Centre, *What Happens when People with Learning Disabilities Need Advice about the Law?* (Bristol, 2013), 2.

28 See Disability Law Service, Accessing Advice, available at: <http://www.dls.org.uk/Advice/> (accessed 31 October 2013).

29 See ARCH Disability Law Centre, Services for Individuals, available at: <http://www.archdisabilitylaw.ca/?q=services-individuals> (accessed 31 October 2013). This centre is based in the Province of Ontario.

30 See Disability Discrimination Legal Service, About Us, available at: <http://www.communitylaw.org.au/clc_ddls/cb_pages/about_us.php> (accessed 31 October 2013). This service is based in the State of Victoria.

31 See National Disability Rights Network, NDRN Member Agencies, available at: <http://www.ndrn.org/en/ndrn-member-agencies.html> (accessed 31 October 2013). This network is the non-profit membership organisation for the federally mandated Protection and Advocacy (P&A) Systems and Client Assistance Programs (CAP). There is a P&A/CAP agency in every state and US territory as well as one serving the Native American population in the four corners region. Collectively, the P&A/CAP network is the largest provider of legally based advocacy services to people with disabilities in the United States.

32 See RAD Deaf Law Centre, available at: <http://royaldeaf.org.uk/Deaf_Law_Centre> (accessed 31 October 2013).

Indeed, arguments to this effect have already been made to justify legal aid cuts in the UK, as follows:

> While the Government has stated that the [Legal Aid, Sentencing and Punishment of Offenders Act] (2013) may have an adverse impact on civil legal aid clients, especially disabled clients who 'may be disproportionately affected' (Ministry of Justice, 2013, p.150), it has defended the changes by arguing that while legal aid is an 'essential part of the justice system ... the fact is it is paid for by taxpayers and resources are not limitless'.[33]

It is certainly possible for accessible public services to coexist with specialist legal services which cater to the specific concerns of people with disabilities – but the more the burden of addressing the legal issues faced by people with disabilities is taken up by civil society, the less incentive there may be to increase the accessibility of public services. This is a quandary which is certainly not exclusive to disability, and indeed, has been raised in many other contexts regarding clinical legal education, including the provision of specialised law clinics for homeless people, older people and immigrants.[34] However, it is one that should not be forgotten in the broader context of increasing access to legal advice and assistance for people with disabilities.

Discourse on accessibility and the legal obligations to provide access in the spheres of information and communication in particular (which are perhaps those most relevant for access to the law) is in its infancy – and a conclusive finding on the application of these obligations is beyond the scope of this chapter. Nevertheless, as international jurisprudence on this issue continues to develop, providers of legal services will have to come to grips with these concerns, and particularly, as stated in the General Comment on Article 9, may have to negotiate with organisations of persons with disabilities in order to understand how legal information and advice can be provided in an accessible manner.

4. Litigation Capacity: Opportunities to Instruct Legal Representation

Once people with disabilities have overcome the barriers to accessing legal advice, they may face additional barriers in terms of the recognition of their legal capacity which significantly impact on their ability to access legal representation, and to challenge perceived rights-violations in court. Most legal systems recognise certain individuals as being incapable of litigating – often based on a standard of 'mental capacity' or decision-making ability, which deems the person not to have

---

33 Norah Fry Research Centre, *What Happens when People with Learning Disabilities Need Advice about the Law?* (Bristol, 2013), 9.

34 See for example, S M Ashar, 'Law Clinics and Collective Mobilization' (2008) 14 *Clinical Law Review* 355.

legal standing to litigate in court on their own behalf, or not to have capacity to instruct a lawyer, or both. Therefore, it is important to consider how legal capacity impacts on the right to litigate and access to individual legal representation, as a potential barrier to accessing justice for people with disabilities.

In the context of litigation capacity and access to justice this separation of mental capacity and legal capacity is crucial. It is worth considering here how the use of mental capacity as a proxy for legal capacity has unfolded in the laws of various jurisdictions in a general sense, before I address the specific issue of litigation capacity in detail. Dhanda outlines three general approaches to the assessment of mental capacity which lead to denials of legal capacity throughout the world.[35] The first type is the status approach, whereby an individual is denied legal capacity based on her status as a disabled person – and sometimes as a person with a specific impairment type, such as a cognitive disability. This approach is based on a presumption of incapacity that is generally predicated on a medical diagnosis of impairment.[36] The outcome approach provides a mechanism for removing or restricting legal capacity based on the perception that the individual has made a bad decision, again, in a manner which is linked to the individual's disability. A common example of this approach is the detention of voluntary patients in psychiatric hospitals following a request to leave, in order to determine if the individual should be involuntarily detained.[37] In this way, Arstein-Kerslake and I support Dhanda's contention that the outcome approach is very similar to the status approach since once the individual is diagnosed as 'disabled' her decision-making skills are automatically questioned.[38]

Under the functional approach, an assessment is carried out to determine whether, at a particular time, the individual understands the meaning and consequences of the decision to be made. The general components of the test are whether the person can use, weigh and retain information in order to make a decision, understand the consequences of the decision and communicate the decision to others.[39] If it is found that the person does not meet the prescribed

---

35 For a discussion of the legal construction of incompetence and explanations of the various approaches, see A Dhanda, 'Legal Capacity in the Disability Rights Convention: Stranglehold of the Past or Lodestar for the Future?' (2006–2007) 34 *Syracuse J. Int'l L. & Com.* 429.

36 An example of the status approach can be found in Ireland, where a 'ward of court' is defined as '*a person who has been declared to be of unsound mind and incapable of managing his person or property*'. See Rules of the Superior Courts, Order 67(I)(1) (S.I. No. 15/1986) (Ireland); see also Lunacy Regulation Act 1871 (c. 22/1871) (Ireland).

37 See for example, section 23, Mental Health Act 2001 (Ireland).

38 See E Flynn and A Arstein-Kerslake, 'Legislating Personhood: Realising the Right to Support in Exercising Legal Capacity' (2014) 10(1) *International Journal of Law in Context* 81 at 86; A Dhanda, 'Legal Capacity in the Disability Rights Convention: Stranglehold of the Past or Lodestar for the Future?' (2006–2007) 34 *Syracuse J. Int'l L. & Com.* 429, 433.

39 See for example section 3(1) e.g. Mental Capacity Act, 2005 (England and Wales).

standard, then the individual's legal capacity is denied for that particular decision. Perhaps the most well-known example of this can be found in the Mental Capacity Act 2005 (England and Wales), which defines a person who is unable to make a decision for himself as someone unable to understand the information relevant to the decision, to retain that information, to use or weigh that information as part of the process of making the decision, or to communicate the decision.[40] Although the standard for the removal of legal capacity appears to be the perceived functioning of the individual in relation to decision-making; practically, the person's mental impairment also plays a major role in the determination. Therefore, Arstein-Kerslake and I argue that the functional approach, although it may appear facially neutral, still indirectly discriminates against persons with disabilities;[41] albeit more subtly than the status approach.

The laws which restrict or remove the legal capacity of persons with disabilities have a direct impact on that individual's legal standing and recognition as a person before the law, which is a core element of ensuring effective access to justice. This section will therefore consider the impact of Article 12 CRPD in a general sense, before addressing how the new thinking in the CRPD might be applied when obtaining and instructing legal representation and being granted legal standing to pursue rights-violations.

The Right to Legal Capacity in Article 12 CRPD

The right to legal capacity is recognised in Article 12 CRPD, which is closely connected to Article 13 on access to justice, as discussed in the previous chapter. Article 12 represents a paradigm shift in understanding the right to legal capacity. Prior to the entry into force of the Convention, there was no international human rights standard that guaranteed to persons with disabilities the enjoyment of legal capacity on an equal basis with non-disabled people. As a result, in many countries around the world, people with disabilities were deprived of their legal capacity – meaning that they were denied the right to make many legally binding decisions – including entering contracts, voting, retaining legal representation and consenting to (or refusing) medical treatment. In many liberal democracies today, it is still considered acceptable to deny people with disabilities the right to exercise their legal capacity, based on the person's 'mental capacity' or decision-making ability. This particularly affects those with intellectual disabilities, psycho-social disabilities, dementia, autism, and other neurological or cognitive disabilities.

Article 12 states as follows:

---

40   Section 2(1), Mental Capacity Act, 2005 (England and Wales).
41   See E Flynn and A Arstein-Kerslake, 'Legislating Personhood: Realising the Right to Support in Exercising Legal Capacity' (2014) 10(1) *International Journal of Law in Context* 81 at 87, citing L A Frolik, 'Plenary Guardianship: An Analysis, A Critique and a Proposal for Reform' (1981) 23 *Ariz. L. Rev.* 599, 604, where the author calls functional assessments of capacity a 'legal fiction'.

1. States Parties reaffirm that persons with disabilities have the right to recognition everywhere as persons before the law.

2. States Parties shall recognize that persons with disabilities enjoy legal capacity on an equal basis with others in all aspects of life.

3. States Parties shall take appropriate measures to provide access by persons with disabilities to the support they may require in exercising their legal capacity.

4. States Parties shall ensure that all measures that relate to the exercise of legal capacity provide for appropriate and effective safeguards to prevent abuse in accordance with international human rights law. Such safeguards shall ensure that measures relating to the exercise of legal capacity respect the rights, will and preferences of the person, are free of conflict of interest and undue influence, are proportional and tailored to the person's circumstances, apply for the shortest time possible and are subject to regular review by a competent, independent and impartial authority or judicial body. The safeguards shall be proportional to the degree to which such measures affect the person's rights and interests.

5. Subject to the provisions of this article, States Parties shall take all appropriate and effective measures to ensure the equal right of persons with disabilities to own or inherit property, to control their own financial affairs and to have equal access to bank loans, mortgages and other forms of financial credit, and shall ensure that persons with disabilities are not arbitrarily deprived of their property.

Article 12(1) reaffirms the status of persons with disabilities as persons before the law, i.e. as individuals possessing legal personality, with legal status and agency. This is confirmed by Article 12(2), which extends the right to enjoy legal capacity on an equal basis with others to all aspects of life. Some might argue that functional assessments of mental capacity (which result in the removal of an individual's legal capacity in respect of a particular decision)[42] conform with Article 12(2), since all adults, regardless of whether or not they have a disability, could, in theory, be subject to a functional assessment of their mental capacity, and have their legal capacity removed for a particular decision if they fail to meet a certain standard of decision-making ability. However, the General Comment

---

42 The functional assessment of mental capacity is broadly understood as a four-part test which assesses an individual's decision-making skills, including the ability to understand information relevant to the decision, to use, weigh and retain the relevant information, to appreciate the consequences of the decision and to communicate the decision to others. For more on the functional test and its problems from a human rights perspective for people with disabilities, see A Dhanda, 'Legal Capacity in the Disability Rights Convention: Stranglehold of the Past or Lodestar for the Future?' (2006–2007) 34 *Syracuse J. Int'l L. & Com.* 429 at 436.

on Article 12 clarifies now that where functional assessments of mental capacity exist, and are disproportionately applied to people with disabilities, they constitute a violation of human rights norms. The Committee contends that Article 12 must be read in conjunction with Article 5 (Equality and Non-Discrimination), and that this reading prohibits the use of functional assessment of mental capacity to justify substitute decision-making, as the functional test is discriminatory (in both purpose and effect) towards persons with disabilities.[43]

The General Comment on Article 12 also clearly states, for the first time in international human rights law, that an individual's mental capacity cannot be used as a reason to deprive that person of legal capacity, even if the deprivation of legal capacity relates to a single decision.

> Legal capacity and mental capacity are distinct concepts. Legal capacity is the ability to hold rights and duties (legal standing) and to exercise these rights and duties (legal agency). It is the key to accessing meaningful participation in society. Mental capacity refers to the decision-making skills of an individual, which naturally vary among individuals and may be different for a given individual depending on many factors, including environmental and social factors ... Under article 12 of the Convention, perceived or actual deficits in mental capacity must not be used as justification for denying legal capacity.[44]

Article 12(3) CRPD contains a novel addition to international human rights norms – a State obligation to provide the supports required to exercise legal capacity. This support can take many forms, including, but not limited to, formal agreements with supporters who assist in certain areas of decision-making. Further explanation of the types of measures which constitute support to exercise legal capacity is provided in the General Comment, which states:

> 'Support' is a broad term capable of encompassing both informal and formal support arrangements, and arrangements of varying type and intensity. For example, persons with disabilities may choose one or more trusted support persons to assist them in exercising their legal capacity for various types of decisions, or may use other forms of support, such as peer support, advocacy (including self advocacy support), or assistance in communication. Support for the legal capacity of persons with disabilities might include measures encompassing universal design and accessibility, – such as requiring private and public actors such as banks and financial institutions to provide understandable information or the provision of professional sign language interpretation –, in order to enable persons with disabilities to perform the legal acts required to

---

[43] Committee on the Rights of Persons with Disabilities, *General Comment on Article 12* (CRPD/C/GC/1) at paras 9, 21 and 28.

[44] Committee on the Rights of Persons with Disabilities, *General Comment on Article 12* (CRPD/C/GC/1) at para 12.

open a bank account, conclude contracts or conduct other social transactions. Support can also constitute the development and recognition of diverse and unconventional methods of communication, especially for those who use non-verbal communication to express their will and preferences.[45]

Article 12(4) then addresses the safeguards required for all measures regarding the exercise of legal capacity. Some argue that this provision allows for some limited forms of guardianship to remain if the appropriate safeguards are in place;[46] however, the Committee on the Rights of Persons with Disabilities has not accepted this argument from any of the countries it has examined to date – even those countries which have interpretative declarations or reservations on Article 12 which state that Article 12 permits some limited forms of substituted decision-making.[47]

The key phrase in Article 12(4), and one which has been used repeatedly by the Committee on the Rights of Persons with Disabilities in its Concluding Observations on the countries examined to date, is that safeguards should be designed to respect the 'rights, will and preferences' of the person. The term 'best interests' does not appear in paragraph four, or in Article 12 at all. Therefore, it is clear that safeguards which are paternalistic in nature, or which envisage the use of substitute decision-making, are not permitted under Article 12. Finally, Article 12(5) refers specifically to the need to respect legal capacity with regard to financial affairs and property – an issue which was subject to extensive debates during the negotiation of the CRPD.

The Committee has repeatedly called for the abolition of regimes of substitute decision-making and their replacement with systems of supported decision-making in each of the 10 Concluding Observations it has issued to date.[48] In each of its

---

45 Committee on the Rights of Persons with Disabilities, *General Comment on Article 12* (CRPD/C/GC/1) at para 15.

46 See Canada's Reservation to the CRPD, Article 12 (11 March 2010). However, the United Nations Committee on the Rights of Persons with Disabilities (CRPD) has recently noted in several of its concluding observations that steps should be taken to replace substituted decision-making with supported decision-making. Consideration of reports submitted by States parties under article 35 of the Convention: concluding observations, Tunisia, Committee on the Rights of Persons with Disabilities (CRPD), 5th Sess., at 4, UN Doc CRPD/C/TUN/CO/1 (11–15 April 2011); Consideration of reports submitted by States parties under article 35 of the Convention: concluding observations, Spain, Committee on the Rights of Persons with Disabilities (CRPD), 6th Sess., at 5, UN Doc CRPD/C/ESP/CO/1 (19–23 September 2011).

47 See for example Consideration of reports submitted by States parties under article 35 of the Convention: concluding observations, Australia, Committee on the Rights of Persons with Disabilities (CRPD), 10th Sess., UN Doc CRPD/C/AUS/CO/1 (2–13 September 2013).

48 See for example Consideration of reports submitted by States parties under article 35 of the Convention: concluding observations, Tunisia, Committee on the Rights of

Concluding Observations on these countries, the Committee expressed concern 'that no measures have been undertaken to replace substitute decision-making by supported decision-making in the exercise of legal capacity'.[49] With respect to all countries, the Committee recommended that the states 'review the laws allowing for guardianship and trusteeship, and take action to develop laws and policies to replace regimes of substitute decision-making by supported decision-making, which respects the person's autonomy, will and preferences'.[50] This approach demonstrates the Committee's acceptance of the need for a support model of legal capacity to be implemented in States Parties to the Convention; and following the publication of the Committee's General Comment more guidance has been provided on the definitions of 'substitute decision-making regimes' and 'supported decision-making' respectively. Substitute decision-making is defined as follows:

> where 1) legal capacity is removed from the individual, even if this is just in respect of a single decision; 2) a substituted decision-maker can be appointed by someone other than the individual, and this can be done against his or her will or 3) any decision made is bound by what is believed to be in the objective 'best interests' of the individual – as opposed to being based on the individual's own will and preferences.[51]

By contrast, the Committee provides a broad interpretation of 'supported decision-making', as 'a cluster of various support options which give primacy to a person's will and preferences and respect human rights norms'.[52] A non-exhaustive list of support options is provided in the General Comment, from relatively minor accommodations, such as accessible information, to more formal measures such

---

Persons with Disabilities (CRPD), 5th Sess., at 4, UN Doc CRPD/C/TUN/CO/1 (11–15 April 2011); Consideration of reports submitted by States parties under article 35 of the Convention: concluding observations, Spain, Committee on the Rights of Persons with Disabilities (CRPD), 6th Sess., at 5, UN Doc CRPD/C/ESP/CO/1 (19–23 September 2011).

49 Consideration of reports submitted by States parties under article 35 of the Convention: Concluding observations of the Committee on the Rights of Persons with Disabilities, Committee on the Rights of Persons with Disabilities: 5th Sess., 4 (11–15 April 2011), available at: <http://www.ohchr.org/EN/HRBodies/CRPD/Pages/Session5.aspx> (accessed 26 April 2013).

50 Consideration of reports submitted by States parties under article 35 of the Convention: Concluding observations of the Committee on the Rights of Persons with Disabilities, Committee on the Rights of Persons with Disabilities, 6th Sess., 5 (19–23 September 2011), available at: <http://www.ohchr.org/EN/HRBodies/CRPD/Pages/Session6.aspx> (accessed 17 May 2013).

51 Committee on the Rights of Persons with Disabilities, General Comment on Article 12 (CRPD/C/GC/1), at para 23.

52 Committee on the Rights of Persons with Disabilities, General Comment on Article 12 (CRPD/C/GC/1), at para 25.

as supported decision-making agreements nominating one or more supporters to assist the individual in making and communicating certain decisions to others.[53]

Importantly, the General Comment also specifically addresses the interaction between Articles 12 and 13 and the impact which recognition of legal capacity has on access to justice, acknowledged in the previous chapter:

> Persons with disabilities must be recognized as persons before the law with equal standing in courts and tribunals, in order to seek enforcement of their rights and obligations on an equal basis with others. States must also ensure that persons with disabilities have access to legal representation on an equal basis with others. This has been identified as a problem in many jurisdictions and must be remedied – including ensuring that individuals who experience interferences with their right to legal capacity have the opportunity to challenge these interferences (on their own behalf or with legal representation) and to defend their rights in court.[54]

Given this strong focus on a universal understanding of legal capacity, the removal of mental capacity as a proxy for legal capacity and the obligation on the State to provide access to the support an individual may require in exercising legal capacity, the following section will consider how this support model could apply in the context of legal representation and litigation capacity.

Legal Capacity and Litigation Capacity: Support to Instruct a Lawyer?

As described above, many States use a functional assessment of mental capacity to deem a person to lack legal capacity, and this also applies to the context of 'litigation capacity'. A prominent example of a functional approach to litigation capacity can be found in England and Wales, which provides for the appointment of the Official Solicitor as a litigation friend of last resort to individuals who lack the mental capacity to litigate, according to the Mental Capacity Act 2005.[55] In other countries, where the status or outcome approaches to mental capacity are used in the general legal framework, individuals can be placed under plenary (full) guardianship, whereby the individual is denied all legal capacity and a substitute decision-maker will make all the person's decisions which are to have legal effect. Partial guardianship is also used in many countries to appoint substitute decision-makers for particular areas of decision-making or specific decisions where an

---

[53] Committee on the Rights of Persons with Disabilities, General Comment on Article 12 (CRPD/C/GC/1), at para 15.

[54] Committee on the Rights of Persons with Disabilities, General Comment on Article 12 (CRPD/C/GC/1), at para 34.

[55] The definition of a lack of mental capacity is provided in section 3 of the 2005 Act. Section 51(2)(e) provides for the appointment of the Official Solicitor to represent an individual who lacks mental capacity before the court.

individual is found to lack mental capacity. In any situation where substitute decision-makers are appointed, this can impact on an individual's access to justice and access to legal representation and the court system in particular, especially where the permission of the substitute decision-maker is required before an issue can be litigated. This is particularly problematic where, as noted in the General Comment on Article 12[56] the individual requires the consent of their guardian or substitute decision-maker in order to challenge the appointment of such guardian, or to challenge a decision made by the guardian regarding the person.

The need to ensure effective access to legal representation, and to the court system, to challenge deprivations of legal capacity is also emerging in recent jurisprudence of the European Court of Human Rights. Series notes that the Court has now set out at least three situations in which a person who is deprived of their legal capacity must be guaranteed direct access to a court to assert their rights, regardless of whether or not their guardian consents.[57] These are where a person wishes to appeal against a deprivation of liberty,[58] where she wishes to seek restoration of her legal capacity[59] or where a person is in conflict with their guardian, and 'when the conflict potential has a major impact on the person's legal situation'.[60] The Court has not yet addressed the issue of litigation capacity *per se* – but this trajectory in its jurisprudence seems to suggest that a person's decision-making skills cannot be used to justify a failure to provide legal representation or to permit access to a court.

A restrictive approach to litigation capacity (which denies individuals who are thought to lack sufficient mental capacity the right to take a case on their own behalf) presents a number of challenges to ensuring effective access to justice. Such an approach can prevent individuals from challenging alleged rights-violations, especially where the person cannot retain their own legal representation. Where an adult guardian or other substitute decision-maker purports to represent the interests of an individual in a case, this presents a conflict of interest, as the guardian's legal representation may not represent the interests of the individual under guardianship. Similarly, if a person who is thought to lack capacity is provided with an alternative to independent legal representation, such as a litigation friend, guardian ad litem, or advocate, there is again no guarantee that these representatives will present the

---

56 Committee on the Rights of Persons with Disabilities, *General Comment on Article 12* (CRPD/C/GC/1), para 34.

57 L Series, 'Legal Capacity and Participation in Litigation: Recent Developments in the European Court of Human Rights' in G Quinn, L Waddington and E Flynn (eds), *European Yearbook on Disability Law* (Volume 5), 103–28.

58 *Shtukaturov v Russia* (App no 44009/05) [2008] ECHR 223 §71, citing *Winterwerp v The Netherlands, Sýkora v The Czech Republic* (App no 23419/07) [2012] ECHR 1960, *Kędzior v Poland* (App no 45026/07) [2012] ECHR 1809, *Mihailovs v Latvia* (App no 35939/10) [2013] ECHR 65

59 *Stanev v Bulgaria* (App no 36760/06) [2012] ECHR 46 §37, §40, *Kędzior v Poland* (App no 45026/07) [2012] ECHR 1809 §85.

60 *D.D. v Lithuania* (App no 13469/06) [2012] §118.

person's views in court – in many jurisdictions, these representatives are mandated to present what they believe to be in the person's 'best interests' rather than seeking the outcome which accords with the person's wishes.

A pertinent example of this can be found in the case of *RP v UK*.[61] In this case a local authority sought an order to remove the baby of a young woman with intellectual disabilities from her care. The woman's solicitor felt that she lacked litigation capacity, and the Official Solicitor was appointed as her litigation friend to instruct her solicitor on her behalf. The Official Solicitor's legal responsibility is to represent the 'best interests' of the client, rather than to communicate the person's wishes to the court.[62] In this case, the Official Solicitor did not oppose the making of the care order in light of the evidence, and as a result RP's solicitor did not contest this evidence or argue against the order in court. Based on the 'best interests' standard, RP was not able to effectively challenge the removal of her child from her care. Unfortunately, the European Court of Human Rights did not take this opportunity to critique the 'best interests' role of the Official Solicitor, but it did hold that 'in order to safeguard RP's rights under Article 6(1) of the Convention, it was imperative that a means existed whereby it was possible for her to challenge the Official Solicitor's appointment or the continuing need for his services'.[63] This example demonstrates how a role which purports to reasonably accommodate people with decision-making disabilities within the court process, such as that of a litigation friend, can actually be counter-productive where it reinforces a 'best interests' approach based on the person's mental capacity, rather than supporting the individual to exercise legal capacity – an argument cogently made by Series previously in reference to the RP case.[64] In the following chapter I will engage in further discussion and critique of the roles of third parties, such as litigation friends, guardians ad litem and advocates in the court process, as possible supports to people with disabilities which can enhance or restrict effective access to justice.

In most jurisdictions, law societies and other professional bodies for lawyers provide guidance to their members on the ethical issue of capacity to instruct, as the consequences of taking instruction from a client deemed not to have sufficient mental capacity can be violation of the rules of professional conduct[65] or a finding

---

61 (App no 38245/08) [2012] ECHR 1796.

62 Office of the Official Solicitor and the Public Trustee, *The Official Solicitor and the Public Trustee: Annual Report 1 April 2011 – 31 March 2012* (London, 2012), 13.

63 (App no 38245/08) [2012] ECHR 1796 §70.

64 L Series, 'Legal Capacity and Participation in Litigation: Recent Developments in the European Court of Human Rights' in G Quinn, L Waddington and E Flynn (eds), *European Yearbook on Disability Law* (Volume 5), 103–28.

65 See for example Solicitors Regulation Authority, *Solicitors Regulation Authority Handbook* (2nd ed., London, 2011), available at: <http://www.sra.org.uk/solicitors/handbook/pdfcentre.page> (accessed 9 May 2013).

of negligence.[66] De Bhailís highlighted that most of these guidance documents recommend that issues regarding the client's litigation capacity are addressed at the outset of the lawyer–client relationship.[67] She also notes that debates on the meaning of 'litigation capacity' are also widespread. Bartlett, Lewis and Thorold suggest that to have the capacity to instruct a lawyer a client must understand the general subject matter of the litigation, and be capable of expressing a clear and consistent view as to the outcome of the case, unencumbered by any decision-making disability.[68] Similarly, these authors suggest that differences of opinion between a lawyer and a client about the prospects of a case or the remedy that should be sought are not viewed as adequate grounds for questioning the client's mental capacity to give instructions.[69]

However, de Bhailís acknowledges that most of the ethical guidance at domestic level on capacity to instruct a lawyer has not kept pace with developments post the UN Convention on the Rights of Persons with Disabilities,[70] which as discussed above, contains a recognition of legal capacity for all persons with disabilities, and does not permit an individual's mental capacity to justify a restriction of legal capacity, in this case, in order to limit access to legal representation. One such example is the New South Wales Law Society. Its guidelines on capacity to instruct advise lawyers that where doubts arise as to whether a client meets the functional test of mental capacity for the particular legal task at hand, the lawyer should conduct an initial assessment of the client's capacity, following the functional test.[71] If after this initial assessment by the lawyer, she is still unsure of the client's mental capacity, this guidance document recommends requesting a clinical assessment of mental capacity from a medical professional, such as a psychologist or psychiatrist, although it emphasises, as do similar guidance documents in other jurisdictions, that medical assessments of mental capacity should only form part of the lawyer's decision as to whether or not the client has, in fact, the requisite capacity to provide legal instructions. However, if the client, as assessed by the lawyer, is found to lack the requisite standard of mental capacity to instruct, solicitors are advised to seek the appointment of a substitute decision-

---

66 *Masterman-Lister v Brutton & Co* [2002] EWCA Civ 1889 from L Series, 'Legal Capacity and Participation in Litigation: Recent Developments in the European Court of Human Rights' in G Quinn, L Waddington and E Flynn (eds) *European Yearbook on Disability Law* (Volume 5), 103–28.

67   C de Bhailís, *People with Disabilities and Access to Legal Representation: Capacity to Instruct a Lawyer* (unpublished LLM thesis, NUI Galway, 2013), 27.

68   P Bartlett, O Thorold and O Lewis, *Mental Disability and the European Convention on Human Rights* (Martinus Nijhoff, 2007), 238–239.

69   Ibid., 239.

70   C de Bhailís, *People with Disabilities and Access to Legal Representation: Capacity to Instruct a Lawyer* (unpublished LLM thesis, NUI Galway, 2013), 27.

71   Law Society of New South Wales, 'When a Client's Capacity is in Doubt: A Practical Guide for Solicitors' (2009), available at: <http://www.lawsociety.com.au/cs/groups/public/documents/internetcontent/023880.pdf> (accessed 15 October 2013).

maker, such as an adult guardian, 'who can stand in the client's place and ensure their best interests are protected'.[72] Again, this applies the 'best interests' standard to clients who lack litigation capacity, which is problematic in ensuring respect for the individual's human rights, as described in the critique of *RP v UK* above, and as addressed by both Series[73] and de Bhailís[74] in their work on this issue.

The New South Wales guidance document also outlines some methods of supporting a client, to 'enhance' the individual's capacity to provide legal instructions.[75] These suggestions are based on guidelines provided by the American Bar Association to its members on working with clients with 'diminished capacity'.[76] In such cases the lawyers are advised to take a number of steps to enhance client capacity including building a relationship of trust and confidence with a client, allowing a support person to be present if that makes the client more comfortable and accommodating various sensory or cognitive impairments.[77] However, the option of terminating the lawyer–client relationship or referring the client to adult guardianship or other forms of substituted decision-making is still available as a last resort.[78]

Clearly, much more work is needed to understand how litigation capacity can be reframed in light of the new understanding of legal capacity and support contained in Article 12 of the UN Convention on the Rights of Persons with Disabilities. To begin, de Bhailís[79] and Series[80] suggest that practical guidance should be available to lawyers to understand how to support and accommodate clients with disabilities in providing instructions, and that systems which substitute for the client's views using a 'best interests' standard are in need of radical reform.

---

72   Ibid., 9.

73   L Series, 'Legal Capacity and Participation in Litigation: Recent Developments in the European Court of Human Rights' in G Quinn, L Waddington and E Flynn (eds), *European Yearbook on Disability Law* (Volume 5), 103–28.

74   C de Bhailís, *People with Disabilities and Access to Legal Representation: Capacity to Instruct a Lawyer* (unpublished LLM thesis, NUI Galway, 2013).

75   Law Society of New South Wales, 'When a Client's Capacity is in Doubt: A Practical Guide for Solicitors' (2009), 18, available at: <http://www.lawsociety.com.au/cs/groups/public/documents/internetcontent/023880.pdf> (accessed 15 October 2013).

76   American Bar Association Commission on Law and Aging, 'Assessment of Older Adults with Diminished Capacity' (2004), available at: <http://www.apa.org/pi/aging/diminished_capacity.pdf> (accessed 15 October 2013).

77   Law Society of New South Wales, 'When a Client's Capacity is in Doubt: A Practical Guide for Solicitors' (2009), available at: <http://www.lawsociety.com.au/cs/groups/public/documents/internetcontent/023880.pdf> (accessed 15 October 2013).

78   Ibid., 9.

79   C de Bhailís, *People with Disabilities and Access to Legal Representation: Capacity to Instruct a Lawyer* (unpublished LLM thesis, NUI Galway, 2013).

80   L Series, 'Legal Capacity and Participation in Litigation: Recent Developments in the European Court of Human Rights' in G Quinn, L Waddington and E Flynn (eds), *European Yearbook on Disability Law* (Volume 5), 103–28.

I would add here that a legal obligation should be placed on lawyers to accommodate the unique forms of communication which people with disabilities may use, and to accept various supports for communication which may enable a person to provide instruction – including the assistance of a trusted support person or advocate. However, there will still be circumstances in which it may not be possible for a lawyer to receive direct instructions, for example, where an individual's will and preferences are still unknown even after significant efforts to discover these have been made. In these cases, I would argue that the support model of legal capacity does not mean that an individual should be refused legal representation, but that any representation provided must be based on the 'best interpretation' of the individual's will and preferences – as understood by the lawyer, or as communicated to her by a person appointed for this purpose.

5. Lawyers' Responses to People with Disabilities

A key barrier identified in multiple reports on access to justice for people with disabilities is the lack of lawyers with sufficient knowledge, training and awareness to fully address the legal issues facing people with disabilities. The issue of legal education and training on the rights of persons with disabilities will be addressed more fully in Chapter 4, but it is worth considering here some of the experiences of those seeking legal advice and the challenges in finding representation which can effectively pursue the person's interests. A report on people with learning disabilities and access to legal services in the UK provided the following findings:

> [S]ome lawyers were skilled in working with people with learning disabilities and adapted their practice to meet the needs of their clients. Using plain language, treating the person with respect and being honest about the possible consequences of taking action were valued by participants in the study. However there were also examples given of where lawyers could not be understood, appeared uninterested or were not able to make a more appropriate referral ... Some legal professionals indicated that they were anxious about working with people with learning disabilities and were uncertain about the issues involved. There is therefore a need for clear advice to lawyers about how to work with people with learning disabilities.[81]

Other common barriers to accessing legal advice identified in an Australian report on access to justice for marginalised groups (including people with disabilities) include fears of retribution, communication difficulties with legal practitioners, lack of information on available options for legal assistance, issues of prejudice, low self-esteem, fear of discrimination, lack of understanding by legal service

---

81 Norah Fry Research Centre, *What Happens when People with Learning Disabilities Need Advice about the Law?* (Bristol, 2013), 56–57.

providers as to the nature of intellectual disability, and lack of awareness on the part of persons with disabilities that legal action may have been taken against them.[82]

The need to adapt legal services to accommodate the needs of people with disabilities is an important point. Writing in the 1980s, Stanley Herr acknowledged the complicating factors which the presence of disability, and intellectual disability in particular, can introduce in the lawyer–client relationship:

> Lawyers have the potential to dominate their developmentally disabled clients and usurp decisions that nondisabled clients would expect to make. This risk stems from several factors. The number of such practitioners is still limited. The clients are frequently impoverished and often depend on free, low-cost, or contingent-fee services to gain access to the justice system. Furthermore, the temptation to be paternalistic is enormous when representing clients with developmental or other mental disabilities ... These images and stereotypes enhance the power of counsel to set the goals of representation, and even to confer 'client' status on some disabled persons but not on others.[83]

Herr also discusses how in interacting with clients with intellectual disabilities, lawyers may be tempted to 'short-circuit' the client-centred counselling process, and may use third parties – including parents, or disability organisations, or simply their own ideologies, to determine what the appropriate outcome for a case might be, rather than spending the time needed to work with the individual client to discover her wishes and use these as the guiding principle for legal advocacy. He describes how this approach was taken to extremes in a particular case on the right to treatment for a client with a mental disability, using the following quote from the lawyer in question: 'I played God. I never met [the named class action plaintiff) or his guardian. And I never needed to do so. I knew what needed to be done'.[84]

From recent reports it appears that the incidences of people with intellectual disabilities directly approaching lawyers to seek legal advice themselves are still extremely rare,[85] and that it is far more likely for family members or carers to seek legal advice on behalf of a person with a disability, or together with them. This complicates the lawyer–client relationship further, as Thorold, Bartlett and Lewis outline: 'The first question is who is the client – the family member, the guardian, the court, or the person with mental disabilities? It is far from obvious that these

---

82   L Schetzer and J Henderson, *Access to Justice and Legal Needs: A Project to Identify Legal Needs, Pathways and Barriers for Disadvantaged People in NSW* (Law and Justice Foundation of New South Wales), 46.

83   S Herr, 'Disabled Clients, Constituencies, and Counsel: Representing Persons with Developmental Disabilities' (1989) 67(2) *The Milbank Quarterly* 352 at 356–357.

84   Ibid., at 357.

85   Norah Fry Research Centre, *What Happens when People with Learning Disabilities Need Advice about the Law?* (Bristol, 2013), 23.

individuals will have interests that are identical, and this should be clarified at the beginning of the relationship'.[86] These issues present complex challenges in ensuring access to legal representation for people with disabilities, and those with intellectual, psycho-social or other cognitive disabilities in particular.

In addition to attitudinal barriers and the complexities of the lawyer–client relationship, cost remains a significant challenge for people with disabilities accessing legal representation. In most jurisdictions, free legal representation is only guaranteed in criminal cases, and increasingly restricted in the context of civil claims. As discussed in Chapter 2, the right to free legal representation in criminal proceedings is also guaranteed by international human rights law, under Article 14 of the International Covenant on Civil and Political Rights.

One notable exception to the lack of free legal representation in non-criminal cases is the process of involuntary detention in a psychiatric institution, which in many countries triggers the automatic appointment of legal counsel, regardless of the means of the individual client.[87] The reason for this exception may well be that the seriousness of such a detention, and its consequent deprivation of the individual's liberty, is so grave as to warrant similar due process rights to criminal proceedings. However, even in these cases, many are critical of the standard of legal assistance provided to those who are involuntarily detained and treated. Michael Perlin states:

> The assumption that individuals facing involuntary civil commitment are globally represented by adequate counsel is an assumption of a fact not in evidence. The data suggests that, in many jurisdictions, such counsel is woefully inadequate – disinterested, uninformed, roleless, and often hostile. A model of 'paternalism/ best interests' is substituted for a traditional legal advocacy position, and this substitution is rarely questioned. Few courts have ever grappled with adequacy of counsel questions in this context.[88]

Perlin suggests as a possible solution a radical overhaul of the right to legal representation in involuntary detention processes, and that an automatic right to legal representation should similarly be available to individuals in psychiatric hospitals who wish to refuse a particular course of treatment. The reality, in many jurisdictions, is far from this ideal, and Perlin's conclusions about the attitudes of lawyers in civil commitment procedures could easily be extrapolated to other types of legal claims, as suggested by Herr above.

---

86 P Bartlett, O Thorold and O Lewis, *Mental Disability and the European Convention on Human Rights* (Martinus Nijhoff, 2007), 241.

87 See for example, P S Appelbaum, *Almost a Revolution: Mental Health Law and the Limits of Change* (Oxford University Press, 1994), 20.

88 M Perlin, 'And My Best Friend, My Doctor/ Won't Even Say What It Is I've Got: The Role and Significance of Counsel in Right to Refuse Treatment Cases' [2005] 42 *San Diego Law Review* 735 at 738.

In times of economic austerity in particular, the availability of free legal representation in civil cases generally becomes more restrictive – in terms of the means test which an individual must pass in order to access representation, and restrictions on the types of legal claims which are eligible, and take priority, in the provision of legal assistance. For example, in the UK, the Legal Aid, Sentencing and Punishment of Offenders Act 2012 removes the availability of legal aid from certain types of proceedings altogether – including private family law cases and personal injury claims, as well as significantly restricting the types of housing, debt, employment and education cases for which a person can access civil legal aid.[89] Reform of legal aid laws can have a disproportionate impact on people with disabilities, who, as discussed above, face many challenges in securing legal representation. The denial of access for people with disabilities to effective legal representation based on cost or the type of legal proceeding, arguably also conflicts with a number of basic human rights principles. As Frances Gibson notes:

> If Article 13 of the CRPD is to have any meaning, then it follows that – in the absence of forums which are simple enough in both procedure and substantive law to allow disabled citizens to have a fair hearing without the assistance of a lawyer – the convention requires states to provide legal aid to people with disabilities who cannot access private legal assistance and that, at a minimum, legal aid should be available for cases involving breaches of the human rights referred to in the treaty.[90]

Such an expansive reading of the right to access justice in the UN Convention on the Rights of Persons with Disabilities to include a corresponding right to legal aid might well be challenged by States Parties. However, Gibson makes a crucial point about the need for radical reform of procedural mechanisms, including courts and tribunals, to accommodate people with disabilities who wish to assert and enforce their legal rights, which will be returned to in the following chapter.

6. Making a Complaint: Criminal and Civil Complaints Mechanisms

This leads to the final aspect of access to law which I will discuss in this chapter – the process of making a civil or criminal complaint about an alleged violation of rights for people with disabilities. There is a certain amount of overlap in terms of barriers to making complaints about rights-violations in the civil context and those which prevent people from reporting crime; however, the challenges which people with disabilities face in reporting crime, being questioned by the police, and in

---

89 See sections 9 and 10, and Schedule 1, Legal Aid, Sentencing and Punishment of Offenders Act 2012.

90 F Gibson, 'Article 13 of the Convention on the Rights of Persons with Disabilities – a Right to Legal Aid?' (2010) 15(2) *Australian Journal of Human Rights* 123 at 131.

the initial stages of criminal investigation, have been widely documented.[91] These include the fear of not being believed by the police, fear of retribution from the perpetrator for reporting the alleged crime and the lack of support and reasonable accommodation for people with disabilities in the reporting, questioning and investigation processes.

A specific concern with disability-motivated hate crime and harassment has emerged in recent years, which coincides in part with greater efforts to deinstitutionalise people with disabilities and integrate people with intellectual and psycho-social disabilities in particular into their local communities. A report by the Equality and Human Rights Commission in England and Wales in 2011 documented the experiences of people with disabilities in reporting disability-based harassment or hate crime and found numerous barriers, including the fact that where people with disabilities had previously come to the attention of police, and were viewed as trouble-makers, they were less likely to be believed, and that in areas where anti-social behaviour was common, concerns about being targeted due to disability were also likely to be disregarded.[92] Problems with identifying perpetrators due to disabilities (e.g. visual impairment) also led to reluctance to report crime, and experience showed reported incidents were less likely to be taken further by police in these circumstances.[93] Where alleged crimes involved family members, close friends or carers, people with disabilities were also less likely to report to the police, often due to fear of damaging the relationship with the individual or losing basic support for daily living.[94]

Internationally, there are some positive examples of supports which can be provided to people with disabilities in their interactions with police to ensure more effective access to justice. As with all aspects of the justice system, accessibility of law enforcement materials (including reporting forms, witness statements), procedures (ensuring the person understands the reporting, questioning or investigation process, and is informed of the next steps, and has a contact person to follow up with) and reasonable accommodation of individuals' needs (including access to sign language, or an advocate) is crucial to ensure equal access to justice for people with disabilities. One specific example of a support for people with disabilities when engaging with the police is the Independent Third Person (ITP) Programme, in the Australian State of Victoria. This Programme provides trained

---

91 See for example S J Modell and M Suzanna, 'A Preliminary Assessment of Police Officers' Knowledge and Perceptions of Persons with Disabilities' (2008) 46(3) *Intellectual and Developmental Disabilities* 183; J R Petersilia, 'Crime Victims with Developmental Disabilities A Review Essay' (2001) 28(6) *Criminal Justice and Behaviour* 655; J McBrien and G Murphy, 'Police and Carers' Views on Reporting Alleged Offences by People with Intellectual Disabilities' (2006) 12(2) *Psychology, Crime & Law* 127.

92 Equality and Human Rights Commission, *Hidden in Plain Sight: Inquiry into Disability-Related Harassment* (London, 2011), 98.

93 Ibid., 97.

94 Ibid., 99.

volunteers who act as ITPs for people with intellectual, psycho-social or other cognitive disabilities who come into contact with the police, by supporting the individual to communicate with the police, providing guidance to the police on how to interact with the person, and advising the police if the person with a disability does not understand their rights at any stage of the process. Responsibility for contacting an ITP lies with the Victoria Police, but an individual with a disability or someone close to them can also request access to an ITP if they wish. ITPs do not replace the role of legal representation, and do not provide legal advice to the person with a disability but are merely present as a formal support for the person to increase the accessibility of the police system.

In a report entitled 'Breaking the Cycle', the Office of the Public Advocate interviewed people with disabilities who had used an ITP in their contact with police, family members, ITPs and professionals about the ways in which this programme could tackle the links between poverty, social isolation and crime, for people with cognitive disabilities.[95] Overall, the experiences of those interviewed were positive, although there were some concerns regarding long-term support for individuals who used the programme, especially those who used the programme more than once, given the short-term nature of the assistance the ITP provides.[96] As a result of this research, the Office of the Public Advocate has committed to implement a two-year pilot advocacy and referral scheme, to link those who use the ITP service to other supports as part of an early intervention strategy in the criminal justice system.[97] This commitment is a positive example of the types of support which can be provided by law enforcement, in partnership with other public bodies to ensure that people with disabilities are reasonably accommodated, and adequately supported through the criminal justice process.

In making a civil complaint, people with disabilities are likely to use a combination of the legal support provided by disability organisations, legal aid clinics, and citizens' advice centres as discussed above. However, two other crucial mechanisms for making these kinds of complaints include the Ombudsman, and equality and human rights infrastructure (i.e. the National Human Rights Institute, equality body, or a specific office with a disability rights mandate, if there is one). The accessibility of these mechanisms to people with disabilities requires consideration, to ensure an effective complaints procedure exists whereby people with disabilities can present their concerns about potential rights-violations, with adequate support to access justice.

In most jurisdictions, an Ombudsman's office exists as a last resort mechanism for complaints about a public authority, once all other efforts to resolve the dispute have been exhausted. People with disabilities might resort to the Ombudsman's

---

[95] Office of the Public Advocate, *Breaking the Cycle: Using Advocacy-Based Referrals to Assist People with Disabilities in the Criminal Justice System* (Melbourne, 2012).

[96] Ibid., 10.

[97] Ibid., 7.

office to complain about discrimination in terms of access to public services, unfair treatment by a public office or state body (including the police force) due to disability, or other unlawful actions, especially where local authorities or public bodies (e.g. the health services) have a direct role in providing support and services to people with disabilities. An Ombudsman's office also typically has the power to conduct investigations on the basis of complaints, especially where an issue might be widespread or systematic, and to make recommendations to public bodies to implement findings, and, ultimately, to report to parliament where recommendations have not been implemented.

Many Ombudsman offices around the world have investigated serious rights-violations concerning people with disabilities. The Ombudsman in Ontario is currently carrying out an investigation into the province's services for people with intellectual disabilities in crisis situations, having received several complaints about people being placed in homeless shelters or prison due to the lack of supports for transitioning between children and adults services – especially for individuals with 'challenging behaviour' or complex support needs.[98] In Ireland, the Ombudsman investigated two systemic disability issues in 2011, concerning the imposition of an upper age limit on the availability of the mobility allowance and the restrictive definition of disability used to determine eligibility for the mobility transport grant, both of which were found to contravene the Equal Status Acts.[99] Recommendations made by the Irish Ombudsman on both issues were subsequently not implemented, which led the Ombudsman to report to the houses of parliament. Unfortunately, following this report, both schemes were discontinued and have not to date been replaced with alternatives.[100]

The Ombudsman in Ireland has also commented in several annual reports on the small numbers of people with disabilities bringing claims to her office, which she suggests, is not reflective of the numbers of individuals who may have a genuine complaint against a public body. In her 2011 report, she stated:

> Yet again, as in previous years the relatively low number of complaints received under the Disability Act, 2005 is disappointing. It is vitally important that people with a disability know their rights on access to services and information and when they are not happy, that they are aware that they have a right of recourse to me as Ombudsman to examine their unresolved complaints.[101]

---

98 Ombudsman Ontario, 'Ontario Ombudsman to Investigate Province's Services for Adults with Developmental Disabilities in Crisis' (Toronto, 2012), available at: <http://www.ombudsman.on.ca/Newsroom/Press-Release/2012/Ontario-Ombudsman-to-investigate-provinces-servic.aspx?lang=en-CA> (accessed 10 November 2013).
99 Office of the Ombudsman, *Annual Report 2012* (Dublin, 2013), 10.
100 Ibid., 11.
101 Office of the Ombudsman, *Annual Report 2011* (Dublin, 2012), 22.

In 2009, the Ombudsman also found that from the low numbers of complaints made to her with regard to her role under the Disability Act, many of the complaints were 'premature' and could not be addressed by the Ombudsman, since the individual had not first made a complaint to the public service provider in question.

> In these cases, when I advise the person that they must do this, they invariably tell me that there is no information available to let them know how to make complaints to the public body concerned. In addition, many individuals tell me that because of their disabilities, they would require assistance to make a complaint but that no such assistance appears to be available from the public bodies concerned.[102]

Given these findings, which are likely to be replicated in many other countries, it is crucial that access to the Ombudsman's office must be strengthened for people with disabilities. In a review of access to justice mechanisms in the Australian state of New South Wales, community legal centre participants suggested that having to make a complaint in writing to the Ombudsman could pose a barrier to those with low levels of English literacy, a factor which also concerns people with disabilities.[103] Therefore, it is important for Ombudsman offices to consider the accessibility of their own complaints mechanisms, as well as highlighting the need for other public bodies to prevent disability discrimination and respect requests for reasonable accommodation.

The equality and human rights infrastructure at domestic level is an important resource for people with disabilities in challenging alleged violations of their human rights. Many of these bodies, similar to the Ombudsman's function, can investigate individual or systemic issues concerning the violation of human rights, but perhaps more importantly, many of these bodies also provide a legal advice and representation service to individuals, including people with disabilities, whose human rights have been violated.[104] This kind of legal support is often vital to a person who would otherwise perhaps not qualify for legal aid, or have the means to challenge the alleged violation in the courts. Reform of domestic equality and human rights infrastructure should therefore pay close attention to how best to protect the human rights of persons with disabilities. These reforms, including the amalgamation of different minority rights commissions/Ombudsman into one central human rights institution have sometimes been controversial as people with disabilities fear the risk of disability rights issues becoming marginalised within a broader institution, losing expertise on disability rights, or the possibility that new

---

102 Office of the Ombudsman, *Annual Report 2008* (Dublin, 2009), 90.

103 L Schetzer and J Henderson, *Access to Justice and Legal Needs: A Project to Identify Legal Needs, Pathways and Barriers for Disadvantaged People in NSW* (Law and Justice Foundation of New South Wales), 46.

104 See for example A Smith, 'The Unique Position of National Human Rights Institutions: A Mixed Blessing' (2006) 28 *Human Rights Quarterly* 904 at 935.

structures will be less accessible to people with disabilities.[105] In order to ensure strong support for the rights of individual people with disabilities, it is important for these broad structures to remain accessible to people with disabilities and continue to provide legal advice, representation and support for disability rights issues.

With the entry into force of the UN Convention on the Rights of Persons with Disabilities, many States Parties, including New Zealand and Spain, have designated some combination of their Ombudsman offices, National Human Rights Institutions and Equality Bodies to form part of an independent mechanism to monitor the implementation of the Convention at domestic level.[106] This new role brings with it the opportunity to re-examine the opportunities which people with disabilities have at domestic level to raise concerns about human rights, and to access legal support, advice and representation to advance their causes.

A final point which is common to all these mechanisms for making civil and criminal complaints is the need for people with disabilities to have effective support in order to access the mainstream complaints mechanisms that exist. For some, this only requires the provision of accessible information and physically accessible venues. Others will need more intensive support, and will look to family members, care staff or others to assist them in accessing these legal services. This requires a great deal of knowledge-dissemination about the availability of public services which provide legal advice or assistance, and, for some, the availability of independent advocates (not necessarily legal advocates or practising lawyers), to assist them in accessing and communicating with lawyers, law enforcement, or other complaints mechanisms.

7. Conclusion

For many of us, the first step in accessing the law is relatively straightforward. We research the information available online, and generally consult a legal practitioner, to determine how we should interact with the legal system in order to assert our rights. In order to ensure these options are fully accessible to people with disabilities, much more work is needed to reframe our thinking about legal services – in terms of the capacity required to instruct a lawyer (and supports necessary to achieve this), the accessibility of legal services in general (including the accessibility of complaints mechanisms and law enforcement), and the ways in which legal services recognise and respond to the individual requirements of people with disabilities. Ensuring access to the law is simply a first step in

---

105 See for example, R Carver, 'One NHRI or Many? How Many Institutions Does It Take to Protect Human Rights? Lessons from the European Experience' (2011) 3(1) *Journal of Human Rights Practice* 1.

106 See for example, G de Beco, 'Article 33 (2) of the UN Convention on the Rights of Persons with Disabilities: Another Role for National Human Rights Institutions?' (2011) 29(1) *Netherlands Quarterly of Human Rights* 84.

addressing the accessibility of the broader legal and justice systems, but a crucial one which must be addressed before considering the options for further reform of the systems and procedures used in the administration of justice, as will be discussed further in the following chapter.

Chapter 4
Access and Participation in Court: Structures, Evidence and Procedures

1. Introduction

While the focus on access to justice throughout this book examines the broad nature of the justice system, the courtroom remains a key location where justice claims are made and adjudicated. For this reason, I focus specifically on the court in this chapter, as a physical space in which justice is administered, and critically examine the processes it uses and their accessibility to people with disabilities. The court system presents a number of inaccessible features – in terms of physical infrastructure, as well as procedural and evidentiary barriers which disproportionately affect people with disabilities. As one of the main spaces in which justice is administered, the symbolic nature of its transparency and ease of access resonates deeply with many groups who have been marginalised in society, including people with disabilities. The accessibility or otherwise of the courts can therefore be considered on a number of levels, which will be discussed throughout this chapter.

First, at the most basic level of access, physical access to court buildings continues to be an issue in many countries for people with disabilities. This is so despite the emergence of legal obligations on courts, as public buildings, to increase their accessibility to people with disabilities, generally under anti-discrimination legislation. The most obvious barriers to access are the architectural features (e.g. steps instead of ramps) which prevent people with disabilities from accessing and using the courtroom in the same way as others in a variety of roles which they may play in the justice system (e.g. lawyer, juror, witness, defendant, judge). The concept of barriers to the physical space in which justice is administered is both a symbolic and a pragmatic challenge to the way in which the justice system responds to people with disabilities.[1]

Second, the accessibility of court procedures also causes problems – and requires more than physical adaptation to fully include people with disabilities. One of the most prevalent examples of this is in respect of communication – ensuring that people with disabilities understand the court procedures and can

---

1 R Bahdi, *Background Paper on Women's Access to Justice in the MENA Region* (International Development Research Centre (IDRC), Women's Rights and Citizenship Program (WRC) and the Middle East Regional Office (MERO), Middle East and North African (MENA) Regional Consultation, 9–11 December 2007, Cairo, Egypt).

effectively communicate with the court, and officers of the court, including court-appointed lawyers or other third parties. Communication can be facilitated through the use of third parties (e.g. sign-language interpreters) or through technological aids, or a combination of both. The role of third parties in facilitating effective communication can sometimes be controversial, especially where the type of communication an individual uses is only understood by very few people, or where third parties have a legal responsibility to represent the person's 'best interests' to the court, rather than their wishes and preferences. Additional challenges in ensuring effective and accessible court procedures may also be faced by lay litigants with disabilities.

Finally, the adaptation of the rules of evidence and procedure to facilitate the effective participation of people with disabilities in a variety of roles in court (such as witness, defendant or juror) is also problematic. Even where procedures are adapted this raises questions about whether those adaptations impact on the integrity of the criminal justice system in particular (particularly whether accommodations for witnesses or jurors with disabilities impinge on the fair trial rights of defendants). In this chapter, I will consider how these key challenges can be met to ensure greater accessibility for, and participation of, people with disabilities who assert their justice claims in court. In keeping with the conceptual framework of intersectionality, I will draw on the experiences of other communities who have been marginalised by the physical and procedural aspects of the courtroom, to provide suggestions for reform.

2. Getting to Court: Challenges in the Physical Design of Spaces for the Administration of Justice

In Ortoleva's article on 'Inaccessible Justice' she provides a poignant example of barriers to accessing the physical space of the courtroom in South Africa:

> Esthe Muller, a South African lawyer and also a wheelchair user, filed suit under the Promotion of Equality and Prevention of Unfair Discrimination Act of 2000 against the Justice Department and the Department of Public Works because of the inaccessibility of the courthouses. Ms. Muller had to be carried down a flight of stairs to enter the courthouse and on another occasion the court had to postpone her cases because she could not get into the room. In September 2004, the South African Equality Court reached a final settlement in which the two government departments admitted that they had failed to provide proper wheelchair access and that this was a form of unfair discrimination against Ms. Muller and other people with similar accessibility needs.[2]

---

2   S Ortoleva, 'Inaccessible Justice: Human Rights, Persons with Disabilities and the Legal System' (2011) 17 *ILSA Journal of International and Comparative Law* 281 at 305–306.

A similar issue of physical access came before the US courts based on the Americans with Disabilities Act 1990. In this case, the applicants George Lane and Beverly Jones were a defendant and a court reporter, respectively, and both had physical disabilities and used wheelchairs.

> Lane alleged that he was compelled to appear to answer a set of criminal charges on the second floor of a county courthouse that had no elevator. At his first appearance, Lane crawled up two flights of stairs to get to the courtroom. When Lane returned to the courthouse for a hearing, he refused to crawl again or to be carried by officers to the courtroom; he consequently was arrested and jailed for failure to appear. Jones, a certified court reporter, alleged that she has not been able to gain access to a number of county courthouses, and, as a result, has lost both work and an opportunity to participate in the judicial process.[3]

In this case the US Supreme Court held by a five to four majority that Congress had properly used its enforcement powers under section 5 of the Fourteenth Amendment in enacting Title II of the Americans with Disabilities Act (ADA) – and that the plaintiffs should not have been discriminatorily denied access to the courts on the basis of disability. The relevant provision of the ADA requires public entities (interpreted to include state and local courtrooms) to make public services accessible to people with disabilities. The Supreme Court's reasoning in this case focused on the Constitutional Due Process clause – which covers, in addition to the right of access to the courts, other commonly understood 'fair trial' rights, such as the right to confront accusers, the meaningful opportunity to be heard and the right to trial by jury. Here the Court found that Title II of the ADA legitimately seeks to enforce a variety of other basic constitutional guarantees and to protect against 'pervasive unequal treatment in the administration of state services and programs, including systematic deprivations of fundamental rights'.[4]

This was a landmark case in many ways, as the US Courts have previously held that other parts of the ADA have impinged on the sovereignty of States. Silvers and Francis note that the use of the term 'including' in the Supreme Court's description of Constitutional due process rights is significant in this ruling,[5] as it suggests that the fundamental rights which the ADA seeks to uphold are a non-exhaustive list, and indeed the Court itself provided some further examples of such rights, including the right to vote, the right to marry and the right to perform

---

3 *Tennessee v Lane*, 541 U.S. 509, 512–14 (2004) at para 7.
4 Ibid., at 524.
5 A Silvers and LP Francis, 'A New Start on the Road Not Taken: Driving with Lane to Head off Disability-Based Denials of Rights' (2007) 23 *Wash. UJL & Pol'y* 33 at 52.

the duties of a juror,[6] issues which resonate with the concepts of substantive and symbolic justice described by Bahdi.[7]

These South African and US examples demonstrate the importance of robust anti-discrimination legislation which places obligations on courts, as public bodies and as an arm of the state's justice system, to accommodate people with disabilities. Given the impact that the ADA in particular has had on disability-based anti-discrimination law in general, I will consider further here its specific contribution to the accessibility of courts, as public entities, providing a public service – namely the administration of justice. Within the ADA, barriers to accessing public services are conceived of as a form of discrimination against people with disabilities, and one that must be remedied. Gould writes convincingly of the need for such legislation that: '[a] combination of socially sanctioned bigotry, benevolent paternalism based upon biased notions of incompetencies, and judicial inflexibility built upon a fear of unexplained differences has often relegated the rights of courtroom participants with disabilities to the bottom rung of judicial apathy'.[8]

Under Title II of the ADA, a public entity, such as a state or local court system, has a duty to accommodate 'qualified individuals with disabilities' to participate in, or receive the benefits of the services, programmes or activities offered by that entity, and must not discriminate on the basis of disability.[9] The duty to reasonably accommodate means that the public service must provide appropriate aids and services where necessary to ensure effective communication between the public entity and people with disabilities in the most integrated setting possible, according to the Department of Justice regulations which accompany the ADA.[10] Examples of these aids and services provided in the regulations include the provision of a sign-language interpreter, the use of technology to facilitate communication, real-time captioning of court proceedings, and the installation of a hearing loop system. Reasonable accommodation also includes the modification of rules, policies or practices, or the removal of architectural, communication or transportation barriers so that the person with a disability can participate in, and receive the benefits of, the public service.[11]

In the courtroom context, in order to determine what kind of adaption is needed, the judge or court administrator is required to 'give primary consideration

---

6 *Tennessee v Lane*, 541 U.S. 509, 512–14 (2004) at 525.

7 R Bahdi, *Background Paper on Women's Access to Justice in the MENA Region* (International Development Research Centre (IDRC), Women's Rights and Citizenship Program (WRC) and the Middle East Regional Office (MERO), Middle East and North African (MENA) Regional Consultation, 9–11 December 2007, Cairo, Egypt).

8 K Gould, 'And Equal Participation for All ... The Americans with Disabilities Act in the Courtroom' (1993) 8 *Journal of Law & Health* 123 at 124.

9 42 U.S.C. § 12132 (1990).

10 28 C.F.R. § 35.150(b) (1993).

11 28 C.F.R. § 35.130 (1993).

to the requests of the individual with disabilities'.[12] This is significant because it reinforces the idea that the individual person with a disability is best placed to know what adaptations are required. It also reaffirms that the ADA's approach to accessing public services is based in anti-discrimination law, and therefore takes the individual as its starting point in determining the adaptations required. Gould contends that the ADA 'demands no less than the integration of courtroom procedures with the active involvement of participants with disabilities'.[13]

This is to be distinguished from the group approach to accessibility, discussed in the previous chapters,[14] whereby in determining adaptations or design of public services, people with disabilities are consulted and actively involved through representative organisations which can provide the views of people with various types of impairment as to what would make the service accessible for them. It should also be acknowledged, following on from the discussion in the previous chapter, that what one person requires to make the court accessible to them (e.g. more lighting for a person with a visual impairment) may mean that the court becomes inaccessible for someone else (e.g. an individual whose disability makes them extremely sensitive to bright light) – and the balancing of different, possibly conflicting, accessibility requirements is a delicate process, and one which should be undertaken carefully by the courts.

While perhaps written more with people with physical and sensory disabilities in mind, the provisions of the ADA are expansive enough to ensure, that regardless of the type of impairment, an individual who requires a public service to be adapted, or needs support to access that service, including court proceedings, could claim a right to be accommodated. For example, a person with autism might make a number of requests about the sensory space, lighting and set-up of the courtroom which would be needed to accommodate participation, and even though courts may not be as familiar with how to accommodate these requests as they are with accommodating people who use wheelchairs, the ADA provides the legal basis for efforts to facilitate the individual's unique requirements. Gould acknowledges that '[t]he Act assumes that appropriate accommodations are possible even if they require greater creativity, flexibility, or ingenuity than the reflexive altering of a physical structure or appointment of a sign language interpreter'.[15] In the following section I will address in further detail how creative approaches to courtroom design can provide a basis for the full inclusion of people with disabilities.

---

12   28 C.F.R. § 35.160(b)(2) (1993).

13   K Gould, 'And Equal Participation for All ... The Americans with Disabilities Act in the Courtroom' (1993) 8 *Journal of Law & Health* 123 at 125.

14   See ch 2 55–58, ch 3 88–90.

15   K Gould, 'And Equal Participation for All ... The Americans with Disabilities Act in the Courtroom' (1993) 8 *Journal of Law & Health* 123 at 134.

Intersectional Approaches to Designing Accessible Courtrooms

Many feminist scholars consider the important symbolism of the courtroom as a physical space in which justice is administered, and the ways in which its architectural design might impact and influence the way in which the law is interpreted, applied and upheld in court. Mulcahy, one of the leading thinkers in this field, posits that the reason for the relative dearth of literature on the internal design of courtrooms might be traced to 'lawyers' obsession with the word',[16] and their reliance on written legal reasoning as the only valid source which can explain the outcome which occurs within a particular space. By contrast, Mulcahy claims that 'the shape of a courtroom, the configuration of walls and barriers, the height of partitions within it, the positioning of tables, and even the choice of materials are crucial to a broader and more nuanced understanding of judgecraft'.[17]

She points to some notable examples – outside the realm of disability – where the physical structure of a courtroom, in addition to other more traditional due process concerns, constituted the breach of the right to a fair trial. In *V v United Kingdom*,[18] the European Court of Human Rights found that the applicant, who was one of two juvenile defendants convicted of the murder of James Bulger, was denied his fair trial rights under Article 6 of the European Convention. Mulcahy takes note of the adaptations to the physical courtroom which were made for the defendant, and the impact which these had on him:

> It was determined that the raising of the dock, undertaken in the hope that it would ensure that the defendant could see what was going on, actually had the effect of increasing his sense of intense discomfort and exposure ... Venables cried throughout most of the trial and claimed to have spent much of the time counting in his head or making shapes with his shoes. Expert evidence on his state of mind suggested that he had felt better after the first three days in the Crown Court, but only because he had stopped listening to the proceedings.[19]

Mulcahy seeks to demonstrate that the interior design of courtrooms makes them far from the open and transparent spaces (at least in terms of accommodating members of the public) that the justice system might claim them to be. While her arguments do not consider the impact of courtroom design on specific groups, such as people with disabilities, there are many examples which build on her theory, and demonstrate that the design of courts send subtle, and sometimes, overt, signals to people with disabilities, among others, that they are not fully welcome or included.

---

16   L Mulcahy, 'Architects of Justice: The Politics of Courtroom Design' (2007) 16(3) *Social & Legal Studies* 383 at 385.

17   Ibid.

18   *V v United Kingdom* [1999] ECHR 171.

19   L Mulcahy, 'Architects of Justice: The Politics of Courtroom Design' (2007) 16(3) *Social & Legal Studies* 383 at 386.

Apart from the obvious, exterior courthouse design which places the court on a raised plinth, accessible only, or primarily, by flights of steps, there are many other subtle examples of the ways in which design can exclude people with disabilities.[20] For example, the use of separate entryways (e.g. a ramp and steps) instead of a universal access point for all court users can subtly suggest a form of exclusion, especially if the ramp brings people to a different entry point into the building, rather than the main entryway.[21] Some courthouses may only have one accessible courtroom, or may provide accessible spaces for witnesses and defendants, but the public gallery or jury space may not be accessible. Similarly, where there are raised platforms for the judges' bench, this too may be inaccessible to some people with disabilities – providing a subtle signal that we do not expect people with disabilities to perform the role of the judge.

Mulcahy and others concede that the design of courts has long been underpinned by the desire to project certain values and images of the justice system – as austere or daunting, reflecting the gravity of the law and the legal system – and that a by-product of these values is the inevitable exclusion of certain groups.[22] Irrespective of whether or not these values are justified in themselves, if we wish to preserve the austerity and grandeur of the physical court structure, this can be done, while ensuring a more accessible space for all participants. As outlined in a US report on court accessibility:

> The use of a raised plinth as a design element to symbolize power and authority dates back to antiquity. Other designs can just as effectively achieve this symbolism. Security can be addressed by other means, such as bollards, planters, or a deeper building setback from the street with an entry plaza. If a high water table is the concern, this too can be addressed by other means, such as improved site drainage or raising the building only the minimum amount required.[23]

Finally, the issue of courtroom design and accessibility returns to the notion of universal design, discussed in the previous chapter.[24] The idea of barrier-free spaces for the administration of justice contains its own, important, symbolism which should be acknowledged, and resonates with Bahdi's concept of the symbolic

---

20 See for example, A Hamraie, 'Designing Collective Access: A Feminist Disability Theory of Universal Design' (2013) 33(4) *Disability Studies Quarterly*.

21 Other examples of common exclusionary practices in courthouse and courtroom design, and examples of good practice in providing access for people with disabilities can be found in US Access Board Courthouse Advisory Committee, *Justice for All: Designing Accessible Courthouses* (Washington DC, 2006).

22 See L Mulcahy, 'Architects of Justice: The Politics of Courtroom Design' (2007) 16(3) *Social & Legal Studies* 383 at 387; P Carlen *Magistrates' Justice* (Martin Robertson, 1976).

23 US Access Board Courthouse Advisory Committee, *Justice for All: Designing Accessible Courthouses* (Washington DC, 2006), 18.

24 See ch 2, 55–58.

component of access to justice.[25] In this respect, Hamraie argues for an approach to universal design which diverges from the narrow, highly individualised, approaches which might stem from traditional anti-discrimination legislation. She contends that 'broad accessibility recognizes that intersectionality compounds environmental misfit and requires a more collective notion of access than barrier-free approaches and individualized accommodations can afford'. An approach to design based on broad accessibility – for people with disabilities as well as other marginalised communities – could therefore contribute to what Weisman terms 'a politics of interdependence',[26] and in the context of the justice system, could lead to a design that is as inclusive as possible, taking on board experiences and perspectives from race, class, gender, age and disability, among other identities.

3. Making Your Voice Heard: Disability and Communication with the Court

People with disabilities generally communicate with the court in one of two ways – either individually (with or without support) or through the assistance of a third party (such as an interpreter, court-appointed advocate or litigation friend). Here I will examine the challenges of communication with the court in general, using examples of third party communication and the challenges people with disabilities can face if they interact directly with the court, both with or without support from others. Following this discussion I will address related issues which touch on communication, such as the right of audience before courts, the rule of personal presence and the experiences of lay litigants with disabilities.

As discussed in the previous section, the courtroom can be an intimidating and challenging environment for many participants, including people with disabilities. Once the physical barriers and design issues are overcome, the next challenge is following the proceedings and being able to communicate effectively with the court. Once inside the court building, courts must ensure that announcements, relevant documentation, explanations of court proceedings, instructions to members of the jury, and all other processes involving the participation of court users, are effectively communicated to those with disabilities. A key preliminary issue is the need for court officials, judges and lawyers to be able to effectively communicate with people with disabilities. This issue has been touched upon in the previous chapter, but is worth considering in further detail here, given its significance for the accessibility of court proceedings.

---

25 R Bahdi, *Background Paper on Women's Access to Justice in the MENA Region,* (International Development Research Centre (IDRC), Women's Rights and Citizenship Program (WRC) and the Middle East Regional Office (MERO), Middle East and North African (MENA) Regional Consultation, 9–11 December 2007, Cairo, Egypt).

26 L K Weisman, 'Redesigning Architectural Education' in J Rothschild (ed), *Design and Feminism: Re-visioning Spaces, Places, and Everyday Things* (Rutgers University Press, 1999), 159–74.

Communication and the Role of Interpreters in Court

Schwartz discusses the importance of lawyers communicating with their deaf clients – and his practical advice could be equally applied to other officers of the court interacting with a deaf person, and may have broader resonance for communicating with people with other kinds of disabilities.[27] He prioritises the need for clear and effective communication, but at the same times cautions against over-simplification, a common mistake when explaining legal procedures to many people with disabilities, as well as deaf people. He discusses a variety of options for communication, including the use of technological devices which enable deaf people to use telephone services, lip-reading and written notes, but focuses predominantly on the use of sign language interpreters and how lawyers should interact with their client if an interpreter is used.

> The lawyer directs comments to the client, not to the interpreter ... The interpreter interprets but does not explain. The lawyer assesses the client's comprehension and explains terminology and procedures when necessary. The interpreter interprets everything, including private conversations in the room and side comments ... The lawyer takes into account the possibility that the client, as a member of a group long stigmatized as 'dumb', may have an oppressed perspective that results in a tendency to say 'yes' when asked 'Do you understand?' even when the client does not understand either the interpreter or the speaker.[28]

This specific guidance can easily be applied to judges, opposing counsel, court clerks and others who interact with deaf people in court, and Schwartz's guidance contains valuable insights which can also be applied to other people with disabilities. In particular, the likelihood of a person who identifies as part of an oppressed minority group responding to judicial or legal authority by giving the answers they expect the other person wants to hear, rather than the response they might give in a different context, is a common challenge which extends beyond the particular experiences of people with disabilities. Nevertheless, the importance of basic principles such as speaking to and interacting directly with the individual, rather than a third party they may use to communicate (such as an interpreter) is a vital starting point for effective communication in court.

In general, the role of sign-language interpreters in a court setting is relatively uncontested. The ADA is an example of national anti-discrimination legislation which provides that sign-language interpreters, where required for deaf witnesses, defendants or litigants, be provided and paid for out of federal or state funding available to the court in question. In many ways, the role of sign-language interpreters is analogous to the role of those who interpret different spoken

---

27 M Schwartz, 'Serving Hearing-Impaired Clients' (1991) 18 *Barrister* 45.
28 Ibid., 46–47.

languages for participants in the courtroom, although laws and policies on the use of sign or spoken interpreters, and determining who should pay the cost for each type of interpretation, varies from country to country. Many countries recognise that as part of the right to a fair trial, criminal defendants in particular have a right to an interpreter where required to understand the proceedings.[29] Traditionally, this was understood to mean a spoken language interpreter, but can easily be applied to ensure that deaf people have access to sign-language interpreters where sign is the person's native language. Constitutional protection or recognition of the status of national sign languages can also help to ensure that outside the narrow context of the criminal trial, deaf people have rights to legal proceedings conducted using sign-language interpreters paid for by the public to ensure effective access to justice.

While generally accepted as necessary to facilitate access to justice, the use of sign-language interpreters is sometimes contested in certain aspects of court procedure. One example of this is the notion that a deaf juror using an interpreter might violate the 'thirteenth person in the jury room' principle.[30] Historically, deaf people (along with those who were blind, had intellectual disabilities or low levels of literacy) were often excluded from jury service. This exclusion and various reform efforts will be discussed further below, but is worth briefly noting here as an example of the ways in which communication can be contested in the courtroom context.

Alternative and Augmented Communication and Facilitated Communication

Another example of communication which may be interpreted by third parties for people with disabilities in court is what is known collectively as 'alternative and augmented communication', or AAC. This term covers a broad range of communication methods which are alternative to spoken communication, such as gestures, forms of sign, communication boards, voice output communication aids, and increasingly, web-based applications (commonly for iPhone or iPad) which enable communication.[31] AAC techniques are used by people with a range of disabilities which lead to their speech not being present or being difficult for others to understand, including intellectual disability, cerebral palsy, acquired brain injury or motor neuron disease. AAC can be 'aided' or 'un-aided' – meaning

---

29 See for example, Human Rights Law Resource Centre, 'The Right to a Fair Hearing and Access to Justice: Australia's Obligations' (Human Rights Law Resource Centre, 2009), available at:
<http://www.hrlrc.org.au/files/hrlrc-submission-access-to-justice-inquiry.pdf> (accessed 4 June 2012), 3.

30 See further, Law Reform Commission, *Report on Jury Service* (Dublin, 2013) LRC 107–2013.

31 D N Bryen and C H Wickman, 'Ending the Silence of People with Little or No Functional Speech: Testifying in Court' (2011) 31(4) *Disability Studies Quarterly*.

that a person can communicate without the assistance of a device (i.e. using sign or gestures), or use a particular communication tool (such as a communication board or app) to interact with others.[32] In general, AAC refers to a structured, tested and accepted form of communication, in which speech and language therapists often specialise, which can be externally validated as a valid representation of the person's thoughts and views.[33] In this sense, it is perhaps quite a professionalised form of communication, whereas individuals who use their own unique ways of communicating, which may not fall within these structured categories, would not identify as users of AAC.

In general, AAC distinguishes itself from what is known as 'facilitated' communication, a technique which was developed primarily for autistic individuals, whereby a facilitator would provide physical assistance (e.g. supporting a person's arm) or emotional support (e.g. sitting with the person) to an individual as she typed on a communication board or keyboard.[34] This form of communication when first introduced was hailed as revolutionary in unlocking the untapped potential of people who were previously regarded as non-communicative,[35] but given the level of support provided by the facilitator, it has generated significant controversy regarding its validity and the potential for the facilitator to manipulate the individual in terms of the messages which are communicated.[36]

In some court proceedings, the use of facilitated communication has been allowed to permit a witness to give testimony, where the judge and jury are satisfied that the responses given by the witness are his or her own, and not influenced by the presence of the facilitator, or the support the facilitator provides. One such example is the US case of *People v Webb*,[37] where a child victim witness gave evidence to a Grand Jury using facilitated communication. On appeal, the court upheld the validity of this form of testimony, stating as follows:

> From a due process standpoint, all parties are concerned that the answers of any witness indeed be his or her own answers, and that the witness understand the question sufficiently to be able to respond. It is, of course, important to ascertain

---

32   See generally, S L Glennen and D C DeCoste (eds), *The Handbook of Augmentative and Alternative Communication* (Cengage Learning, 1997).

33   See also J Light, 'Toward a Definition of Communicative Competence for Individuals using Augmentative and Alternative Communication Systems' (1989) 5(2) *Augmentative and Alternative Communication* 137.

34   M P Mostert, 'Facilitated Communication since 1995: A Review of Published Studies' (2001) 31(3) *Journal of Autism and Developmental Disorders* 287.

35   D Biklen, *Communication Unbound: How Facilitated Communication is Challenging Traditional Views of Autism and Ability/Disability* (Teachers College Press, 1993).

36   J W Jacobson, J A Mulick and A A Schwartz, 'A History of Facilitated Communication: Science, Pseudoscience, and Antiscience Science Working Group on Facilitated Communication' (1995) 50(9) *American Psychologist* 750.

37   157 Misc.2d 474 (1993) 597 N.Y.S.2d 565.

that the answer of the witness is not guided, controlled, suggested, or changed by the facilitator. Apparently, the facilitator does not speak during the question and answer process between the questioner and the witness. Additionally, in this case, the facilitator was equipped with headphones through which 'white noise' was produced, so as to make it difficult or impossible for the facilitator to hear the questions.[38]

In this particular case the witness responded to questions by typing on a keyboard, letter by letter, spelling out the words of each answer, while the facilitator supported the individual's wrists. In permitting the use of facilitation, or indeed the use of less controversial forms of AAC, the courts have on occasion made analogies to the use of interpreters (of spoken or sign language) to justify this form of support for witness testimony.[39] Independent verification of the validity of the communication methods have been sought by the courts in different ways, for example, by asking the facilitator to leave the room while the question is asked, and to return only to support the person to communicate the answer.[40] However, scientific criticism of facilitated communication remains, and indeed, although AAC and facilitated communication can, to varying degrees, support an individual to communicate with the court, there are many forms of unique communication which individuals use that do not easily lend themselves to interpretation within the strict rules of procedure and processes imposed in the court setting.

Baggs makes a powerful argument about the failures of the non-disabled world (and this would include the court system) to learn how to communicate with disabled people – always requiring the individual with disability to learn or acquire a method of communication that non-disabled people understand, rather than interacting with the person in their chosen form of communication, which may be quite challenging. Commenting on her own preferred communication and the notion of personhood, she says:

> However the thinking of people like me is only taken seriously if we learn your language, no matter how we previously thought or interacted ... It is only when I type something in your language that you refer to me as having communication ... I find it very interesting, by the way, that failure to learn your language is seen as a deficit, but failure to learn my language is seen as so natural that people like me are officially described as mysterious and puzzling, rather than anyone admitting that it is themselves who are confused, and not autistic people or other cognitively disabled people who are inherently confusing.[41]

---

38   Ibid., at 476.
39   See for example, *People v Augustin*, 112 Cal. App. 4th 444 (Cal. Ct. App. 2003) and *People v Miller*, 530 N.Y.S.2d 490 (City Ct. Rochester Cty. 1988).
40   See for example *In re Luz P.*, 595 N.Y.S.2d 541 (N.Y. App. Div. 1993).
41   A M Baggs, *In My Language* (2007), available at: <http://www.youtube.com/watch?v=JnylM1hI2jc> (accessed 13 November 2013).

Baggs' experiences are a convincing argument that courts, and other aspects of the justice system, need to be more creative in recognising the diverse communication methods people with disabilities use that can facilitate them to provide testimony – and adapting court procedures and rules of evidence where necessary to accommodate this, without undermining key principles of the right to a fair trial, as will be discussed further below.

Beyond Interpreters: The Role of Independent Advocates in the Court Process

In the context of access to justice, the term 'advocacy' is usually assumed to refer to legal advocacy in the court process. The responses of lawyers to clients with disabilities has already been discussed in the previous chapter,[42] and this section will consider a different kind of advocacy, primarily focusing on the role of independent non-legal advocates, who are often state-appointed with a legislative mandate to support people with disabilities in the assertion and enforcement of their rights. This may include accompanying a person and supporting them to communicate their views as part of a court process, and the statutory advocates who perform this role may also have some conflicting commitments, including a requirement that the advocate communicate to the court the course of action which she believes to be in the 'best interests' of the represented person (even where this conflicts with the individual's wishes), or the possibility of being appointed a substitute decision-maker for a person with a disability by the court.

My focus here on non-legal advocacy in the court process is predominantly on the role of independent representative state-appointed advocates, rather than the many different forms of community and voluntary advocacy which exist and provide vital support to people with disabilities (e.g. self advocacy,[43] citizen advocacy,[44] peer advocacy,[45] family advocacy[46] or political advocacy/lobbying[47]). This is not to undermine the importance of these various forms of advocacy, but rather reflects the reality that state-appointed advocates are more likely to play a prominent role in court processes involving people with disabilities than any of

---

42 See ch 2, section 5.

43 For more, see D Goodley, *Self Advocacy in the Lives of People with Learning Disabilities* (Open University Press, 2000), 81.

44 See further W Wolfensberger and H Zauka (eds), *Citizen Advocacy and Protective Services for the Impaired and Handicapped* (National Institute for Mental Retardation, 1973).

45 See for example, C M Rhoades, P L Browning and E J Thorin, 'Self-Help Advocacy Movement: A Promising Peer-Support System for People with Mental Disabilities' (1986) 47 *Rehabilitation Literature* 2–7.

46 See N Pike, 'The Neglected Dimension: Advocacy and the Families of Children with Learning Difficulties' in B Gray, and R Jackson (eds), *Advocacy and Learning Disability* (Jessica Kingsley Publishers, 2002), 152.

47 See R K Scotch, 'Disability as the Basis for a Social Movement: Advocacy and the Politics of Definition' (1988) 44(1) *Journal of Social Issues* 159.

these other, more organic, forms of advocacy. The possible exception to this rule is the involvement of parent or family advocates and their crucial role particularly in the initial stages of bringing a case to court. This issue has been addressed somewhat in the previous chapter.[48] However, it should also be acknowledged that parent or family advocates may have a different view from the person with a disability at the centre of a court process[49] about what the desired outcome might be, and for this reason, I will focus here on the role of those appointed by the court, or another state body, with the mandate to be 'independent' and to communicate the person's views to the court.

For the purpose of this discussion I use the term 'state-operated' advocacy services to describe the role played by professional, independent, non-legal, representative advocates. This definition of state-operated advocacy includes systems such as the Independent Mental Capacity Advocate introduced in England and Wales under the Mental Capacity Act 2005, the Office of the Public Advocate in Victoria, Australia and the National Advocacy Service in Ireland.[50] In general, although advocates within these systems are employed or funded by state bodies or local authorities, they are required to be independent in the performance of their functions – since much of their work may involve challenging State failures to uphold the rights of persons with disabilities. In most cases, individuals with disabilities have a legislative or administrative entitlement to this type of advocacy if they meet the eligibility criteria – and such advocacy is often focused on crisis situations, and only available as a last resort, where all other attempts to resolve the individual's circumstances have failed.[51]

Annual reports from various state-operated advocacy services demonstrate that independent advocates are often appointed to people with disabilities during a court process. In the Irish context, a legal aid circular was developed on foot of a High Court judicial review case concerning the rights of parents with intellectual disabilities to receive support throughout childcare proceedings to ensure their human rights were respected.[52] The 2007 circular provides for the appointment of an 'appropriate person', funded by the Legal Aid Board, to support an individual with 'impaired capacity' to understand the proceedings, outside the provision of independent legal representation, to assist the person in instructing counsel and to

---

48 See ch 3, section 3 and 67–72.

49 For a particularly pertinent example of this, see the 'Jenny Hatch' case: *Ross v Hatch*, 113 LRP 31633 (Va. Cir. Ct. 08/12/13).

50 The Personal Advocacy Service in Ireland is currently operating on a non-statutory basis as the National Advocacy Service. The Citizens Information Act 2007 envisages the establishment of a Personal Advocacy Service on a statutory footing, with legislative entitlements to an advocate in certain circumstances and statutory powers for PAS advocates to carry out their functions.

51 See generally E Flynn, 'Making Human Rights Meaningful for People with Disabilities: Advocacy, Access to Justice and Equality before the Law' (2013) 17(4) *International Journal of Human Rights* 491.

52 *Legal Aid Board v Judge Brady and Case Stated* 2005/474 JR.

communicate with the court.[53] In practice, advocates from the National Advocacy Service (NAS) have generally been appointed as 'appropriate persons' in these cases. The following case study is provided by NAS as an example of how its advocates operate in these situations:

> Pamela is a woman recently diagnosed with an intellectual disability. For a range of reasons the HSE were looking for temporary care orders for her children. Pamela was extremely distressed and confused about what was going on and what role she could play in the court process. The advocate met with Pamela to get to know her and worked with her, contacting her solicitor to inform them about NAS and advocacy practice; preparing and supporting Pamela before she attended meetings, during meetings with her solicitor and during court hearings. Pamela finds these meetings very stressful. The advocate also supported Pamela to raise her opinions in relation to reports associated with the court process, to engage as much as possible and to input as effectively as she can ... So far Pamela has had a positive and engaging relationship with her solicitor and barrister where she is able to express and input her opinions and perspective; she has also been able to attend the court and discuss the process that is going on around her.[54]

The NAS Annual Report states that '[t]he quality of NAS involvement in these cases has been praised by judges, solicitors and barristers' but also raises a concern that this type of advocacy work is particularly time-consuming and resource-intensive, but only accounts for a small amount of the service's overall case load.[55]

A similar kind of support during court processes is provided by Independent Mental Capacity Advocates (IMCAs) in England and Wales. However, there are some important distinctions between this and the NAS in Ireland, which primarily concern the legislative framework within which IMCAs operate – namely, the Mental Capacity Act 2005. According to this Act, IMCAs can only be appointed to an individual who is thought to lack mental capacity for the relevant decision,[56] and in general are only appointed where the person is unbefriended – i.e. where there is no other individual who can act as an advocate for that person, apart from paid carers.[57] Finally, while the IMCA has a responsibility to support the person with a disability to understand the nature of a decision which is to be made about him or her,[58] and to assist them in challenging this decision if the person wishes to do so,[59] there is a conflicting requirement which underpins the legislative framework,

---

53 Legal Aid Board Circular 2/2007.
54 Citizens Information Board, *National Advocacy Service for People with Disabilities Annual Report 2012* (Dublin, 2013), 8.
55 Ibid.
56 Section 35(1), Mental Capacity Act 2005.
57 Section 39(1), Mental Capacity Act 2005.
58 Section 36(2), Mental Capacity Act 2005.
59 Section 36(3), Mental Capacity Act 2005.

which requires all interventions made with a person who lacks capacity to be done in that person's 'best interests'.[60]

The Act envisaged the appointment of IMCAs in cases where a 'best interests' decision is being made about a person who lacks capacity, which involves serious medical treatment being administered to the person,[61] or a decision about where the person will live.[62] IMCAs must be appointed where a person is deprived of their liberty, if the person or their representative requests an advocate, or if the supervisory body (usually a local authority) believes that without the help of an advocate, the person, or their representative, would be unable to exercise their rights.[63] However, as Series notes, the data for the years 2010–2012 provided by the UK Department of Health suggests that, although the numbers of referrals to IMCAs are gradually increasing,[64] the appointment of an IMCA is very unlikely to lead to a formal complaint or application to the Court of Protection to challenge a best interests substitute decision made about a person who lacks capacity.

In 2012, less than 0.5 per cent of IMCA referrals resulted in a formal complaint to the Court of Protection.[65] As Series suggests, this is unlikely to mean that in 99.5 per cent of cases where an IMCA was appointed, the person did not want to make a formal complaint, or that the person did not wish to challenge the best interest decision which had been made on their behalf.[66] The low level of complaints following from an IMCA appointment is particularly concerning in light of the fact that many IMCA referrals are made because a person has been deprived of their liberty, and IMCAs were envisaged as an important safeguard within the Act which could enable a person to challenge their de facto detention. Moreover, there is very little independent empirical research or evaluation available internationally on the experiences of people with disabilities who are appointed independent representative advocates as part of a state-operated, or statutory advocacy service. If we are to take the values of the CRPD seriously,[67] then it is important to actively seek information on people with disabilities' experiences of independent representative advocacy – especially where advocates are being appointed to support individuals to assert their rights, including through contentious and often complex court processes.

---

60   Section 39(1), Mental Capacity Act 2005. See also section 4, Mental Capacity Act 2005, which provides a definition of 'best interests'.
61   Section 37, Mental Capacity Act 2005.
62   Sections 38–39, Mental Capacity Act 2005.
63   Sections 39A-D, Mental Capacity Act 2005.
64   L Series, 'How Often Do IMCAs Challenge Decision-Makers? Not Very', available at: <http://thesmallplaces.blogspot.ie/2013/03/how-often-do-imcas-challenge-decision.html> (accessed 25 November 2013).
65   Ibid.
66   Ibid.
67   As discussed in ch 2, Article 4(3) CRPD requires the active involvement of persons with disabilities and their representative organisations in the development of law, policy and programmes affecting them.

The courts have only relatively recently begun to recognise the validity of an independent (non-legal) representative advocate's role as a support to people with disabilities in the court process. Where this involvement has been permitted in the court process, early findings indicate that it can lead to positive results – both for the court in terms of understanding and hearing the person's wishes, and for the individual to feel that they have more of a say in the court process and can follow the proceedings.[68] However, if the involvement of state-appointed representative advocates in the formal court process is to increase, thought must be given to whether this role falls within the remit of a general statutory advocacy service to people with disabilities, or whether this support should be provided by the courts service directly, as an entitlement of people with disabilities in the court process.

Next Friends and Guardians ad Litem: Supporting Communication or Substituting Decisions?

The more common, formally-recognised roles for third party supporters to people with disabilities in the court process are roles such as the 'next friend' or guardian ad litem. In both cases, the individuals appointed to these roles represent a person in court, often in circumstances where the person themselves is not present in the courtroom. Historically, there was a distinction between these roles, as 'next friend' represented a plaintiff, whereas the guardian ad litem represented a defendant.[69] This distinction in roles as representing plaintiff or defendant is no longer present in modern legal frameworks, although there is a tendency for the term 'next friend' to be used in relation to an individual who represents an adult with a disability,[70] and guardians ad litem are most commonly used in cases involving children (with or without disabilities).[71] However, the terms are often used interchangeably, and as a rule refer to the representation of individuals not thought to be capable of representing themselves in court.

Series describes the role filled by such representatives as akin to that of a 'litigation guardian' – since the next friend or guardian ad litem is appointed to represent a person's 'interests' in legal proceedings.[72] She also acknowledges the tension in the use of the term 'interests' – sometimes the guidance to such

---

68 See for example, Citizens Information Board, *National Advocacy Service for People with Disabilities Annual Report 2012* (Dublin, 2013), 8.

69 See G B Fraser, 'Independent Representation for the Abused and Neglected Child: The Guardian Ad Litem' (1976) 13 *Cal. W.L. Rev.* 16 at 27.

70 See for example, K X Metzmeier, 'The Power of an Incompetent Adult to Petition for Divorce through a Guardian or Next Friend' (1994) 33 *U. Louisville J. Fam. L.* 949. See further, *Sinnott v Attorney General* [2001] 2 I.R. 545.

71 See C T Cromley '[A]s Guardian Ad Litem I'm in a Rather Difficult Position' (1998) 24 *Ohio NUL Rev* 567.

72 L Series, 'Legal Capacity and Participation in Litigation: Recent Developments in the European Court of Human Rights' in G Quinn, L Waddington and E Flynn (eds), *European Yearbook on Disability Law* (Volume 5), 103–28.

representatives is that they should represent the individual's 'best interests' (this is particularly likely where children are represented), rather than the person's wishes. The person's interests can be represented or communicated to the court by a next friend or guardian ad litem directly; alternatively, individuals in these roles can instruct a legal representative for the person who presents the issues in court. While a family member, friend or advocate might fill this role, they will not necessarily do so, and it is often performed by professionals who are not usually the individual's guardian in relation to other matters. In some cases the next friend or guardian ad litem will instruct legal representation for the individual as well as providing their own evidence to court about the course of action they believe is in the person's interests.

While originally envisaged as a possible support to a vulnerable person in court proceedings, there are mixed views about the effectiveness of next friends and guardians ad litem in supporting a person with a disability to articulate their own views and present these to the court and to counsel. Series notes as follows:

> The role of litigation guardian can, however, become problematic where a dispute arises between the litigation guardian and the person they represent regarding what outcome or remedy should be sought, and how and when cases may be settled. In such circumstances, it is possible that a litigation guardian may argue a case that supports a measure which the person themselves opposes, or may at least refuse to oppose such a measure.[73]

This tension between representing the person's perceived 'interests' and supporting the individual to express their own views is particularly problematic in light of the human rights norms contained in the CRPD, especially in Article 12, which contains the right to support to exercise legal capacity for persons with disabilities, as discussed in the previous chapter.[74]

Similar critiques regarding the tension between 'best interests' and 'expressed wishes' can be found from the experiences of children who are appointed guardians ad litem in child custody cases. A study by Ruegger found that many children who expressed their views to guardians ad litem in confidence were unaware that these views would be disclosed in the guardian's report to the court, and that their parents would learn of their views, which might later be used against them.[75] This study also indicated a lack of awareness among children that their guardian ad litem might recommend a course of action to the court that was not in accordance with the child's wishes.[76] This leads Ruegger to question whether guardians ad litem are, perhaps deliberately, at times, avoiding potential with the children they

---

73 Ibid.
74 Ch 3, section 4.
75 M Ruegger, 'Seen and Heard but How Well Informed? Children's Perceptions of the Guardian ad Litem Service' (2001) 15(3) *Children & Society* 133 at 140.
76 Ibid.

represent by minimising the aspect of their role which requires them to report their own independent assessment to the court, and instead emphasising their role in communicating the child's views to the court.[77]

This approach of having your interests represented by a third party in court (often implying that the individual will not be present in court) can be contrasted with the rule of personal presence,[78] which has been articulated by the European Court of Human Rights, as well as many domestic courts, as an essential component of the right to a fair trial. This concept applies to both the civil and criminal contexts, and the European Court of Human Rights has in its more recent jurisprudence begun to articulate how it can apply to cases where an individual's legal capacity is being determined. In general, the Court has found that an oral hearing is necessary for the effective administration of justice,[79] where the person at the centre of the process has the opportunity to personally provide their perspective.[80] Some exceptions to this rule can be made on appeal if the matter is a purely technical or legal one,[81] or in relatively minor cases where there is no issue as to the credibility of witnesses,[82] but in general the presumption in favour of personal presence is extremely strong.

In the context of cases where a decision regarding the individual's legal capacity is being made, it is clear that the individual is an important source of information and should be present – although in many countries adult guardianship orders can be made by courts without ever meeting the person under guardianship.[83] Arguments may be made about the person's health or state of mind – suggesting that it would be too distressing for the person to attend court, or that they would not be in a position to give valid evidence to the court. However, the European Court has strongly rebutted these presumptions, stating in *Salontaji-Drobnjak v Serbia* that 'a simple assumption that a person suffering from schizophrenia must be excluded from the proceedings is not sufficient'.[84]

This was affirmed by the Court in *X and Y v Croatia*, where it held that 'judges adopting decisions with serious consequences for a person's private life under Article 8 ECHR, such as those entailed by divesting someone of legal capacity, should in principle also have personal contact with those persons'.[85] In *Shtukaturov v Russia*, the Court found that it was a breach of the principle of adversarial proceedings enshrined in Article 6 ECHR to make a decision to

---

77 Ibid., at 141.
78 See L Series, 'The Rule of Personal Presence: Implications for the Court of Protection', available at: <http://thesmallplaces.blogspot.ie/2013/10/the-rule-of-personal-presence.html> (accessed 10 February 2014).
79 *Koottummel v Austria* [2009] ECHR 2033.
80 *Ekbatani v Sweden* [1991] 13 EHRR 504.
81 *Schlumpf v Switzerland* [2009] ECHR 36.
82 *Suhadolc v Slovenia* [2011] ECHR 836.
83 See for example New York Surrogate Court Procedure Act Art. 17A.
84 *Salontaji-Drobnjak v Serbia* [2009] ECHR 1526.
85 *X and Y v Croatia* [2011] ECHR 1835 at §84.

deprive the plaintiff of legal capacity on the basis of documentary evidence alone, and stated that the applicant's presence in court should have been required to allow him present his own case.[86]

While requiring that individuals with disabilities who are central to a legal case are personally present in court is an important step, it will remain a relatively superficial requirement unless adequate supports are provided to make the courtroom and legal processes accessible, as discussed above. Even where the person is present, their views may be in large part communicated to the court via third parties – including lawyers, advocates, next friends, or guardians ad litem, as discussed above. It is also important to acknowledge that the individual's presence is not the same as a right of audience before the court – the person will, in general, only be permitted to give evidence when called upon, and will not have as much of an opportunity to interact with the court as other parties, particularly the legal representatives, may have.

Self-Represented Litigants with Disabilities and Communication with the Court

Some people with disabilities may by choice, or through lack of alternatives (including inability to secure legal representation), act as 'litigants in person' (also known as 'lay litigants', 'pro se litigants' or 'self-represented litigants'), meaning that they present their own case to the court, without having instructed legal representation to do so on their behalf. Much of the literature reports an increasing number of litigants in person from the 1970s onwards; in various countries the increases have been traced at different times to a variety of factors, including cuts to legal aid, the development of smaller, less formal, courts of first instance (e.g. small claims courts) and administrative tribunals which are easier to follow without legal representation.[87] Little is known about the numbers of people with disabilities who act as litigants in person, but it is clear that some take on this role, either by choice or necessity. However, without the appropriate support, it can be exceptionally difficult for disabled litigants in person to achieve a satisfactory outcome for their case. Colker's analysis of cases taken by people with disabilities under the Americans with Disabilities Act in the United States suggests that those who are litigants in person are less likely to be successful in these cases.[88]

Some supports have been recognised by the courts as valid in assisting litigants in person to effectively present their cases. The primary example of this is the role

---

86 *Shtukaturov v Russia* (App no 44009/05) [2008] ECHR 223 §73.

87 See for example, G Appleby, 'The Growth of Litigants in Person in English Civil Proceedings' (1997) 16 *Civil Justice Q.* 127, and E Richardson, T Sourdin and N Wallace, 'Self-Represented Litigants: Literature Review' (Australian Centre for Justice Innovation, Civil Justice Research Online, 2012).

88 R Colker, 'Winning and Losing under the Americans with Disabilities Act' (2001) 62 *Ohio St. LJ* 239 at 258.

of a 'McKenzie friend' – named after the first case in which it was recognised.[89] This English case concerned a divorce, where the plaintiff was no longer able to pay his legal representation, but wished to have the assistance of a volunteer, who was not licensed to practice law in the relevant court, but was willing to sit with the plaintiff, and support him by writing notes including suggestions for questions to pose in cross-examination. This conduct attracted the attention of the judge in the case who ordered the assistant to leave the court, but on appeal the right of litigants in person to 'reasonable assistance' was upheld, although the determination of what was reasonable remained with the trial judge. Those fulfilling the role of McKenzie friend may or may not have legal knowledge or experience, have an existing relationship with the litigant, and are generally not paid for their assistance.[90] For people with disabilities, the assistance of a McKenzie friend could take a similar form to the advocate support in court processes described above, although if the individual is a litigant in person, the McKenzie friend will not play a role in helping the person to express their views to their legal representation, as none will be present.

New innovative supports for people with disabilities in the court process, similar to the roles of non-legal advocates and McKenzie friends, are currently being developed, following the entry into force of the CRPD. One example of this is the role of 'court friend' which is proposed in the Assisted Decision-Making (Capacity) Bill in Ireland. Section 60 specifies that the Public Guardian may appoint a court friend to assist a person in a court procedure concerning a declaration of that person's mental capacity.[91] A court friend must be appointed for a person who has not instructed a legal practitioner and has no other supporter who can assist them in the case.[92] The court friend must be given access to records concerning the person which are relevant to the case (but not health records unless the court friend is a medical practitioner).[93]

In addition to attending court with a relevant person, a court friend is empowered to 'promote the interests of the relevant person in court' if the relevant person is not attending court.[94] While the Bill also establishes a general principle that the relevant person should attend court, certain exceptions are provided for, for example, if the court determines that it would not cause injustice if the person were not to attend, or if it would adversely affect the person's health, or if the person is unwilling to attend.[95] No further clarity is provided on what constitutes

---

89 *McKenzie v McKenzie* [1970] 3 WLR 472.
90 See E Richardson, T Sourdin and N Wallace, 'Self-Represented Litigants: Literature Review' (Australian Centre for Justice Innovation, Civil Justice Research Online, 2012), 11.
91 Section 60(1), Assisted Decision-Making (Capacity) Bill 2013.
92 Section 14(9), Assisted Decision-Making (Capacity) Bill 2013.
93 Section 60(3)–(4), Assisted Decision-Making (Capacity) Bill 2013.
94 Section 60(5), Assisted Decision-Making (Capacity) Bill 2013.
95 Section 107(1), Assisted Decision-Making (Capacity) Bill 2013.

the 'interests' of a person – so it is not yet clear whether court friends can form their own views of what might be in a person's interests and present this to the court, or whether the court friend should simply present the relevant person's wishes to court. The use of the term 'interests' here, however, seems to indicate that court friends have a mandate beyond simply presenting the relevant person's views to the court.

One key challenge with this role is that it does not permit or envisage that an individual might have both a court friend and a solicitor, since court friends can only be appointed where the person has not instructed legal representation. The experience of the National Advocacy Service in Ireland in performing a role similar to that of 'court friend', and supporting people with disabilities through court proceedings, suggests that it is invaluable that the person have both a court friend-type support, and legal representation – so that the court friend does not become a substitute for effective legal representation, particularly where the proceedings are so serious, since they may lead to a deprivation of the individual's legal capacity. Similarly, if the person has no legal representation, and does not attend court, it seems that the court friend will play a role similar to that of legal representation, although there is no guarantee that court friends will have experience of legal practice and may face significant challenges in presenting the individual's case to court.

This is particularly concerning in light of the limited availability of legal aid in these cases[96] – as it will be difficult for many people subject to a hearing to establish their legal capacity to qualify for legal aid, and there is no automatic right to representation in these cases despite the potentially significant impact which a restriction or denial of legal capacity has on an individual's autonomy and freedom. This is potentially problematic, as Series notes in the context of guardians ad litem or litigation guardians,[97] as it creates a conflicting role for the court friend – on the one hand, to assist the relevant person to communicate their wishes to the court, and on the other, to make arguments to the court about the course of action which is in the person's 'interests'. These issues demonstrate that while non-legal supports to assist people with disabilities in court are vital – there are relatively few examples of such roles where the assistant's sole purpose is to support the person to express their views, and often crosses the boundary from support to 'substituted decision-making' – creating conflicts with the principles of the CRPD in terms of the support people with disabilities require to exercise legal capacity.

---

96   Section 32, Assisted Decision-Making (Capacity) Bill 2013.
97   L Series, 'Legal Capacity and Participation in Litigation: Recent Developments in the European Court of Human Rights' in G Quinn, L Waddington and E Flynn (eds), *European Yearbook on Disability Law* (Volume 5), 103–28.

Amicus Curiae for Disability Rights: Supporting Equal Participation in Court?

Beyond legal representation and non-legal assistance in court, another key procedural support is the role of 'amicus curiae' – meaning 'friend of the court', a role often played by equality bodies, national human rights institutions, the Ombudsman or NGOs, who provide information to a court – often on regional or international human rights standards or comparative legal analysis which may be useful to the court in making its decision regarding the rights of persons with disabilities. There are many examples of the impact which strong, human rights-based amicus briefs have had on court decisions – particularly in the emerging jurisprudence on legal capacity and deinstitutionalisation from the European Court of Human Rights. One pertinent example is the amicus brief of Interights in the case of *Stanev v Bulgaria*.[98] Interights' amicus brief provided important context for the court on the right to community living in Article 19 CRPD and international trends to provide support in the community to people with psycho-social disabilities, such as the plaintiff, as an alternative to institutionalisation.[99] These arguments were clearly helpful to the court in finding a violation of the rights contained in Articles 3, 5 and 6.

However, it is often the case that a well-meaning NGO or human rights body provides such a brief to the court in cases involving people with disabilities in which arguments, contrary to its intentions, can be used to justify a violation of that individual's rights. There are some examples of amicus curiae briefs where arguments have been advanced on behalf of plaintiffs with disabilities which in fact contradict international human rights law standards. For example, in an amicus brief prepared by the European Group of National Human Rights Institutions for the European Court of Human Rights, an argument was made that a functional assessment of mental capacity is consistent with the right to legal capacity under Article 12 CRPD.[100] This is now clearly contradicted by the UN Committee's General Comment on Article 12 which highlights the discriminatory impact and disproportionate effect of functional tests of mental capacity on people with disabilities.[101] Similarly, in a US case, *Delling v Idaho*,[102] several amicus briefs were submitted, by a group of criminal law and mental health professors, the American Psychiatric Association[103] and the Constitutional Accountability

---

98   *Stanev v Bulgaria* [2012] ECHR 46.

99   Interights, *Written Submission of Interights: Stanev v Bulgaria (App no 36760/06)*, pending before the Grand Chamber (2010).

100   European Group of National Human Rights Institutions, *Amicus Brief re DD v Lithuania (App no 13469/06) (2008)*, 10.

101   Committee on the Rights of Persons with Disabilities, *General Comment on Article 12* (CRPD/C/GC/1) at paras 13 and 21.

102   *Delling v Idaho* 568 US (2012).

103   *Delling v Idaho, Amicus Brief of American Psychiatric Association and American Academy of Psychiatry and the Law*, No. 11–1515 (2012).

Center (among others), arguing that the availability of a defence of insanity was constitutionally required. This conflicts with the findings of the UN Office of the High Commissioner for Human Rights, which argues in an issues paper that the CRPD mandates the abolition of any 'defence based on the negation of criminal responsibility because of the existence of a mental or intellectual disability'.[104]

There is a significant divergence in the literature as to the potential usefulness of amicus briefs and their impact on the ultimate decisions of courts. Studies suggest that briefs on highly technical matters, which provide new information and context for the court, are more likely to be considered,[105] and may be influential – whereas others suggest that a strong amicus brief can remedy the weaknesses in a poor merits brief,[106] or where the plaintiff's legal representation has not presented a particularly strong argument. However, the authorship, collaborative nature of the brief, evidence base and quality of the legal argumentation all play a role in determining whether an amicus brief will be relied upon by the court.[107] While amicus briefs can therefore add value to disability rights cases and help to ensure more effective access to justice, they are clearly not a substitute for accessible court procedures, providing the client with full information and support, including legal representation, and other advocacy support, where necessary to achieve access to justice.

4. Disability Bias in the Courtroom: Judgments, Evidence and Procedure

Bias, myths, stereotypes and derogatory or offensive language regarding people with disabilities have long been documented in the justice system. Indeed, there is scarcely an example of a high-profile disability rights case, even in the last decade, which does not make some assumptions about individuals based simply on diagnosis of disability, or use terms such as 'suffering', 'confined' or 'vulnerable' to describe people with disabilities.[108] With this statement, I do not intend to belittle the experiences of people with disabilities taking cases before the courts – who may well describe themselves in these terms, but merely wish to highlight the pervasive myths and stereotypes which abound about people with disabilities in

---

104 Office of the High Commissioner for Human Rights, *Thematic Study by the Office of the United Nations High Commissioner for Human Rights on Enhancing Awareness and Understanding of the Convention on the Rights of Persons with Disabilities* (UN, 2009), 15.

105 See for example, J D Kearney and T W Merrill, 'The Influence of Amicus Curiae Briefs on the Supreme Court' (2000) 148(3) *University of Pennsylvania Law Review* 743.

106 S Krislov, 'The Amicus Curiae Brief: From Friendship to Advocacy' (1963) 72 *Yale L.J.* 694, 711.

107 K J Lynch, 'Best Friends-Supreme Court Law Clerks on Effective Amicus Curiae Briefs' (2004) 20 *JL & Pol.* 33.

108 For example, in *Stanev v Bulgaria* [2012] ECHR 46, the applicant was described as 'suffering' from schizophrenia, at §35.

the argumentation put forward during court processes. Often these terms are used by the plaintiff's own counsel, and the fact that reliance on stereotypes of people with disabilities as frail, vulnerable or 'in need' is deemed necessary to procure a successful outcome for a plaintiff seems remarkable in the 21st century. Based on existing studies, there is clearly a need for greater awareness-raising, education and training of all involved in the administration of justice in order to ensure more effective access to justice.

Prejudice towards people with disabilities in the justice system is particularly prevalent in the context of intellectual and psycho-social disabilities. Perlin demonstrates the extent of discriminatory attitudes of jurors towards defendants with mental disabilities (especially those with mental health issues) in death penalty cases.[109] This bias that is replicated across the criminal justice system, as confirmed in research by Garvey[110] and Gibbons et al.,[111] who demonstrated that jurors were more likely to believe that defendants with intellectual disabilities were guilty, as compared with non-disabled defendants. McConnell and Llewellyn also point towards worrying evidence of children being unnecessarily removed from parents with intellectual disabilities based on misguided or prejudicial conceptions of parenting ability which are sanctioned in the court process.[112] Similarly, the weight attributed by the courts to medical evidence regarding decision-making skills of individuals with a particular diagnosis of disability, as used to justify deprivations of legal capacity, has been much criticised, as many scholars demonstrate that such evidence does not have the objective scientific standpoint which it claims.[113]

These forms of bias and stereotypes can be addressed using a number of complementary strategies. As will be discussed in more detail in the following chapter, legal education is in need of significant reform to ensure that those representing, defending and adjudicating on the rights of people with disabilities have greater awareness of and sensitivity towards disability issues. Given the paternalistic history and legacy of the medical model of disability which has dominated the legal system, it is also important to think more creatively about how evidence of the lived experience of disability can be presented in the courtroom

---

109 M L Perlin, 'The Sanist Lives of Jurors in Death Penalty Cases: The Puzzling Role of Mitigating Mental Disability Evidence' (1994) 8 *Notre Dame JL Ethics & Pub. Pol'y* 239.

110 S P Garvey, 'Aggravation and Mitigation in Capital Cases: What do Jurors Think?' (1998) 98 *Columbia Law Review* 1538.

111 F X Gibbons, L L C Sawin and B N Gibbons, 'Evaluations of Mentally Retarded Persons: "Sympathy" or Patronization?' (1979) 84 *American Journal of Mental Deficiency* 124.

112 D McConnell and G Llewellyn, 'Stereotypes, Parents with Intellectual Disability and Child Protection' (2002) 24(3) *The Journal of Social Welfare & Family Law* 297.

113 See for example, D Morgan and K Veitch, 'Being Ms B: B, Autonomy and the Nature of Legal Regulation' (2004) 26 *Sydney Law Review* 107; F Freyenhagen and T O'Shea, 'Hidden Substance: Mental Disorder as a Challenge to Normatively Neutral Accounts of Autonomy' (2013) 9(1) *International Journal of Law in Context* 53.

context. Courts often invite expert reports on technical issues of relevance to the legal dispute in question – and the weight of medical evidence, where this may be prejudicial to the arguments advanced by people with disabilities as they seek to enforce their rights, could be tempered by recourse to evidence which is more representative of the experiences of people with disabilities.

Peers with disabilities are rarely, if ever, asked to provide expert evidence to courts to support judges or jurors in making a determination about an individual's rights. Naturally, the courts should first recognise that the individual in question is the most qualified to give evidence on their own views and experiences, and should be supported to do so as appropriate. However, where the court seeks additional information and perspectives, in many contexts, peers, as well as family members and friends, can offer valuable insights into an individual's experience – and importantly, this perspective can differ radically from the assessments of professionals, particularly medical professionals, as to the best course of action in order to protect an individual's human rights. Peer support in mental health[114] and autism,[115] to name just two areas, has proven particularly valuable in providing alternatives to the options which the justice system more commonly selects (e.g. institutionalisation and deprivation of legal capacity), particularly where a person is experiencing a crisis. These examples demonstrate the need for greater openness in the justice system to the multiplicity of perspectives on disability, and the need for greater emphasis on hearing directly from those with a lived experience of disability, rather than an over-reliance on medical expertise as the most trusted source of information about people with disabilities' lives.

5. Remedying Disability Bias Through Adaptations to Evidence and Procedure

Another important strategy for addressing disability bias in the court system is the adaptation of rules of evidence and procedure in order to accommodate the testimony of people with disabilities themselves. However, objections to the adaptation of evidence and procedure are often made, based on the need for strict due process, and respect for the rights of defendants, in particular in the criminal process. Nevertheless, some innovative adaptations of the criminal process have been made, particularly to accommodate the testimony of witnesses with intellectual and psycho-social disabilities in cases of sexual abuse. One such example is the Investigation and Testimony Procedural Act 2005 in Israel, which permits defendants, victims and witnesses with cognitive or mental disabilities to

---

114 P Solomon, 'Peer Support/Peer Provided Services Underlying Processes, Benefits, and Critical Ingredients' (2004) 27(4) *Psychiatric Rehabilitation Journal* 392.

115 P Whitaker, P Barratt, H Joy, M Potter and G Thomas, 'Children with Autism and Peer Group Support: Using "Circles of Friends"' (1998) 25(2) *British Journal of Special Education* 60.

give evidence in a modified court procedure for certain types of serious crimes (e.g. sexual offences, aggravated assault, human trafficking, manslaughter and murder). While concerns about the impact of this reform on the due process rights of non-disabled defendants might be raised, its constitutionality has not yet been challenged before the Israeli Supreme Court. In addition, the fact that the accommodations are available equally to victims and defendants could help to alleviate concerns about fairness or due process in the criminal justice system.

The 2005 Act was lobbied for by civil society on the basis of a pilot project implemented by an NGO called Bizchut, the Israel Human Rights Center for People with Disabilities, based on this organisation's experience in supporting people with disabilities, generally as victims and witnesses, primarily during criminal prosecutions for sexual and violent crimes. The Act applies both to police investigations and to testimony in court. Similar to other innovative practices to make the justice system more accessible to victims, and to children, the Act requires the involvement of 'therapeutic professionals' (e.g. psychologists and social workers) with experience of working with people with intellectual and psycho-social disabilities, who can intervene in the questioning, and provision of evidence by people with disabilities, to redirect the questioner, or enable the court to better understand the answers and evidence provided by the person with a disability. It is important to emphasise in this context that these cases are adjudicated only by judges, and that there is no jury.

Ziv describes the new methods of questioning, testimony and cross-examination as outlined in the 2005 Act as follows:

> Instead of an unmediated and direct impression of a witness by a judge, there is external intervention in this interaction. Testimony by a person with a mental or cognitive disability can be supported, directed, and interpreted by experts from therapeutic disciplines, who are vested with extensive authority. These experts can point to the way a witness should be addressed, what questions she may or may not be asked, how to frame the questions, what her responses mean (or do not mean), what her body language insinuates, etc. In general, these experts provide a type of interpretation to the testimony, by casting it against distinctive behavioral patterns of persons with similar disabilities.[116]

This form of adaptation to the rules of evidence and procedures in criminal cases involving people with disabilities has the potential to be highly contested. However, challenges to the purported objectivity of the law of evidence in 'fact-finding' for legal proceedings are widespread, in critical disability studies as well as feminist and critical race theory. Positivist legal scholars contend that the laws of evidence exist to discover the truth of the set of facts at the heart of the legal question in a manner that preserves the integrity of the justice system, relying on

---

116 N Ziv, 'Witnesses with Mental Disabilities: Accommodations and the Search for Truth' (2007) 27(4) *Disability Studies Quarterly*.

objectivity and rationality.[117] In effect, this represents the idea that we can determine exactly 'what happened' by seeing and hearing the testimony of witnesses. Several empirical studies of witness testimony and jury verdicts demonstrate, however, that this attempt at objectivity is not borne out in practice – in fact, determinations of guilt and innocence, among others, are often made based on highly subjective value judgments.[118]

Given this subjectivity, the challenge remains in terms of accommodating witnesses and defendants such as persons with disabilities who may not provide the kind of testimony which is most prized within the justice system – i.e. testimony which is heavily reliant on the demonstration of rational, objective memory and recollection skills, which shows 'credible' behaviour patterns with which decision-makers (judge and jurors) can empathise, and demonstrates that the individual can reliably communicate consistent information even under the pressure of intense cross-examination. As many critical scholars emphasise, these laws of evidence and features of what is considered reliable witness testimony do not reflect the lived realities of many different societal groups, including women, members of ethnic minorities, and people with disabilities.[119]

One approach to the adaptation of evidence and procedure is to offer the same supports to people with disabilities regardless of whether they appear as victims, witnesses or defendants – and in this way, perhaps it is possible to maintain the integrity of the criminal justice system and the traditional due process rights of the defendant, such as the right to confront accusers, the meaningful opportunity to be heard, and the right to a fair trial. Similar adjustments have been made to ensure more child-friendly justice systems (including the possibility to testify via video-link),[120] and to better accommodate victims within the criminal justice system (such as the development of victim impact statements[121] and victim-friendly courts).[122] These adaptations have been made in general without significant

---

117 See for example, M MacCrimmon, 'The Social Construction of Reality and the Rules of Evidence' (1991) 25 *University of British Columbia Law Review* 23, 36–50.

118 See for example S D Penrod, S M Fulero and B L Cutler, 'Expert Psychological Testimony on Eyewitness Reliability Before and After Daubert: The State of the Law and the Science' (1995) 13(2) *Behavioral Sciences & the Law* 229.

119 See for example, D Nicolson, 'Gender, Epistemology and Ethics: Feminist Perspectives on Evidence Theory' in M Childs and L Ellison (eds), *Feminist Perspectives on Evidence* (Cavendish, 2000), 13–37; A Ornstein, '"My God!": A Feminist Critique of the Excited Utterance Exception to the Hearsay Rule' (1997) 85 *California Law Review* 159

120 G Doherty-Sneddon and S McAuley, 'Influence of Video-Mediation on Adult–Child Interviews: Implications for the Use of the Live Link with Child Witnesses' (2000) 14(4) *Applied Cognitive Psychology* 379.

121 E Erez and L Rogers, 'Victim Impact Statements and Sentencing Outcomes and Processes: The Perspectives of Legal Professionals' (1999) 39(2) *British Journal of Criminology* 216.

122 T J Nhundu and A Shumba, 'The Nature and Frequency of Reported Cases of Teacher Perpetrated Child Sexual Abuse in Rural Primary Schools in Zimbabwe' (2001)

constitutional challenges in terms of the due process rights of the accused, so it is perhaps possible to make similar adjustments, for both victims and defendants with disabilities, in order to ensure more effective access to justice.

A separate but related issue is that of fitness to plead or competence to testify. This relates again to the discussion of legal capacity in the previous chapter.[123] Indeed, although making adaptations to evidence and procedure for defendants with disabilities may be possible in order to ensure access to justice, some may argue that adaptations will not be used as many of the intended defendants will often be found not fit to plead.[124] While a detailed analysis of the applicable rules on competence to testify and fitness to plead is outside the scope of this chapter, it is clear in light of Article 12 CRPD that our understanding of criminal responsibility, and its interaction with certain kinds of disabilities, is in need of reform, to better recognise the legal agency of persons with disabilities, while providing the necessary supports for individuals to engage with the criminal process in order to ensure a fair trial.[125]

In the judicial system, judges, prosecutors and opposing counsel could also learn from the approach suggested in the previous chapter for lawyers representing people with disabilities,[126] in order to ensure accurate communication and the right to a fair trial. The Judicial College in the UK provides guidance in its Equal Treatment Bench Book, for the adjudication of cases involving people with intellectual and psycho-social disabilities as victims, witnesses or defendants. This guidance includes recommendations to take regular breaks, not to ask the same question repeatedly as this may give the impression that the answer given is not believed and that a different answer is required, and to ask concrete, rather than abstract, questions. The bench book also reminds judges and prosecutors to bear in mind the need to 'Allow a witness to tell their own story and do not ignore information which does not fit in with assumptions as there may be a valid explanation for any apparent confusion (e.g. the witness may be telling the correct story but using one or more words in a different context at a different level of understanding)'.[127] This reminder to acknowledge the different 'ways of knowing' and different styles of communication in witness testimony provides a good starting point for considering how court rules on evidence and procedure might be

---

25(11) *Child Abuse & Neglect* 1517, which discusses victim-friendly courts in Zimbabwe for child sexual abuse cases.

    123   Ch 2, section 4.

    124   T P Rogers, N J Blackwood, F Farnham, G J Pickup and M J Watts 'Fitness to Plead and Competence to Stand Trial: A Systematic Review of the Constructs and their Application' (2008) 19(4) *The Journal of Forensic Psychiatry & Psychology* 576.

    125   See for example, T Minkowitz, 'Norms and Implementation of CRPD Article 12' presentation at Committee on the Rights of Persons with Disabilities Day of General Discussion on Article 12, 21 October 2009, available at: <http://www.panusp.org/wp-content/uploads/2013/02/Article-12-Minkowitz.pdf> (accessed 10 December 2013), 3.

    126   Ch 3, sections 3 and 5.

    127   Judicial College, *Equal Treatment Bench Book 2013* (London), 6.

adapted to better accommodate people with disabilities and ensure more effective access to justice.

6. Beyond Evidence: Increasing the Participation of People with Disabilities in Determining Justice – the Role of Disabled Jurors

Adaptations to the rules of court procedure may also be necessary to facilitate the effective participation of people with disabilities in a number of key roles within the justice system from which they have previously been excluded. One prominent example of this is the opportunity for people with disabilities to participate on juries, in countries where a jury system is an integral component of the justice system. Many statutes have listed certain impairments as characteristics which will disqualify an individual for jury service, such as lack of literacy, blindness, deafness (sometimes extending this prohibition to persons who do not use speech), intellectual and psycho-social disability. For example, in Ireland, the Juries Act 1976, which was somewhat ironically enacted to remedy the historical exclusion of women from jury service, provides the following list of persons 'incapable' and therefore ineligible to serve on a jury:

> A person who because of insufficient capacity to read, deafness or other permanent infirmity is unfit to serve on a jury.
>
> A person who suffers or has suffered from mental illness or mental disability and on account of that condition either
>
> (a) is resident in a hospital or other similar institution, or
>
> (b) regularly attends for treatment by a medical practitioner.[128]

This was reformed in 2008, and the first part of the definition of ineligibility based on capacity to read, deafness, or other permanent infirmity was replaced with the following wording: 'Persons who have – (a) an incapacity to read, or (b) an enduring impairment, such that it is not practicable for them to perform the duties of a juror'.[129] The second part of the definition of ineligibility for persons with mental illness or mental disability was not however amended by the 2008 Act.

These provisions were challenged in a 2010 case by a deaf woman who was deemed ineligible for jury service, and the judge in that case found that the use of a sign-language interpreter could violate the prohibition in common law against

---

128 Section 7 (Schedule 1), Juries Act 1976.
129 Section 64, Civil Law (Miscellaneous Provisions) Act 2008.

the inclusion of a 13th person in the jury room.[130] However, subsequent cases in the Irish courts have taken a different perspective, with Judge Carney finding in 2010 that requiring sign-language interpreters to swear an oath of confidentiality similar to that sworn by jurors would be sufficient to preserve the integrity of the jury process.[131] In comparative jurisdictions, varying approaches have been taken to this issue, with the English courts maintaining the prohibition against 'strangers' in the jury room,[132] whereas the US courts have acknowledged that the use of a sign-language interpreter is appropriate to facilitate the participation of a deaf juror,[133] and since the passage of the Americans with Disabilities Act, it has not been permissible to explicitly exclude people with disabilities from eligibility for jury service. On a global scale, while challenges to the exclusion of jurors with physical and sensory disabilities have been somewhat successful, fewer challenges to ineligibility of individuals for jury service on the grounds of intellectual or psycho-social disability, or levels of literacy, appear to have been taken.

The Irish Law Reform Commission has critiqued the current system of ineligibility for jury service in Ireland in light of the UN Convention on the Rights of Persons with Disabilities and made a number of recommendations for reform. With respect to jurors with physical and sensory disabilities, the Commission recommended amending the 2008 Act to state that 'a person is eligible for jury service unless the person's physical capacity, taking account of the provision of such reasonably practicable supports and accommodation that are consistent with the right to a trial in due course of law, is such that he or she could not perform the duties of a juror'.[134] Similarly, in the context of mental health and intellectual disability, it recommended that the 1976 Act be amended to reflect that 'a person is eligible for jury service unless, arising from the person's ill health, he or she is resident in a hospital or other similar health care facility or is otherwise (with permissible and practicable assisted decision-making supports and accommodation that are consistent with the right to a trial in due course of law) unable to perform the duties of a juror'.[135] Finally, in the context of reading and linguistic ability, the Commission suggested that 'in order to be eligible to serve, a juror should be able to read, write, speak and understand English to the extent that it is practicable for him or her to carry out the functions of a juror'.[136]

---

130 *Clarke v County Registrar County Galway*, Courts Service of Ireland and Attorney General (2006 No.1338 JR), High Court, 14 July 2010, *The Irish Times*, 15 July 2010; and High Court 13 October 2010 (date of order).

131 *The People (DPP) v O'Brien (Application of Dunne)*, Central Criminal Court, 29 November 2010.

132 *Regina v A Juror* (Jeffrey McWhinney), Woolwich Crown Court, U19990078, 9 November 1999, Smith Bernal Reporting Ltd.

133 See for example, *People v Guzman*, 555 N. E. 2d. 259.

134 Law Reform Commission, *Report on Jury Service* (LRC 107–2013) (Dublin, 2013), 59.

135 Ibid., 63.

136 Ibid., 68.

The Law Reform Commission suggested that no individual assessment of capacity would be required as a rule for any juror but that jurors would be informed of their obligations and encouraged to come forward if they felt that due to their disability they would be unable to carry out the functions of a juror.[137] In all cases, it would be the responsibility of the judge to ultimately determine whether an individual juror could adequately perform her duties, and in so doing, the judge should apply the presumption of capacity and the requisite standard of juror competency expected of all who are eligible for jury service.[138] The report also acknowledged that having a disability that requires extensive accommodation and support to carry in order to perform jury service could constitute 'good cause' for a juror to request to be excused.[139] The Commission also recommended that, where there was a conflict between the obligation to provide a fair trial and the principles contained in the UN CRPD, fair trial duties would take precedence.[140]

In opening up jury service to accommodate persons with disabilities, questions will inevitably be raised about the impact which this might have on fair trial rights – especially for defendants in criminal cases. However, Bleyer, McCarty and Wood argue that in light of the disability equality imperative:

> Courts must open their doors as well as their jury boxes and consider with care how to accommodate a range of impairments while ensuring a fair trial. Judges must make sensitive determinations about each individual's ability to serve, based on a thorough knowledge of accommodations and the nature of the case at hand. They must weigh the competing rights of people with disabilities to serve against the rights of defendants and litigants to a fair and impartial jury trial.[141]

These authors suggest five possible ways for developing a more inclusive jury. The first requires checks and balances to ensure that disabled people are not excluded from the lists where potential jurors are sourced.[142] This can pose a problem as discussed further in Chapter 6 since many of these types of databases (e.g. electoral lists, census data, tax registries) do not include all people with disabilities who might be eligible to serve on a jury. Another approach is to include non-discrimination statements in the legislative and regulatory frameworks governing jury service – to prevent any blanket exclusions of potential jurors on the basis of a specific disability.[143] This would seem to echo the approach suggested by the Irish Law Reform Commission. The third route proposed is to clarify what eligibility

---

137 Ibid., 63.
138 Ibid.
139 Ibid., 60.
140 Ibid.
141 K Bleyer, K S McCarty and E Wood, 'Jury Service for People with Disabilities' (1994) 78 *Judicature* 273 at 273.
142 Ibid.
143 Ibid., at 274.

for jury service involves, and to make juror qualifications transparent and easily attainable, while meeting the requirement for a fair trial.[144] Fourth, exemptions from jury service must be clearly outlined, and should be sufficiently flexible to allow people with disabilities to opt out of jury service if it would impact negatively on their health, while maintaining the desired representativeness in the jury system.[145] Finally, it is suggested that introducing legislative mandates to reasonably accommodate jurors with disabilities is necessary to achieve substantive equality and to incentivise greater participation by people with disabilities in jury service.[146]

In addition to these suggestions, one of the more implicit barriers that jurors with disabilities may face is the fact that in most jurisdictions, litigators have such a degree of flexibility in selecting potential jurors that people with disabilities, although not explicitly excluded from jury service, are often not actively selected from the pool of potential candidates.[147] While legal remedies may not be sufficient to combat this problem, greater awareness-raising and training on disability equality, particularly within the legal profession, as suggested in Chapter 5, can perhaps help to address the issue. Taken together, these suggestions should help to make juries more representative of the diversity within our communities and society at large, and to include the perspectives of people with disabilities in key deliberations about how justice is done through our court system.

7. Conclusion

It is clear from the discussion undertaken in this chapter that there is much work to be done in order to increase the accessibility and usability of the justice system for persons with disabilities, beginning with the court process. Some basic issues, such as access to the physical infrastructure in which justice is administered, and the need to secure a right of audience, or personal presence of people with disabilities before courts, remain to be addressed in many different countries across a whole range of legal procedures. Facilitating the effective participation of people with disabilities in the court process in a wide range of roles, including as lawyers and judges (to be addressed further in the next chapter), as well as those of plaintiff, witness, defendant and juror, remains a core challenge in the efforts to create an accessible and inclusive justice system, as demonstrated throughout this chapter. These challenges can be addressed in part through the provision of additional supports to communicate throughout the court process, as well as adaptation to the

---

144 Ibid.
145 Ibid.
146 Ibid.
147 See for example, A Weis, 'Peremptory Challenges: The Last Barrier to Jury Service for People with Disabilities' (1997) 33 *Willamette L. Rev.* 1, and M J Crehan, 'The Disability-Based Peremptory Challenge: Does It Validate Discrimination against Blind Prospective Jurors' (1997) 25 *N. Ky. L. Rev.* 531.

rules of evidence and procedure – which, as discussed earlier in the chapter, must be accomplished in a manner which also respects the rights of all parties to the proceedings, with particular regard to the rights of defendants in criminal trials.

There is also much to be learned from an intersectional analysis of the accessibility and transparency of the justice system – and particularly, drawing on examples of good practice from gender and age-based innovations in access to justice, in order to build a courtroom system and process which is fully inclusive of people with disabilities and sensitive to their lived experiences. As stated at the outset of this chapter, the perceived and actual exclusion of people with disabilities from the justice system, particularly the courtroom process, has the symbolic,[148] as well as practical significance, as countries continue to progress in the domestic implementation of international human rights norms, such as the right to access justice contained in Article 13 CRPD.

---

148 R Bahdi, *Background Paper on Women's Access to Justice in the MENA Region* (International Development Research Centre (IDRC), Women's Rights and Citizenship Program (WRC) and the Middle East Regional Office (MERO), Middle East and North African (MENA) Regional Consultation, 9–11 December 2007, Cairo, Egypt).

Chapter 5
Incorporating Disability in Legal Education and Practice: A Call for Consciousness-Raising

1. Introduction

As demonstrated in the previous two chapters, the interaction between lawyers, judges, justice officials and people with disabilities leaves a lot to be desired in terms of ensuring an inclusive and accessible justice system. In the previous chapters I discussed how reforms might be constructed, starting with access to legal information, advice and representation (Chapter 2), and ensuring greater accessibility of court structures and processes (Chapter 3). Another approach to the problem is to examine the legal education system and the training of future legal practitioners and judges, to determine whether the actors in question have the appropriate tools to understand the experience of people with disabilities and adjudicate questions of their human rights, as well as whether people with disabilities themselves face additional barriers if they wish to enter one of the legal professions.[1]

While, as indicated in the previous chapters, an accessible justice system requires that all professionals, not just lawyers, but law enforcement, social workers, professional representative advocates and others, respect the rights of persons with disabilities, this chapter will focus predominantly on the training and education of lawyers and legal professionals, as a more comprehensive analysis of the training of all professionals involved in the administration of justice is beyond the scope of this research. Nevertheless, many of the recommendations which are made in the context of legal education and training could be replicated throughout other professions involved in the administration of justice.

In addition, the approach of the academy to issues of disability rights could also be strengthened across a wide range of disciplines, not just law, where disability remains a marginal issue, if it is discussed at all; including philosophy, literature, engineering, architecture, and many others.[2] Again, a more detailed discussion of

---

1   See generally, S Ortoleva, 'Inaccessible Justice: Human Rights, Persons with Disabilities and the Legal System' (2011) 17 *ILSA Journal of International and Comparative Law* 281.

2   For more on this, see A Lawson, 'The Ivory Tower and the Real World: Academia and the Convention on the Rights of Persons with Disabilities', Reykjavik, Nordic Network

the inclusion of disability in all academic disciplines is beyond the scope of this book, although in the broad sense, since disability by its nature is such a cross-cutting issue as part of the diversity of humanity, it is difficult to imagine a single discipline where disability is irrelevant. Therefore, as a general recommendation, it can be argued that greater attention should be paid to disability discourse in all aspects of academic education – as well as greater inclusion and reasonable accommodation of students and teachers with disabilities in higher education.

In this chapter, I will address three key issues, beginning with general legal education in third level – including both undergraduate and postgraduate legal education, and its inclusiveness of disability (both in terms of disabled students and faculty and teaching issues of disability rights). A wide range of issues in teaching and learning will be addressed, including admission onto courses, assessment, reasonable accommodation, academic freedom and course content, drawing, where possible, on the experience of including other marginalised communities in legal education. Second, I will consider the specific issue of clinical legal education, an approach which is perhaps more common in US law schools than in other common law systems, but is nonetheless gaining traction worldwide, and consider whether clinical approaches are sufficiently cognisant of disability rights issues (including university-run legal clinics which are specifically aimed at persons with disabilities). Finally, I will consider professional education and training of legal professionals such as solicitors, barristers, attorneys and judges. This discussion will include an examination of ongoing training and continuing professional development opportunities for legal professionals to increase their knowledge and understanding of disability rights.

2. Teaching and Learning the Law: Experiences of Disabled Students and Faculty in Legal Education

People with disabilities may have related experiences as both students and teachers in higher education – and in this context, in legal education. In this section I will first examine the experiences of students with disabilities in gaining access to legal education at third level, and negotiating the reasonable accommodations required to enable them to pursue their chosen course of study with a particular focus on different ways of learning, evaluation and assessment. Following this, I will discuss the related experiences of university educators with disabilities in the field of legal education. Throughout this discussion, it will become apparent that there is a divide in the approach to legal education on either side of the Atlantic – with the US approach, in which law is primarily a field of postgraduate study, being characterised as more vocational, with its primary objective to prepare students for legal practice; whereas a broader approach is taken in Ireland and the UK, with legal education being available at undergraduate level, but where further separate

---

of Disability Research Conference, 27–28 May 2011.

professional or vocational education is required before students can commence legal practice. This description of the divergence of approaches is undoubtedly over-simplistic, but nonetheless, provides a useful starting point for the purpose of the following discussion.

Ortoleva acknowledges the barriers which students with disabilities face in gaining access to legal education as follows:

> Law schools tended not to admit applicants with disabilities and even to this day, law school entrance exams are not accessible to those applicants. Employment is limited by many factors, including that bar exams present challenges to many because of inaccessibility of the exam, attitudinal barriers posed by employers, unavailability of reasonable accommodations, and other factors.[3]

Lawson also highlights that students with disabilities in third level education, including law students, are less likely to apply to enter higher education and experience higher drop-out rates than non-disabled students, citing a lack of awareness, and availability of, reasonable accommodation as one of the primary causes for this.[4]

Anti-Discrimination Legislation: Enabling Access to Higher Education

In accessing legal education and throughout one's studies, the key underlining legal principle for students with disabilities is that of non-discrimination, as discussed in previous chapters. In general, third level institutions such as universities are prohibited by statute from discriminating against 'otherwise qualified' students with disabilities who meet the entry requirements for accessing legal education. In addition, educational institutes are generally obliged to 'reasonably accommodate' students with disabilities (or to make reasonable modifications or adjustments) to enable them to pursue their course of study. Such accommodations can range from the physical accessibility of university buildings to additional time for exams, the provision of a scribe, personal assistant or note-taker, assistive technology, the availability of course materials in accessible formats, or alternative methods of evaluation and assessment. Standards and legal obligations vary across jurisdictions and may also be dependent in part on whether the educational institution in question is public or private.

---

3 S Ortoleva, 'Inaccessible Justice: Human Rights, Persons with Disabilities and the Legal System' (2011) 17 *ILSA Journal of International and Comparative Law* 281 at 303.

4 A Lawson, 'The Ivory Tower and the Real World: Academia and the Convention on the Rights of Persons with Disabilities', Reykjavik, Nordic Network of Disability Research Conference, 27–28 May 2011.

Smith,[5] however, argues that, given the nature and purpose of the academy, third level educational institutions, and law schools in particular, should be held to a high standard in terms of their inclusiveness for students and faculty with disabilities, rather than relying on a narrow interpretation of the applicable law. He states:

> The legal framework establishes a floor, not a ceiling, for law school administrators and legal educators. To fulfill their dual roles as educational institutions and professional schools, law schools, and the law school administrators and legal educators who run them, must go beyond the minimum requirements imposed by law. Decision makers should interpret expansively both 'disability' and 'reasonable accommodation'. A wide range of accommodations and services should be made available to, but not forced upon the disabled law student without regard to whether she requested them.[6]

I return here again to the Americans with Disabilities Act (ADA) as an example of non-discrimination legislation which addresses the issue of how inclusive third level education in general, and legal education in particular, must be of students with disabilities. Since its enactment in 1990, debates on its interpretation in the higher education context, particularly in legal education, have been widespread.[7] The use of the term 'otherwise qualified individual' in the ADA and in many other anti-discrimination statutes throughout the world seems to indicate that the student in question must, *despite* her disability, be eligible for entry onto a particular third level course.[8] However, the introduction of reasonable accommodation in second level education has also meant that certain students have benefited from supports in attaining their eligibility for third level study – which means the definition of 'otherwise qualified' individual becomes more muddied and complex.

Alternative Pathways to University Education: Access and Inclusion Programmes

In the past two decades in particular, many jurisdictions have developed alternative pathways to third level education for students from disadvantaged backgrounds, and/or students with disabilities. These opportunities include 'access' programmes, whereby students are not required to meet the same eligibility as the general intake for a particular mainstream university course (including law degrees) but can be

---

5 K H Smith, 'Disabilities, Law Schools, and Law Students: A Proactive and Holistic Approach' (1999) 32 *Akron L. Rev.* 1.

6 Ibid., at 3.

7 See for example, L F Rothstein, 'Introduction to Disability Issues in Legal Education: A Symposium' (1991) 41 *Journal of Legal Education* 301.

8 See for example, S J Adams, 'Because They're Otherwise Qualified: Accommodating Learning Disabled Law School Writers' (1996) 46 *Journal of Legal Education* 189.

admitted if they reach a lesser standard of academic achievement, combined with evidence of the impact which the relevant disadvantage or disability has had on their educational performance to date.[9] Similarly, certain universities have developed specific programmes to specifically include students with intellectual disabilities, who would not meet the general eligibility requirements for entry into courses on offer to other students, to participate in lifelong learning and have access to a mainstream university experience – although often these courses are not accredited in the same way as other university offerings, and may not include all subject areas, or be open to students interested in studying law.[10]

These alternative pathways should be considered as part of any strategy to increase the participation and intake of students with disabilities who wish to study law, but should be carefully designed to ensure they facilitate meaningful and effective participation, and do not segregate students with disabilities or place a lesser value on their educational achievements than on those available to students who enter university through one of the more established pathways. While these alternatives can form an important element in facilitating access to university for law students with disabilities, they should also not be seen as a replacement for, or alternative to, improving access for these students through the universal, mainstream pathways to higher education. Therefore, in the following section, I will discuss in more detail how the general entry criteria and universally available courses for law students can be adapted to better accommodate students (and teachers) with disabilities, and facilitate their effective participation in higher education.

Adapting Law School Curricula: What Are 'Essential Components' of Legal Education?

Other debates which have emerged in higher education following the entry into force of anti-discrimination statutes around the world include the ongoing discussion about what counts as a disability and scepticism about whether students over-identify as being disabled in order to benefit from the supports available.[11] These issues will not be addressed in detail here, except to mention that they should

---

9 In Ireland, for example, access programmes to third level education are provided for students from socio-economically disadvantaged backgrounds (HEAR – higher education access route) and students with disabilities (DARE – disability access route to education). For more information see <http://www.accesscollege.ie/> (accessed 1 January 2014).

10 See for example, D Corby, W Cousins and E Slevin, 'Inclusion of Adults with Intellectual Disabilities in Post-Secondary and Higher Education: A Review of the Literature' (2012) *Lifelong Learning and Community Development* 69–86. For a practical overview of third level education opportunities for adults with intellectual disabilities in the United States, see <http://www.thinkcollege.net/> (accessed 1 January 2014).

11 See for example, M Kelman, *Jumping the Queue: An Inquiry into the Legal Treatment of Students with Learning Disabilities* (Harvard University Press, 1997).

also be contextualised by the evidence that many students with disabilities are often reluctant to identify as disabled at third level,[12] and that limited supports are available for many, depending on the university's resources, attitudes of faculty and administrative staff, and the flexible or rigid application of course requirements.

In the early years of integration of students with disabilities into legal education, questions were raised about whether the adaptation of coursework, assessment (including exams) and evaluation to facilitate students with disabilities might risk compromising the integrity or quality of legal education, or have an adverse impact on the qualifications of law school graduates. Another way of approaching this issue might be to ask what really constitutes the 'essential components' of legal education, which cannot be changed, as opposed to the aspects of that education which can be modified, adapted or omitted, to accommodate students with particular disabilities? For example, is the use of the Socratic method (particularly common in US law schools) an 'essential component' of legal education? Can the same be said of the ability to effectively manage exam stress without the need for accommodations in the form of assessment (e.g. extra time, a quieter exam space, or support with preparation)?

Many have argued that, since wide-ranging accommodations may not be available in the 'real world' once the student graduates,[13] educational institutions should exercise caution and enter into a dialogue with the student about the levels of accommodation which can be provided, to ensure that the student is adequately prepared for employment after graduation. However, such an approach which aims to reduce the accommodations provided seems premised on the notion that education, and in this instance, legal education, is purely vocational in nature, and if the student in question could not survive in legal practice then they should not be accommodated to obtain a legal education. Perhaps where legal education takes a purely, or predominantly vocational approach (for example, in Ireland and the UK, professional training for solicitors or barristers, or in the United States, law school), the principle of reducing individual students' reliance on certain supports not available post-graduation may have some validity. Similarly, if the provision of supports facilitates the tokenistic inclusion of students with disabilities who are not met with the same expectations in terms of academic achievement as their non-disabled students, then it should be met with caution.

However, if one takes a broader approach to the purpose of legal education, based on the notion that what is required is simply an ability to gain a deeper understanding of the operation of the law in all its political, economic, social and cultural contexts,[14] then it follows that greater flexibility in the provision of

---

12   See L F Rothstein, 'Introduction to Disability Issues in Legal Education: A Symposium' (1991) 41 *Journal of Legal Education* 301 at 305.

13   K H Smith, 'Disabilities, Law Schools, and Law Students: A Proactive and Holistic Approach' (1999) 32 *Akron L. Rev.* 1 at 78.

14   See for example S C Halpern, 'On the Politics and Pathology of Legal Education (Or Whatever Happened to That Blindfolded Lady with the Scales)' (1982) 32 *J. Legal*

reasonable accommodation to students with disabilities should be granted. In this context, it is important also to acknowledge that pursuit of legal practice is not the only possible outcome for law student in terms of employment, as of course many law students go on to enter different professions. Since legal education, particularly at undergraduate level, as it is most commonly provided in Ireland, the UK and many other European countries, generally takes this broader pedagogical approach, it is appropriate that a high standard of reasonable accommodation and flexibility in the determination of the 'essential components' of the course be provided. Clearly, reasonable accommodation is required in all aspects of the educational experience – not just the formal curriculum and assessment, but in all aspects of the academic experience – including ensuring the accessibility of group work projects, study visits, field trips and internships, so that these aspects of university education are also made accessible to law students with disabilities.

Smith provides some important criteria to consider in determining what is an 'essential function' or objective of legal education and, therefore, to determine whether or not a particular accommodation is 'reasonable', while cautioning that deference should be given where possible to the individual educator's judgment, especially when considering the required pedagogical approach. These include the pedagogical impact of the accommodation required, the academic freedom of the instructor to determine the content of the course, skills required and methods of evaluation, the cost and benefit of the accommodation, the potential impact (including possible harm) for the disabled student as well as non-disabled students (e.g. a decrease in resources which could be spent on other educational materials).[15]

Jolly-Ryan goes even further than Smith in arguing for a move away from focusing on individual student deficits in legal education, as she contends that it is legal educators who experience teaching disabilities in their inability to communicate information effectively to students who are 'non-traditional learners'.[16] She attributes this narrow-minded approach to a number of factors – including the fact that most legal educators in US law schools are drawn from a small number of elite schools, and were themselves students who thrived in the status quo of legal education, making them reluctant to acknowledge the need for change in pedagogical approaches.[17] The stigma associated with disability, and learning disabilities in particular, is another underlying factor, along with scepticism about the diagnosis of what Jolly-Ryan describes as non-verbal

---

Education 32 383; D L Rhode, 'Missing Questions: Feminist Perspectives on Legal Education' (1992) 45 *Stan. L. Rev.* 45 1547; C Menkel-Meadow, 'Feminist Legal Theory, Critical Legal Studies, and Legal Education or the Fem-Crits Go to Law School' (1988) 38 *J. Legal Educ.* 61.

15 K H Smith, 'Disabilities, Law Schools, and Law Students: A Proactive and Holistic Approach' (1999) 32 *Akron L. Rev.* 1 at 72–78.

16 J Jolly-Ryan, 'Disabilities to Exceptional Abilities: Law Students with Disabilities, Nontraditional Learners, and the Law Teacher as a Learner' (2005) 6 *Nev. LJ* 116.

17 Ibid., at 124.

learning disabilities (e.g. dyslexia), particularly where these have not become apparent prior to entering legal education. She also provides an interesting critique of traditional law school teaching methods, arguing for example that the Socratic method, while it may benefit individual students who learn well verbally, has been proven to be ineffective for many groups of learners, including women, minorities and students with a wide variety of learning styles.[18]

Jolly-Ryan also explores the benefits which law students with disabilities can bring both to the classroom and to legal practice, arguing that a change in the way we teach the law is beneficial for all learners, not just students with disabilities. She also highlights some of the specific talents which students with a wide range of abilities and skills, including students with disabilities, bring to the learning and practice of law, citing examples of creative thinking, more visual approaches to understanding the law (for students who are not verbal learners), and perhaps most importantly, the development 'of empathy and a sense of justice to serve clients and the public in an exceptional manner'.[19]

Her recommended strategies for more inclusive learning in the law school classroom include quite basic requirements, such as providing clarity on the course, materials and assessment at the outset, providing study and note-taking guides, using a multi-sensory approach to teaching and providing frequent evaluation and feedback.[20] In her later work she has also argued for the adoption of a universal design approach to teaching law, particularly through the effective use of new technologies.[21] The adoption of more creative approaches to assessment (including the introduction of more practical assignments, clinical legal education and opportunities for students to relate their legal education to their own experiences) can also benefit students with disabilities, as well as the general law student population.

Teaching the Law: Experiences of Legal Educators with Disabilities

As for students with disabilities, legal educators with disabilities also need the same basic guarantees of equality, non-discrimination and the provision of reasonable accommodation in order to encourage an inclusive and barrier-free work environment. Since historically, many people with disabilities experienced segregated education, it is only in relatively recent decades that legal educators with disabilities (and those with 'invisible' disabilities who openly identify as disabled) have become more visible in our classrooms. Some examples of positive action to encourage more people with disabilities to enter academia have been introduced in certain jurisdictions, and this can benefit the diversity of legal education. For

---

18 Ibid., at 125.
19 Ibid., at 131.
20 Ibid., at 148–52.
21 J Jolly-Ryan, 'Bridging the Law School Learning Gap Through Universal Design' (2012) 28 *Touro L. Rev.* 28 1393.

example, following the legislative provision for positive discrimination on the ground of disability in the Equality Act 2010,[22] employers in England and Wales can subscribe to a 'guaranteed interview scheme' also known as the 'two ticks' scheme[23] for people with disabilities, meaning that if a person identifies as disabled in a job application, and meets the minimum criteria for the position, they can be guaranteed an interview. Many universities, including law schools, adhere to this scheme and the guarantee of an interview, while obviously not guaranteeing the disabled person a job, can be beneficial to increase the opportunities for a diverse academic workplace.

Once in post, law teachers with disabilities may require a range of reasonable accommodations which can also impact on students – for example, a blind lecturer may require assignments to be submitted electronically, and may need additional support to access course materials not available in accessible formats. The experience of learning from a teacher with a disability, or learning with other students with disabilities can also help to ensure that law students develop an appreciation for reasonable accommodation and accessibility which they may carry throughout the rest of their careers.

Other adjustments which might be made to the teaching of law could benefit students and teachers with disabilities equally. For example, Lawson recommends the introduction of centralised university budgets for reasonable accommodation requests made by staff or students.[24] She argues that, while individualised funding for reasonable accommodation demonstrates a person-centered approach, it can have a disproportionate impact on the first person to request a particular accommodation (e.g. transcription of an inaccessible textbook), as the funding for this will be taken from an individual's budget, but the resource developed can be shared with all those who subsequently request accessible materials.

In order to contribute to a more inclusive academic environment, Lawson also highlights the importance of valuing all forms of contribution made by academics in the pursuit of disability rights and equality. This includes encouraging further inter-disciplinary and multi-disciplinary research and teaching (both widening existing discipline boundaries and mainstreaming disability issues across a broad range of disciplines), developing valuable, respectful partnerships between the university and disabled people's organisations, and valuing academic engagement with the broader community, including through activism.[25] These activities represent a broader set of academic values, and can be encouraged for both faculty and students, including through assessment and performance evaluation,

---

22   Section 13(3), Equality Act 2010 (England and Wales).
23   For more information about these schemes, see <https://www.gov.uk/looking-for-work-if-disabled/> (accessed 2 January 2014).
24   A Lawson, 'The Ivory Tower and the Real World: Academia and the Convention on the Rights of Persons with Disabilities', Reykjavik, Nordic Network of Disability Research Conference, 27–28 May 2011.
25   Ibid.

opportunities for experiential learning and promotion, and recognition of the impact of academic or scholarly achievements.

Similarly to law students with disabilities, disabled law teachers require equal access to opportunities to progress in their careers – including opportunities for promotion within the academy, and the benefits of membership of the academy, such as the opportunity to take sabbaticals. Criteria for promotion or progression generally involve ranking against an agreed set of academic indicators or outputs – such as numbers of peer reviewed publications, external research grants secured, development of innovative teaching methods and evaluation of teaching approaches, as well as demonstration of academic leadership, contributions to administration and management. These criteria are usually rigorously applied and often do not contain space for reasonable accommodation. However, in the context of gender equality, some positive developments have been achieved, such as adjusting research benchmarking exercises to take account of time spent on maternity leave.[26] Similar approaches could be introduced in the context of disability – as well as perhaps recognising that other criteria should be evaluated in making promotion decisions – including contributions beyond the academy in the fields of civic engagement and collaboration with advocacy organisations and activists.

Disability and Invisibility in Course Content: Legal Education

While there is quite a significant body of literature on how to teach students with disabilities about the law, and how to ensure a more inclusive legal academy, relatively little has been written about how to teach the general law student population about disability rights, or to think critically about the application of the law to issues concerning people with disabilities. Lawson has commented on the limited coverage of disability rights issues in core human rights textbooks aimed at undergraduate law students.[27] For example, two core human rights texts: Steiner, Alston and Goodman's *International Human Rights in Context: Law, Politics and Morals*[28] and Alston and Goodman's *International Human Rights*,[29] contain only minor references to disability rights although both were published following the entry into force of the UN Convention on the Rights of Persons with Disabilities.

---

26 See for example, A McDonald, 'Levelling the Playing Field: Maternity Leave, Paternity Leave and the REF', *Impact of Social Sciences Blog* (London School of Economics), 7 November 2011, available at: <http://blogs.lse.ac.uk/impactofsocialsciences/2011/11/07/levelling-the-playing-field/> (accessed 10 January 2013).

27 Ibid.

28 H J Steiner, P Alston and R Goodman (eds), *International Human Rights in Context: Law, Politics and Morals* (2nd ed., Oxford University Press, 2008).

29 P Alston and R Goodman (eds), *International Human Rights* (Oxford University Press, 2013).

Similarly, Rehman's *International Human Rights Law*,[30] when first published in 2003, did not contain any discussion of disability rights, although the most recent edition, published in 2010, has been updated to include a chapter on the rights of persons with disabilities.

Given that 'disability law' has only relatively recently emerged as a field of study in legal education, it is not surprising that in a general education, law students may seldom learn about the human rights concerns of people with disabilities. Cases involving plaintiffs with disabilities may be covered to a limited extent in core subjects such as Torts, Contract, or Constitutional law, but for any detailed consideration of disability rights issues, the selection of more elective modules – such as mental health law, or labour law, may be required – and more specialised modules on disability rights may only be available in postgraduate, rather than undergraduate, legal education. Indeed, law students are often more likely to study disability in the context of medical negligence, personal injuries, social welfare, health law or social care law than in equality law or human rights. Such an approach could well instill a medicalised view of disability among law students, rather than a more holistic, human-rights based approach or social model of disability.

In comparing disability with gender and race in arguments about the centrality or marginal nature of these topics to a general education, Berubé aptly states in his foreword to Linton's seminal polemic, *Claiming Disability*, 'for some reason, *even though disability law might someday pertain to me*, I could not imagine it as central to the project of establishing egalitarian civil rights in a social democracy'.[31] He describes how through the forceful scholarship of Linton and others, as well as through his personal experience of becoming a father to a disabled child, he reframed his ideas about the centrality of disability to all areas of study, but particularly, the humanities, concluding: 'and perhaps, just perhaps, if disability is understood as central to the humanities, it will eventually be understood as central to humanity – in theory and in practice, in sickness and in health, in cultural studies, as in public policy'.[32] So too, it might be said, can an understanding of disability as part of human diversity enhance the law student's learning of the scope and application of human rights law.[33]

More choices and opportunities are emerging in recent years, particularly in postgraduate legal education, for students with an interest in disability law. The

---

30 J Rehman, *International Human Rights Law* (2nd ed., Pearson Education Limited, 2010), ch 17 – rights of the persons with disabilities.

31 M Berubé, 'Foreword' in S Linton, *Claiming Disability: Knowledge and Identity* (New York University Press, 1998), x–xi. Emphasis in original.

32 Ibid., xi.

33 A Arstein-Kerslake and G Quinn, 'Restoring the "Human" in "Human Rights": Personhood and Doctrinal Innovation in the UN Disability Convention' in C Gearty and C Douzinas (eds), *The Cambridge Companion to Human Rights Law* (Cambridge University Press, 2013), 36.

Soros Open Society Foundation has made available scholarships for students from developing countries to study disability law and human rights in globally-recognised masters programmes.[34] More human rights and equality law courses are including modules on disability, as well as opportunities for law students to combine their legal education with disability studies, or to undertake clinical legal opportunities which focus on serving the interests of people with disabilities.[35] The availability of disability law courses via distance-learning, including those funded by development aid programmes as part of ongoing commitments to enhance democracy and the rule of law, can also contribute to the continuous training and development of lawyers, law students and disability activists.[36] The issue of ongoing training and awareness-raising for legal professionals on disability rights will be addressed further towards the end of this chapter.

3. Clinical Legal Education and Disability Rights: Learning by Doing

Although first conceived in the 1930s by Jerome Frank,[37] university-based law clinics began to flourish from the 1960s in the United States on an express realisation that many indigent and marginalised groups could not access the legal system and thus vindicate their rights and entitlements. The widespread introduction of Student Practice Orders to enable advanced law students participate openly in the lower levels of the administrative apparatus, and indeed lower courts, was seen as a key to giving life to clinics.[38] Clinical legal education is also growing in popularity in European countries such as Ireland and the UK, although, without the advent of legal instruments enabling law students to undertake legal practice prior to obtaining professional legal qualifications, it can be more difficult for students to engage in direct courtroom advocacy for clients, although they may

---

34 See Open Society Foundations, *Disability Rights Scholarship Programme*, available at: <http://www.opensocietyfoundations.org/grants/disability-rights-scholarship-program/> (accessed 2 January 2014).

35 See for example Office of the Human Rights Commissioner, *Report of the Consultation on the Focus of the Second Phase of the World Programme for Human Rights Education* (Geneva and New York, 2009) A/HRC/12/36.

36 See for example, M L Perlin, 'An Internet-Based Mental Disability Law Program: Implications for Social Change in Nations with Developing Economies' (2006) 30 *Fordham Int'l LJ* 435. Other examples of ongoing training include the European Academy of Law's training programmes on the CRPD, see for example <http://www.era-comm.eu/dalaw/> (accessed 10 January 2014).

37 J Frank, 'Why Not a Clinical Lawyer-School?' (1933) 81(8) *University of Pennsylvania Law Review and American Law Register* 907.

38 G S Grossman, 'Clinical Legal Education: History and Diagnosis' (1973) 26 *J. Legal Educ.* 162.

still do significant client contact work.[39] There are many different aspects of clinical legal education which can be used to enhance disability rights – from providing information, advice and ultimately representation to individual clients, to supporting legal practitioners in the development of their cases, to developing amicus briefs or other third party interventions for domestic and regional courts, and establishing partnerships with NGOs to address the rights-violations identified by civil society organisations.

As discussed in Chapter 3, these clinics provide a valuable service to individuals, as well as to the administration of justice;[40] although they should not be seen as justification for State failure to provide adequate legal support, including advice and representation, to people with disabilities. Law clinics also serve to enhance the clinical educational experience of law students, ensuring that students enter the world of practice with some experience and knowledge of how the law operates. Professor Frank – the originator of the idea of law clinics – emphasised that the 'law in action' is how and where to study law.[41] Therefore, clinical legal education is not just about acquiring skills, but it is also about gaining a deeper understanding of the nature of the law in its various habitats. Through it students gain a certain 'situation sense' which helps them better apply the law in the interests of their clients and justice.

Clinical legal education provides a unique opportunity to train a new generation of lawyers in how to approach disability rights issues. Scholars writing about the experiences of law students in clinics describe the key shifts in attitude which can occur when students are faced with the lived reality of others which is so different from their own. Since, as discussed in the previous section, it is only in relatively recent decades that people with disabilities have even had the opportunity to attend law school, working in a law clinic on disability rights issues might be the first time that many law students have direct contact with people with disabilities in a professional capacity.

This can have a transformative impact on students' understanding of the effect of the legal system on people with disabilities. Quigley finds this outcome to be common in the experiences of students in her law clinic, quoting one student as follows: 'The judge saw my client as less able to care for her kids than their father just because her income is limited to a disability payment, while he has a good-paying job. My client is real upset and she keeps saying she doesn't see the system as fair. I have to say that I agree with her.'[42] Quigley describes these transformations in attitude as 'disorienting moments' in students' learning, and

---

39 See for example, R J Wilson, 'Western Europe: Last Holdout in the Worldwide Acceptance of Clinical Legal Education' (2009) 10 *German Law Journal* 823.

40 Ch 3, section 3.

41 J Frank, 'Why Not a Clinical Lawyer-School?' (1933) 81(8) *University of Pennsylvania Law Review and American Law Register* 907.

42 F Quigley, 'Seizing the Disorienting Moment: Adult Learning Theory and the Teaching of Social Justice in Law School Clinics' (1995) 2 *Clinical L. Rev.* 37.

argues that clinical legal educators should not merely accept these as the natural by-product of a clinical course, but use these moments to teach students about social justice.

However, not all law students are immediately 'transformed' by their experiences in serving people with disabilities. Massey and Rosenbaum describe the following example:

> Michelle admitted to a classmate that there are some special education students who are intellectually capable and only need help because of their physical disabilities. She thought those students probably should be served because they have the capacity to learn and do something in the future. But she felt that services for students with more limited abilities are not economically justified.[43]

This kind of statement equally presents the opportunity for teaching and learning social justice – particularly for students who have not previously been exposed to the lived experience of people with disabilities. Quigley acknowledges that

> Most law students come to the course without significant exposure to the victims of injustice and almost none come to the course with experience representing a person trying to wring a just result from an often unresponsive legal system. When the learners are confronted with their clients' very real suffering and frustration, the learners' necessarily abstract understanding of social justice often prevents assimilation of the experience.[44]

These examples demonstrate that care should be taken in the design of law clinics to serve people with disabilities to ensure that an empowering approach is taken to addressing their human rights concerns, rather than reinforcing the stereotypes of dependency and vulnerability which risk further stigmatising people with disabilities. There are a number of ways in which this can be achieved. One can be to develop partnerships with people with disabilities and disabled people's organisations (DPOs) in designing the curriculum and determining how cases will be selected for the students to work on, as well as deciding the kinds of legal argument which will be pursued, to ensure that empowering approaches are chosen, rather than those which further reinforce dependency and victimisation. Often, in order to achieve a preferred outcome for an individual client with a disability, a legal argument premised on the individual's particular vulnerability is advanced. If this approach is followed as an inherent philosophy by a particular

---

[43] Cited in P A Massey and S A Rosenbaum, 'Disability Matters: Toward a Law School Clinical Model for Serving Youth with Special Educational Needs' (2004–2005) 11 *Clinical L. Rev.* 271.

[44] F Quigley, 'Seizing the Disorienting Moment: Adult Learning Theory and the Teaching of Social Justice in Law School Clinics' (1995) 2 *Clinical L. Rev.* 37 at 53.

legal clinic, it could risk undermining broader strategic litigation which seeks to advance disability rights in a positive frame.

Stone and Priestley also discuss the complexity of relationships between disabled people's organisations and academics or researchers, which provides a useful perspective on how partnerships between DPOs and university law clinics might be developed. They suggest that, since throughout history people with disabilities felt that they were always the object of research, and did not have control over research findings by academics, it is important to develop a relationship which is an equal partnership – not one where either partner is perceived as a 'pawn' of, or a parasite on, the other.[45] Another approach to ensure a more positive framing of disability law clinics can be to integrate knowledge of human rights law, and of disability studies, into the training of students in law school clinics. Lawson argues that increased inter-disciplinarity (blending disability studies, law and related disciplines) in teaching, research and academic leadership is the best way to ensure that the academy plays an active role in realising the UN Convention on the Rights of Persons with Disabilities at grassroots level.[46]

Law clinics serving people with disabilities can take a variety of approaches to advance equality – including by direct client interaction and ultimately representation, selecting cases for strategic litigation on issues of the public interest, development of amicus briefs in key human rights cases at domestic, regional or international courts and drafting submissions for law and policy reform on disability issues in a variety of domestic and international arenas. All of these provide valuable opportunities for contributing to the disability rights agenda – however, it must be reaffirmed, as discussed in Chapter 3,[47] that the vital work of clinics should not undermine the need for clear rights to legal aid and State provision of accessible legal services to people with disabilities to enable them to advance and enforce their rights. Nevertheless, as discussed in the previous section, consciousness-raising on disability rights should be an integral part of the education and training of new lawyers, and clinical legal education presents an ideal opportunity to bring the lived experience of disability into the law school classroom.

4. Legal Training and Disability Consciousness-Raising in Legal Practice

As discussed in Chapter 1, the symbolic dimension of access to justice is such that if people with disabilities do not see members of their community in positions of

---

45 E Stone and M Priestley, 'Parasites, Pawns and Partners: Disability Research and the Role of Non-Disabled Researchers' (1996) *British Journal of Sociology* 699.

46 A Lawson, 'The Ivory Tower and the Real World: Academia and the Convention on the Rights of Persons with Disabilities', Reykjavik, Nordic Network of Disability Research Conference, 27–28 May 2011.

47 Ch 3, section 3.

power in the justice system – in the role of lawyers (both prosecutors and defence lawyers), judges, expert witnesses, etc. then they may lose confidence in the ability of the justice system to fairly address their concerns.[48] In increasingly diverse societies, there is also a public interest in ensuring greater representativeness of people with a wide range of backgrounds, cultures, genders, religious beliefs, etc. in positions of authority in the justice system. Moreover, the way in which professional legal training (post-university) is constructed does not generally take account of the accessibility challenges affecting people with disabilities, and the availability of reasonable accommodation may be more restricted in this context than in the law school setting.

Unless professional training programmes for lawyers, judges and other justice officials are thoroughly reformed, in keeping with the principle of equality of opportunity and in recognition of the value of a diverse legal profession, then the risk remains that any inclusion of people with disabilities will be tokenistic at best, and this could undermine the valuable contribution which people with disabilities can make in these roles. In addition to dismantling barriers imposed on people with disabilities who seek to enter these roles, it is also important to provide ongoing training and sensitisation on disability rights issues to those who make up the justice system – including the judiciary, law enforcement, court officials and lawyers. For the purpose of this discussion, I will focus on the professional training and continuing development of legal practitioners and the judiciary, although many of these observations and recommendations for reform could also apply to other roles within the justice system.

As identified above, general legal education at the pre-professional stage can benefit from reform to increase its accessibility to students with disabilities. Nevertheless, some important steps forward have been taken in recent decades with a reconceptualisation of the pedagogical goals of law schools, and the increasing recognition of the need to provide reasonable accommodation to law students with disabilities. However, the reluctance to adapt admissions procedures and eligibility tests for entry into the legal profession for persons with disabilities presents an even greater challenge.

Admission to Practice: Entrance Examinations and Lawyers with Disabilities

Heywood describes a specific case in the late 1990s[49] where the New York State Board of Law Examiners failed repeatedly to grant a request for reasonable accommodation (involving the allocation of additional time) to a candidate who had difficulty reading the bar exam questions because of a learning disability. In this case the examiners refused the request on the basis that there was not

---

48   Ch 1, section 3.3.
49   S S Heywood, 'Without Lowering the Bar: Eligibility for Reasonable Accomodations on the Bar Exam for Learning Disabled Individuals under the Americans with Disabilities Act' (1998) 44 *Ga. L. Rev.* 603.

sufficient evidence of a learning disability – despite medical evidence from the applicant's doctors and the fact that similar accommodations had been granted to her during her law school study. The candidate subsequently succeeded in a court case in obtaining the relevant accommodations – partly because similar accommodations were made to enable candidates who were blind or visually impaired to sit the bar exam.[50] He writes that despite the increasing numbers of similar reasonable accommodation requests, the courts have not developed a consistent approach to the application of the Americans with Disabilities Act on these issues, stating that 'the outcomes of these cases often hinge on the court's particular interpretation of the ADA's regulations or, seemingly, the degree of sympathy that the court has for the plaintiff's condition'.[51]

Similarly, Herr discusses the invasive nature of questions which candidates for the bar exam are asked which require them to disclose their disabilities, including psycho-social disabilities, and which might lead to a failure to process an admission, even where a candidate has passed the written test.[52] While strategic litigation and negotiation with bar examiners led to some reforms in the Maryland bar examination for candidates with psycho-social disabilities, Herr argues that more widespread national reform is required to eliminate discrimination against bar candidates with disabilities. The justification provided by examiners for continuing to make inquiries about candidates' mental health treatment histories include the desire to protect the public, and the reputation of the legal profession, from malpractice actions taken against lawyers with psycho-social disabilities who are negligent in the performance of their duties as legal representatives, where such negligence may be linked to the presence of a disability.[53] However, Herr concurs with Eth, that 'the prejudice arising from a history of psychiatric diagnoses or treatment far outweighs its value as a predictor of future competence as an attorney'.[54]

In other contexts, persons with disabilities are more explicitly excluded from taking up positions in the justice system – particularly as judges or jurors. The specific issue of jury service has already been addressed in Chapter 4,[55] and therefore here I will concentrate on exclusions of people with disabilities from

50   970 F. Supp. 1094 (S.D.N.Y. 1997), reh'g denied, 2 F. Supp. 2d 288 (S.D.N.Y 1997), and aff'd in part, vacated in part, 156 F.3d 321 (2d Cir. 1998) (affirming that the plaintiff was disabled under the ADA and RA).

51   S S Heywood, 'Without Lowering the Bar: Eligibility for Reasonable Accommodations on the Bar Exam for Learning Disabled Individuals under the Americans with Disabilities Act' (1998) 44 *Ga. L. Rev.* 603 at 605.

52   S S Herr, 'Questioning the Questionnaires: Bar Admissions and Candidates with Disabilities' (1997) 42 *Vill. L. Rev.* 635.

53   Ibid., 638.

54   Interview with Dr Spencer Eth, Clinical Director of the Department of Psychiatry at St. Vincent's Hospital, in Englewood, NJ (23 November 1996), cited at fn. 27 in ibid., 640.

55   Ch 4, section 6.

the judiciary. A particularly pertinent example can be found in India, where within the federal system, state governments could take different approaches to the eligibility of certain persons with disabilities for the role of judge. The Indian Persons with Disabilities (Equal Opportunities, Protection of Rights and Full Participation) Act 1995 provides a 3 per cent quota (known as a 'reservation') in public service positions (including the judiciary) for people with physical disabilities (1 per cent each for people who are blind, deaf or have mobility impairments).[56] When certain candidates who were blind were not accepted into the judiciary following the required examination and interview, the applicability of the national standard in the Act began to be challenged through strategic litigation. In a 2005 case, the applicant, a blind lawyer, was excluded from consideration allegedly because he had not practised as an advocate for the four years immediately prior to his application, although he had previously practised as an advocate for 10 years.[57] The court found that since he had already completed the examination and interview for the position of civil judge, the results of this process should be released and if he had successfully completed these requirements, his previous experience would ensure his eligibility, and he should be appointed to the position.

However, in 2009, the Madras High Court suggested to the Tamil Nadu State government that it could exempt the judiciary from the requirement to comply with section 33 of the 1995 Act, based on the following reasoning: 'A Judge may be physically handicapped, but he is supposed to hear the case and write the judgment. If a person has total hearing impairment, such as deaf or his is blind [sic], it is not clear, how such person can function as a Judge of a Court to hear cases and then deliver Judgment'.[58] The Tamil Nadu State Home Department developed such an exemption for persons with 'complete blindness and complete hearing impairment' in an order of August 2012.[59] The constitutionality of such an exemption has not yet been tested, although a 2013 case reaffirmed that candidates with mobility impairments were not to be excluded from eligibility for the judiciary as a result of this exemption.[60] This example demonstrates the difficulty in ensuring equal access to positions of power within the justice system for people with disabilities. In the Indian context, no discussion of reasonable accommodation for judges with disabilities has been raised, which may be linked to the fact that no requirement to provide reasonable accommodation is included in the current legislative framework as part of the prohibition on discrimination.

---

56 Section 33, Persons with Disabilities (Equal Opportunities, Protection of Rights and Full Participation) Act 1995.

57 *B Veerakumar v The Secretary* on 3 January 2005 (Madras High Court).

58 WP 27089 of 2008, Court order dated 15.4.2009, as cited in *G. Christian v. Government Of Tamil Nadu* on 18 April 2013 (Madras High Court).

59 G.O.Ms.No.642, Home (Cts-I) Department, dated 31.8.2012.

60 *G Christian v Government Of Tamil Nadu* on 18 April 2013 (Madras High Court).

Of course, the exclusion of persons with disabilities from certain roles in the justice system – such as prosecutors, defence counsel, or judges – is not always so explicit. More often, it is an implicit understanding that people with disabilities will simply not be able to perform the 'essential functions' of these roles, rather than an explicit prohibition on their eligibility, which is responsible for the low numbers of people with disabilities taking up such positions. However, this provides us with an interesting opportunity to reconsider what the 'essential roles' of legal practitioners and judges might be – and whether, with the provision of reasonable accommodation, they could be performed by people with disabilities.

Accommodating Legal Practitioners with Disabilities: The Essential Functions of Lawyering and Judgecraft?

In presenting a rationale for excluding (implicitly or explicitly) people with disabilities from roles in professional legal practice, the following arguments might be made. Some might argue that it is 'essential' that a judge be able to look into the faces of the plaintiff or defendant as they provide their testimony, or hear their words as spoken, rather than as interpreted through sign language. Others might suggest that is it necessary for counsel to be able to physically stand in court when called on by a judge to do so, or to be able to read legal documents such as briefs, in a certain format within a short period of time. As I discuss above, a lawyer with a learning or 'print' disability which causes difficulty in reading information in certain formats may be skilled in delivering oral argument. With the increasing diversification in roles played by lawyers in professional practice, there should be room to provide reasonable accommodation where necessary if the client wishes to benefit from the particular skills which a lawyer with a disability may have. Therefore, in order to combat both explicit and implicit exclusions of people with disabilities from such roles, a further exploration of the 'essential functions' of the posts is called for.

Familant provides the following provisional list of 'essential functions' of lawyering, drawn primarily from the American Bar Association Model Rules of Professional Conduct:

- being able to think like a lawyer (spotting issues, reasoning by analogy, solving problems).
- being organized and being able to perform tasks in a reasonable time period.
- paying attention to detail.
- being able to communicate well, both orally and in writing.
- being punctual.
- having ambition and self-motivation.
- being an advocate for the client, as well as for the legal system.
- being able to deal with stress.

- being able to maintain the required amount of billable hours.
- being able to perform 'independent, unsupervised legal analysis, research, and writing'.[61]

He also argues that the concept of 'essential functions' of employment contained within the Americans with Disabilities Act (as a domestic example) is related only to the tasks which an employee must perform, and not the manner in which they are performed.[62] This means that it is irrelevant whether the task is performed with or without accommodations, as long as such accommodation does not cause undue hardship to the employer. A key debate here in both the context of the bar examination and in legal practice is whether speed (specifically the ability to read quickly, and respond quickly to the legal arguments presented) is necessarily an essential function required of a practising lawyer. Rothstein suggests that speed, or the ability to complete tasks within narrow time constraints, is not generally an essential function in this respect, as 'in most situations what is being tested is knowledge, issue identification, ability to apply rules of law correctly, analytical and logical reasoning, and the ability to articulate this information in an understandable way'.[63]

Another concern is whether the ability to cope with stress is a similarly 'essential' function of practising the law – especially since what are considered acceptable levels of stress or pressure may be so subjectively defined. Perlin describes how even where lawyers with disabilities have overcome the initial procedural barriers and been admitted to the practice of law, the use of disciplinary and ethical procedures can demonstrate further layers of discrimination, particularly against lawyers with psycho-social disabilities.[64] Despite the fact that lawyers, and indeed judges, as a profession, experience relatively high levels of mental illness, substance abuse and suicide, Perlin recounts that the numbers who disclose a psycho-social disability remains extremely low.[65] This is in part, he suggests, due to the threat of sanction in disciplinary procedures, where, in a number of cases, a more stringent approach is applied to attorneys with mental disabilities than to defendants in criminal cases.[66] He suggests that the first step towards remedying the current system's attitudes towards lawyers and judges with psycho-social disabilities is to first acknowledge the levels of disability within the legal profession, and second, to move away from a culture of blaming the individual for

---

61 B M Familant, 'The Essential Functions of Being a Lawyer with a Non-Visible Disability: On the Wings of a Kiwi Bird' (1998) 15 *TM Cooley L. Rev.* 517 at 540–541.

62 Ibid., at 536.

63 L F Rothstein, 'Bar Admissions and the Americans with Disabilities Act' (1994) *Housing Law* 34 at 38.

64 ML Perlin, 'Baby, Look inside Your Mirror: The Legal Profession's Willful and Sanist Blindness to Lawyers with Mental Disabilities' (2007) 69 *U. Pitt. L. Rev.* 589.

65 Ibid., at 593.

66 Ibid., at 597; *Florida Bar v Clement*, 662 So. 2d 690 (Fla. 1995).

their disability, towards an approach based on therapeutic jurisprudence, which can combat these 'sanist' prejudices.[67]

Professional Legal Training: Accommodating Trainees with Disabilities

In order to move towards a more inclusive legal profession, it is important not only to dismantle barriers for those who wish to gain entry to the profession, and to reasonably accommodate practising lawyers, but also to reconceptualise post-university legal training to ensure it is accessible to people with disabilities. Given the history of stigma and discrimination, it is not surprising that many law graduates seeking a traineeship (in countries where this is a prerequisite for legal practice) are reluctant to disclose disabilities in their applications for training contracts. Lipskar even questions whether law schools should have to disclose whether or not their graduates received accommodations to potential legal employers.[68] However, most guides for law graduates in securing professional employment suggest that upfront disclosure is key, especially since the individual will need to establish early on what accommodations will be available to enable her to carry out the required tasks.

In jurisdictions where a period of professional legal training is required for law graduates, prior to admission for the legal profession, such as the UK, Ireland, Australia and Canada, little research is available on lawyers with disabilities' experiences of the training process. However, some general observations can be made about these training processes which may be particularly relevant for people with disabilities. Research in Canada on law graduates with disabilities seeking 'articling' placements found that most graduates with disabilities did not even apply to private law firms, as '[t]hey reasoned that they would not be hired, and they preferred to seek articles with institutions that had proven records on equity issues'.[69] Experience in the UK suggests that the larger corporate law firms may be more suited for trainees with disabilities than small private firms, as the corporate firms have sufficient resources to provide the reasonable accommodations which people with disabilities may request.[70] While this is certainly an advantage, it is important to ensure that such firms are being truly inclusive of lawyers with disabilities and valuing them for their skills, rather than providing an opportunity for a trainee with a disability in order to demonstrate evidence of 'diversity', while

---

67 M L Perlin, 'Baby, Look inside Your Mirror: The Legal Profession's Willful and Sanist Blindness to Lawyers with Mental Disabilities' (2007) 69 *U. Pitt. L. Rev.* 589 at 606.

68 L B Lipskar, 'Learning Disabilities and the ADA: A Guide for Successful Learning Disabled Students Considering a Career in the Law' (2000) 3 *U. Pa. J. Lab. & Emp. L.* 647.

69 A McChesney, R Nolan, M Schmieg and N Druckman, *Advancing Professional Opportunities and Employment Accommodation for Lawyers and Other Law Graduates Who Have Disabilities* (Reach, 2001) at 31.

70 F MacDaeid, 'Disability and a Career in the Law' (2011) *Chambers Student Newsletter* 566.

not offering similar opportunities to practising lawyers with disabilities who seek full-time employment upon completion of their training.

Legal training is often based on a hierarchical system which places trainees at the bottom of the social structure, and expects that trainees will work the hardest, for the longest hours, for the least reward, among their colleagues in a professional law firm.[71] For trainees with disabilities, the requirement to work extremely long hours, without the opportunity to complete training part-time or to benefit from flexible work options (including working from home), can mean that participating in legal training without accommodations is not an option. McChesney et al. suggest that, in Canada, many private law firms 'rationalize their failure to accommodate on the basis of accessibility needs for clients and availability of staff for court appearances'.[72] In the context of gender equality, or the acknowledgment that a work–life balance can enhance productivity, this attitude is particularly disappointing, as McChesney's research also found that even when firms offered 'part-time' options – this usually amounted to 'a controlled 35–40 hour week', as 'less than that probably wouldn't work'.[73] This makes legal training, and professional practice, a far less viable option for lawyers with family responsibilities as well as those with disabilities.

Another concern which flows from the hierarchical nature of legal training is that trainees, in addition to their legal duties, are generally assigned a high level of administrative or routine tasks which are not a core component of their legal education, but they are nonetheless expected to complete – including photocopying, delivering files, and other similar tasks. McChesney et al. suggest that 'the assignment of routine duties (a.k.a. grunt work) does not, according to Law Society guidelines, provide an appropriate quality of education. A student's time committed to such tasks should be kept within limits compatible with the educational goals of articling'.[74] In addition, these tasks may present certain specific challenges for trainees with disabilities – as a trainee who uses a wheelchair may not be able to deliver files to inaccessible offices, or a blind trainee may not be able to make photocopies. This may mean that these tasks are therefore assigned to other trainees, or administrative staff, in order to reasonable accommodate trainees with disabilities – which can in turn cause problems if disabled trainees are perceived to have a lighter work-load than others. For this

---

71 See for example H Sommerlad and P Sanderson, 'The Legal Labour Market and the Training Needs of Women Returners in the United Kingdom' (1997) 49(1) *Journal of Vocational Education and Training* 45; L Jewel, 'Bourdieu and American Legal Education: How Law Schools Reproduce Social Stratification and Class Hierarchy' (2008) 56 *Buffalo Law Review* 1156.

72 A McChesney et al., *Advancing Professional Opportunities and Employment Accommodation for Lawyers and Other Law Graduates Who Have Disabilities* (Reach, 2001) at 34.

73 Ibid., at 34.

74 Ibid., at 35.

reason, it is perhaps time to reconceptualise legal training as a whole, so that the majority of any trainee's time and work is devoted to legal duties which enhance their professional knowledge and skills, rather than routine administrative tasks, which, while important, are not necessarily a core component of legal education.

Ongoing Training and Continuing Professional Development for Lawyers

Once a lawyer has completed her legal education and initial training, the question of opportunities for ongoing training and continued professional development arises. Even if course content on disability rights is made widely available in mainstream legal education for the next generation of lawyers, there will still be a need for the provision of ongoing training to currently practising lawyers and other legal professionals, including judges, on these issues. As the law on disability equality is constantly evolving at national and international levels, regular, up-to-date training becomes even more essential. Opportunities for targeted training on disability issues for legal professionals can be scarce – although in recent decades, more specific training modules have been made available to legal professionals in both developed and developing countries.[75]

Many of these training opportunities have even been designed in partnership with people with disabilities, academics, researchers and disability activists. While this is clearly an important step forward, the challenge remains that the legal profession, and many of its branches, can be resistant to new ways of thinking about disability rights – especially where these conflict with existing legal doctrines. One pertinent example is judicial resistance to the abolition of adult guardianship and other forms of substitute decision-making – whereby judges continue to use principles such as 'parens patrie' to justify imposing restrictive, protective measures on people with disabilities they deem not capable of exercising their legal capacity, even where the legislative mechanisms for placing someone under guardianship have been abolished.[76]

This experience suggests that a number of inter-connected approaches are needed to progress ongoing training and development for legal professionals. First, the development of peer training by professionals, including judges, who have benefited from an inclusive legal education and are familiar with disability rights discourse. Second, greater emphasis on partnerships between the legal

---

75 See for example, M L Perlin, 'An Internet-Based Mental Disability Law Program: Implications for Social Change in Nations with Developing Economies' (2006) 30 *Fordham Int'l LJ* 435. Other examples of ongoing training include the European Academy of Law's training programmes on the CRPD, see for example <http://www.era-comm.eu/dalaw/> (accessed 10 January 2014).

76 See for example A F Johns, 'Guardianship Folly: The Misgovernment of Parens Patriae and the Forecast of Its Crumbling Linkage to Unprotected Older Americans in the Twenty-First Century – A March of Folly or Just a Mask of Virtual Reality?' (1997) 27 *Stetson L. Rev.* 1.

community and people with disabilities, including through developing ongoing training in collaboration with disabled people's organisations. Finally, the continued investment of training in the next generation of legal professionals – to ensure that issues which concern disability rights are mainstreamed throughout the university curriculum. This will ensure that students learn about the concerns of people with disabilities while studying contract or constitutional law, and not just when they take specialised courses on disability and equality.

5. Conclusion

The development of an inclusive, disability-sensitive, and responsive legal profession at all levels of the justice system is clearly crucial in ensuring effective access to justice for people with disabilities. Such an approach is also in the interests of the legal academy and legal professions, especially since these institutions claim to uphold values of justice, equality and fairness. Greater inclusion and participation of people with disabilities can be achieved by providing conditions that enable people with disabilities to enter the profession and take up valued positions of responsibility within it, as well as developing educational and training opportunities to enhance the knowledge of non-disabled legal professionals regarding the 'justice' claims which people with disabilities make. This parallel approach should ensure that, when people with disabilities feel aggrieved and turn to the justice system to assert and enforce their claims, they are met by individuals and by a system that understands and can accommodate their concerns.

Chapter 6
Participatory Justice, Deliberation and Representation in Public and Political Life

1. Introduction

Iris Marion Young's contention that deliberative democracy provides the best opportunity for negotiating justice claims, is a useful starting point for a discussion about securing justice for people with disabilities in the political sphere. She argues:

> Deliberation is most likely to arrive at a fair distribution of resources, just rules of co-operation, the best and most just division of labor and definition of social positions, if it involves the open participation of all those affected by the decisions. With such participation, people will persuade, ideally, only if they phrase their proposals as appeals to justice, because others will call them to account if they believe their own interests endangered. With such participation, people will most likely introduce relevant information. Democratic decisionmaking tends to promote just outcomes, then, because it is most likely to introduce standards of justice into decisionmaking processes and because it maximizes the social knowledge and perspectives that contribute to reasoning about policy.[1]

As discussed in Chapter 1, the claims to justice made by persons with disabilities are not confined to the legal or judicial sphere.[2] Lord et al. clearly state that 'access to justice' involves access to all the places and spaces in which justice is administered.[3] While the focus of much of this text has been on access to the law and the legal system, it is worth considering the extent to which people can secure justice through participation in political and public life. Specifically, this requires a consideration of justice claims by people with disabilities in the legislative sphere – and the extent to which electoral and parliamentary processes are inclusive of persons with disabilities. Political participation can be considered as both an individual and a collective endeavour – I will consider both forms of participation throughout this chapter.

---

1 I M Young, *Justice and the Politics of Difference* (Princeton University Press, 2011), at 93.
2 Ch 1, sections 2 and 3.
3 J Lord, K N Guernsey, J M Balfe, V L Karr and N Flowers (eds), *Human Rights. Yes! Action and Advocacy on the Rights of Persons with Disabilities* (Human Rights Resource Center, 2009), ch 12, para 12.1.

The issue of participation in political and public life is addressed in a specific article of the UN Convention on the Rights of Persons with Disabilities (Article 29), and is considered of such paramount importance in assessing the overall inclusiveness of a justice system that it is worth examining in this chapter. Many people with disabilities are denied the right to vote as a result of a determination of legal incapacity and subsequent placement under adult guardianship or other forms of substituted decision-making regimes. Similarly, in a number of jurisdictions, many people with disabilities may be prohibited from voting or running for political office. While these deprivations of legal capacity, and related denials of rights to participate in political life, most often affect people with intellectual and psycho-social disabilities, in many jurisdictions they have a broader impact, and the relationship between these rights violations and access to justice must be addressed. In this chapter I will examine these issues with a view to providing some guidance for reform from an international and comparative perspective.

2. Pursuing Justice in the Political Sphere: Lobbying for Legislative Change

While we might perceive that most claims for justice which people with disabilities make can only be realised in the courts, the reality is in fact that some of the most important advances in the field of disability rights have been made through the legislative process. One of the first and most broad-ranging anti-discrimination laws for people with disabilities – the Americans with Disabilities Act – was developed as a result of a strong disability rights campaign for legislative change. Therefore, the potential for deliberation on claims for justice in the legislative or parliamentary process is significant – and requires two key components to be truly effective.

The first is that the deliberative process must be open and receptive to hearing the claims and concerns of civil society – including people with disabilities themselves. The other key component of an effective legislative deliberation links back to the concept of symbolic justice:[4] essentially, that people with disabilities have the possibility of entering these deliberative spheres as political participants and elected representatives, not just as representatives of civil society or disabled people's organisations. Many scholars have also highlighted the importance of having champions within the parliamentary process, or other positions of power, for securing effective legislative change. In the context of disability, these champions might be persons with disabilities themselves, individuals with a

---

4 R Bahdi, *Background Paper on Women's Access to Justice in the MENA Region* (International Development Research Centre (IDRC), Women's Rights and Citizenship Program (WRC) and the Middle East Regional Office (MERO), Middle East and North African (MENA) Regional Consultation, 9–11 December 2007, Cairo, Egypt).

personal or family connection to disability, or other allies committed to social justice and equality.

One example of effective legislative reform with the collaboration of a parliamentary champion is the role of Senator Tom Harkin (among others) in the enactment of the Americans with Disabilities Act. Weicker acknowledges Harkin's seminal role in steering the Bill through difficult debates, stating that: 'He performed yeoman's service in guiding the bill through the legislative storms. Under his leadership, significant revisions were made to the bill prior to its reintroduction in the Senate. These modifications made the bill more specific and somewhat more moderate'.[5] Bagenstos also credits Harkin with leading the charge against perceptions of people with disabilities as inherently vulnerable and necessarily dependent individuals, and insisting that the prohibition of discrimination contained in the ADA would rather result in a decrease in public expenditure on disability programmes which reinforced dependency, rather than recognising the potential contribution people with disabilities could make on the open labour market, if provided with reasonable accommodation.[6] Senator Harkin himself has spoken often about his personal and family experience of disability – particularly his relationship with his brother Frank, who is deaf.[7] This experience perhaps helps to add legitimacy to his role as a political champion advocating the prohibition of discrimination on the basis of disability.

The opportunity for deliberation which the legislative process provides can, as Iris Marion Young describes, provide a space for people to assert their claims to justice. In the context of disability, there are some relevant examples of parliamentary processes and other deliberative exercises which have proved significant in advancing claims to justice. One such example is the pre-legislative scrutiny in the Irish Parliament which was undertaken prior to the publication of the Assisted Decision-Making Capacity Bill 2013. In 2012, the Oireachtas Committee for Justice, Defence and Equality held a series of hearings from a broad range of civil society organisations to gather views on what the Bill should look like.[8] These hearings followed an open call for submissions to the Committee, and the transcripts from the hearings, as well as a huge volume of submissions received, were included by the Committee in its final report on the proposed legislation. Many of the groups who presented at oral hearings convened by the Justice

---

5   L P Weicker Jr, 'Historical Background of the Americans with Disabilities Act' (1991) 64 *Temp. LR* 64 387 at 391.

6   S Bagenstos, 'The Americans with Disabilities Act as Welfare Reform' (2003) 44 *William and Mary Law Review* 921.

7   See for example, T Harkin, 'The Americans with Disabilities Act Ten Years Later: A Framework for the Future' (1999) 85 *Iowa L. Rev.* 1575.

8   Oireachtas Press Release, *Committee on Justice, Defence and Equality continues hearings on proposed Mental Capacity Legislation* (February 2012), available at: <http://www.oireachtas.ie/parliament/mediazone/pressreleases/2012/name-6931-en.html> (accessed 10 March 2014).

Committee in 2012 had also participated in a civil society coalition for legal capacity reform, involving organisations in the fields of disability, mental health and older people, which had produced a set of Essential Principles for Irish Legal Capacity Law.[9] In its final report, the Justice Committee made a ground-breaking recommendation that a shift away from the 'best interests' model of substitute decision-making was required and suggesting that the drafters adopt the support model of legal capacity, embedding respect for the will and preferences of the individual at the core of the new legislation, echoing some of the suggestions of the civil society coalition which drafted the Essential Principles.[10] While this process was significant, it should be noted however that none of the groups invited to present to the Committee were disabled people's organisations (DPOs), i.e. groups entirely controlled by and composed of persons with disabilities themselves.

As I discuss further below,[11] when people with disabilities are enabled to stand for election to parliament, this can incentivise the creation of inclusive deliberation within the legislative process on reforms affecting people with disabilities. Campbell argues that a key function which people with disabilities can play as legislators is the enforcement of inclusive approaches to policy-making, within and beyond the context of disability.[12] She points to the involvement of people with disabilities themselves in the development of the Community Care (Direct Payments) Act 1996 in England and Wales as a positive example of inclusive legislation and policy-making, where legal principles were developed based on the direct input of disabled people:

> In collaboration with Civil Servants, Members of Parliament, Social Service Practitioners, the disabled people's movement were considered to be the experts in our own situation. As a result we were given a central role in the planning of a social infrastructure that was to fundamentally change the nature of the relationship between disabled people and our personal care provider. So, POWER CHANGED HANDS. In the process the creative tension produced the constructive empowerment of disabled people that we all talk about, but rarely achieve.[13]

---

9 Amnesty Ireland and Centre for Disability Law and Policy, *Essential Principles for Legal Capacity Reform* (2012), available at: <http://www.nuigalway.ie/cdlp/documents/principles_web.pdf> (accessed 10 March 2014).

10 Oireachtas Joint Committee on Justice, Defence and Equality, *Report on Hearings in Relation to the Scheme of the Mental Capacity Bill* (May 2012), available at <http://www.oireachtas.ie/parliament/media/michelle/Mental-capacity-text-REPORT-300412.pdf> (accessed 15 March 2013).

11 Section 3 below.

12 J Campbell, 'Excellence in Policy-Making – The Future Challenge?' paper presented at the 'Towards Excellence: Top Tips for Policy Making from the Department of Health Policy Collaborative' Conference, Britannia Hotel, Docklands, London, 17 March 2005.

13 Ibid., 5.

This shift in power is what is so critical to the development of ideas of 'justice' in the political sphere by people with disabilities, and is, as Campbell acknowledges, and as discussed above with respect to other legislative processes (in Ireland, India and the United States for example), often lacking, especially when it comes to hearing the voices of people with disabilities themselves, rather than families, carers, researchers and service providers.

Inclusion in the Deliberative Process: Parliament and Community Partnerships

Another mechanism for greater involvement of civil society organisations, and disabled persons' organisations (DPOs) in particular, in legislative deliberations on the justice claims of persons with disabilities, is the development of formal government–community partnerships in the drafting process of law reform. This approach has been particularly emphasised in the development of new legislation on legal capacity and supported decision-making, and there are some prominent examples of successful community–state partnerships in Canadian provinces on this issue. One of the most well-known statues in the field of supported decision-making is the Representation Agreement Act in British Columbia, which was drafted by a broad-based community coalition – including the representative organisations of people with intellectual disabilities, mental health service users and older persons' services. A member of parliament at the time, Val Anderson, described the Bill as 'a people's Bill, with government's co-operation'.[14] The legislation was developed and drafted over a four-year period by the Project to Review Adult Guardianship, founded by the Alzheimer Society, the Association for Community Living, the Coalition of People with Disabilities and the Community Legal Assistance Society and funded by the Law Foundation of British Columbia. This group facilitated provincial discussions on what the new law should contain, and developed principles to underpin the new legal framework. It was succeeded by the Community Coalition for the Implementation of Adult Guardianship – still in operation at the time of writing, which wrote the draft Bill presented to and accepted by government, and continues to oversee the implementation of the Representation Agreement Act, including by establishing a community resource centre where individuals can access easy to understand information about the process of creating a representation agreement.[15]

A similar process was undertaken in India with the drafting of the Persons with Disabilities Bill (2011 and 2012),[16] with the appointment by the Ministry of Social Justice and Empowerment of a committee with strong civil society participation,

---

14 Cited in C Gordon, 'The Representation Agreement Act in British Columbia: The Right to Supported Decision-Making in Canada' presented at the Zero Project Conference, Vienna, Austria, 22–23 January 2012, 8.

15 Ibid., 12.

16 See A Dhanda 'The Rights of Persons with Disabilities Bill 2011: Justificatory Note on the Proposed Bill' (Centre for Disability Studies, NALSAR University, 2011).

to develop a draft of the new Bill in partnership with government representatives. While civil society in this process did not have as much control over the final Bill (yet to be published at the time of writing)[17] as their comparators in the British Columbian example, this partnership is another example of how a more inclusive and participatory approach can be taken to the development of legislation which sets out the justice claims of people with disabilities.

Representation and the Legitimate Voice: Who Speaks for People with Disabilities?

However, naturally there are complexities involved in the participation and representation of people with disabilities in deliberative processes – in both the parliamentary sphere and the broader political arena. First, the issue of who gains access to these deliberative processes, and who is perceived as representing the interests of disabled people (in general) or specific groups of people with disabilities, is a key concern. Much has been written about the fact that the first advocacy groups for people with disabilities were more composed of parents, siblings, charitable individuals and professionals, than representative of persons with disabilities themselves.[18] Even when the concept of organisations composed of people with disabilities emerged, many of the groups which claimed to be such organisations were found not to be so by the people with disabilities who joined. Rachel Hurst, a disabled woman who went on the chair the British Council of Disabled People, describes her experience upon joining one such local group in the mid 1970s:

> I joined GAD [Greenwich Association of Disabled People], which although it had been called an organisation of disabled people since its inception in 1975, it certainly was not by any stretch of the imagination. In fact, by the time I actually joined them officially in 1978 or 1979, there were three of us who were tokens. My first introduction to the movement was through the television programme about the Berkeley CIL. That was in 1980. And it was like heaven, absolute heaven. And I immediately got in touch with them.[19]

---

17 The Ministry of Social Justice and Empowerment produced a draft Bill in 2012 based on the Committee's proposals, but not incorporating all of the Committee's suggestions. See Ministry of Social Justice and Empowerment, *Draft Rights of Persons with Disabilities Bill 2012* (Delhi, 2012). The final Bill to be introduced in parliament has not been made public at the time of writing.

18 See generally, T Shakespeare, 'Disabled People's Self-Organisation: A New Social Movement?' (1993) 8(3) *Disability, Handicap & Society* 249; J Campbell and M Oliver (eds), *Disability Politics: Understanding Our Past, Changing Our Future* (Psychology Press, 1996).

19 J Campbell and M Oliver (eds), *Disability Politics: Understanding Our Past, Changing Our Future* (Psychology Press, 1996), 51.

Other disabled activists in Britain around the same time also describe the dominance of the charitable model in organisations set up to advocate for people with disabilities – and the extent to which these groups were controlled and operated by non-disabled people. Joe Hennessy describes a local co-ordinating body for disabled people having 'dowager duchesses – large ladies in floppy hats and floppy bosoms – running the organisation'[20] and Millie Hill reported that similar organisations in London were being 'led primarily by non-disabled retired gentlemen who really felt that they were doing good work by helping these poor disabled people'.[21]

Although new disability service providers were beginning to emerge in the UK in the 1970s and 1980s which emphasised self-help and encouraged people with disabilities to achieve their potential, Anna Rae describes how little control people with disabilities had in these new, supposedly more progressive organisations: 'It started to bother me that individual achievement was being emphasised, no matter what other problems people were struggling with. Nothing was going outwards to what we would now call disabling barriers; there was no concern with what was happening outside in the external world we were having to struggle with'.[22] Many people with disabilities who felt their concerns were not being addressed within existing disability organisations and service providers then moved on to set up their own organisations, based on the concept that groups which advocated for justice for disabled people should be controlled by, and accountable to, disabled people.

The phenomenon of disability service providers, family organisations and other groups for, rather than comprised of, people with disabilities being perceived by political decision-makers as the appropriate organisations to represent the 'justice' concerns of people with disabilities continues to the present day. For example, the National Disability Strategy Implementation Group in Ireland (a partnership between government officials and civil society, established by the Minister for Disability, Equality, Mental Health and Older People in 2011) contains a subgroup of disability stakeholders – predominantly, these are umbrella organisations which include disability service providers and families among their membership, as well as those who exclusively represent disability service providers, such as the National Federation of Voluntary Bodies and the Not-for-Profit Business Association.[23]

The National Disability Strategy Implementation Plan states that the group also contains members who have lived experience of disability, and an independent chairperson.[24] While the inclusion of people with disabilities in the group must be welcomed, it should be noted that these individuals are not named in the Implementation Plan, nor is it clear how many of them participate in the group.

---

20   Ibid., 50–51.
21   Ibid., 51.
22   Ibid., 47.
23   Department of Justice and Equality, *National Disability Strategy Implementation Plan 2013–2015* (Dublin, 2013), pp. 4–5.
24   Ibid., 5.

Another concern is that the supports available to ensure the effective participation of people with disabilities in this group are not detailed in the Implementation Plan (e.g. whether accessible information must be provided and how far in advance of meetings, whether presentations and discussions at meetings are accessible to all, and what, if any, opportunities these members have to dictate how meetings will work, etc.). Nor is it clear what power these individuals can have in the process, or who they represent, beyond themselves. Again, although this represents an important step forward in developing participatory deliberative processes for the implementation of legislation and policy and a forum where the justice claims of people with disabilities can be heard, more action is needed to ensure that the participation of people with disabilities in this group is truly effective, and to ensure greater representatives and accountability of the group to the broader community of people with disabilities in Ireland.

A similar example can be found in the Indian Committee established by the Ministry of Social Justice and Empowerment to prepare a Draft of the Persons with Disabilities Bill in 2011. The majority of the NGO representatives on this Committee came from service providers to people with disabilities, or advocacy organisations for people with disabilities who also play a role in the direct provision of services, such as the Ability Foundation, the National Institute for the Mentally Handicapped and the Society for Disability and Rehabilitation Studies, and it was chaired by Dr Sudha Kaul, Vice Chairperson of the Indian Institute of Cerebral Palsy.[25] The relative dearth of representation from organisations completely controlled by persons with disabilities on the Committee may be partially attributed to the lack of such organisations at the national level in India. Nevertheless, the Committee sought to combat the lack of direct representation of people with disabilities on the Committee by organising a series of consultative fora in several locations around the country over a two-year period,[26] to gather the views and perspectives of people with disabilities themselves, and use these to inform its final report and recommendations to government.

Globally, there is still a dearth of organisations exclusively controlled by people with intellectual, psycho-social and other cognitive disabilities (such as dementia) who can claim to be nationally representative of their particular communities, and who are properly equipped and supported to participate in deliberative processes. There are some notable exceptions, such as the World Network of Users and Survivors of Psychiatry, but many of the organisations of people with intellectual disabilities for example (including many national People First organisations)

---

25 Ministry of Social Justice & Empowerment, *Office Memorandum – Sub: Constitution of a Committee to draft a new legislation to replace the Persons with Disabilities (Equal Opportunities, Protection of Rights and Full Participation) Act, 1995. ('PwD Act')* (New Delhi, 2010).

26 See Committee appointed by Ministry of Social Justice and Empowerment, *The Rights of Persons with Disabilities Bill 2011 – Final Report* (Centre for Disability Studies, NALSAR University, 2011), 39–49.

include, or have a majority of non-disabled people on their boards and governing structures – as well as hiring them to provide administrative and financial support.[27] The absence of such organisations can be addressed in part through the provision of government and philanthropic funding for the development of truly representative disabled people's organisations, and the full inclusion of individuals from these communities in cross-disability organisations, with the provision of adequate support to ensure they can participate fully in these deliberative processes.

In the absence of strong, independent representative organisations of people with disabilities, policy-makers and political decision-makers will consult others – including disability service providers, academics and medical professionals – in deliberative processes concerning the rights of persons with disabilities. For example, in the pre-legislative scrutiny of the Scheme of the Mental Capacity Bill 2008 by Ireland's parliamentary justice committee, the Committee heard oral evidence from 12 organisations,[28] but no organisation composed solely of disabled people was present. It is particularly noteworthy that no representatives of the communities which it is anticipated will be most affected by the Bill – i.e. people with intellectual, psycho-social and other cognitive disabilities – gave evidence to the Committee. There are of course relatively few organisations in the Irish context that could claim to solely represent people with disabilities and not others, such as family members or disability service providers, and it may be that the Committee felt the perspectives of disabled people were adequately represented by the NGOs present. Nevertheless, in future deliberative processes on this legislation it is hoped that greater involvement from the direct representatives of disabled people will be sought.

Reproducing disabling hierarchies in deliberative processes?
These examples of increasing involvement of people with disabilities in parliamentary and other deliberative political processes raise another key concern: the potential for reproducing hierarchies of the disability movement through efforts to include people with disabilities in political and legislative reform. Campbell and Oliver's research demonstrates that when organisations controlled by and accountable to people with disabilities began to emerge in Britain, it was those made up of people with physical and sensory disabilities which seemed to

---

27   See for example S Aspis, 'Self-Advocacy for People with Learning Difficulties: Does it Have a Future?' (1997) 12(4) *Disability & Society* 647; F Branfield, 'What Are You Doing Here? "Non-Disabled" People and the Disability Movement: A Response to Robert F. Drake' (1998) 13(1) *Disability & Society* 143.

28   Oireachtas Joint Committee on Justice, Defence and Equality, *Report on Hearings in Relation to the Scheme of the Mental Capacity Bill* (May 2012), available at: <http://www.oireachtas.ie/parliament/media/michelle/Mental-capacity-text-REPORT-300412.pdf> (accessed 14 March 2013).

lead the field,[29] and, as Goodley described,[30] it took at least another decade before any attempts to develop self-advocacy among people with intellectual and psycho-social disabilities were made.

Humphrey describes how the right to self-identify as disabled has the logical corollary of accepting as legitimate other people's self-definitions of disability – but after decoding transcripts of interviews with disabled people's organisations, she points to three emerging themes as follows: 'a self-defined disabled person may be suspected of not being disabled when they harbour a non-apparent impairment, and/or express views which diverge from the prevailing consensus, and/or simultaneously belong to one of the other self-organized groups. These themes, in turn, suggest the operation of hierarchies of impairments, orthodoxies and oppressions, respectively'.[31] In particular, Humphrey points to the marginalisation of people with intellectual and psycho-social disabilities within the broader disability movement, as well as people with disabilities who also identify as a member of other minorities due for example to their race, gender, or sexual orientation.

> For one thing, people with learning or mental health difficulties may speak with a different voice, given the qualitatively different stigmata attached to different impairments and given the fact that the social model has been developed by those with physical impairments, so that their contributions may be interpreted as deviating from prevailing orthodoxies. For another, people who belong to another oppressed group may be all too visible in their difference, but their blackness or gayness may be construed as detracting from their contributions as disability activists, given the propensities of each group to prioritize its own specific identification-discrimination nexus.[32]

The reproduction of hierarchies within the disability movement can compromise the development of truly representative cross-disability organisations, which encompass the multiple and intersecting layers of identity we all hold. However, some scholars suggest that, given the diversity of the disability community, the development of a coherent national organisation of disabled people which is truly representative across all types of impairment and individual experience is an impossible task. Ghai adheres to this view in her writing about the Indian disability movement:

---

29 J Campbell and M Oliver (eds), *Disability Politics: Understanding Our Past, Changing Our Future* (Psychology Press, 1996).

30 See generally, D Goodley, *Self-Advocacy in the Lives of People with Learning Difficulties: The Politics of Resilience* (Open University Press, 2000).

31 J C Humphrey, 'Researching Disability Politics, Or, Some Problems with the Social Model in Practice' (2000) 15(1) *Disability & Society* 63 at 67.

32 Ibid., at 68.

Since individual aspects of disability matter, their clubbing together as one creates tensions. These homogenizing experiences prevent the recognition of cross-disability distinctions, and their specific realities and necessary responses to them. To seek rationality and symmetry within them would be to replicate the fallacy of modernist premises.[33]

Nevertheless, there are some positive examples of cross-disability collaboration in activism and advocacy for legislative change – including in the development of the Americans with Disabilities Act described above,[34] and indeed more recently at an international level, the drafting of the UN Convention on the Rights of Persons with Disabilities.[35] However, it must be acknowledged that many attempts at the development of truly representative and inclusive cross-disability groups in domestic contexts have failed, including, in the Irish context, the dissolution of two such organisations: the Forum of People with Disabilities and People with Disabilities in Ireland.[36] Critiques of the failure to fully include people with intellectual, psycho-social and other cognitive disabilities in positions of power within similar structures (with the appropriate supports to effectively fulfil these roles) have been made by some commentators,[37] while others acknowledge that since people with disabilities are not a homogeneous group, any attempt to reach common ground for campaigning can be a frustrating and complex exercise.[38] Other critiques include the blurring of lines between service provision and advocacy work, as well as the potential conflicts of interest which alliances with organisations of parents and siblings of persons with disabilities, and disability service providers, may present in the work of cross-disability organisations.[39]

---

33 A Ghai, 'Disability in the Indian Context: Post-Colonial Perspectives' in M Corker and T Shakespeare (eds), *Disability/Postmodernity: Embodying Disability Theory* (Continuum, 2002), 88 at 98.

34 S Caras, 'Disabled: One More Label' (1994) 9(1) *Disability and Society* 89.

35 R Kayess and P French, 'Out of Darkness into Light? Introducing the Convention on the Rights of Persons with Disabilities' (2008) 8(1) *Human Rights Law Review* 1.

36 The Forum of People with Disabilities was dissolved in 2008, and People with Disabilities in Ireland in 2011. See E Flynn, *From Rhetoric to Action: Implementing the UN Convention on the Rights of Persons with Disabilities* (Cambridge University Press, 2011), 320–322, 352–355.

37 M Cooper, 'The Australian Disability Rights Movement Lives' (1999) 14(2) *Disability & Society* 217.

38 J C Humphrey, 'Researching Disability Politics, Or, Some Problems with the Social Model in Practice' (2000) 15(1) *Disability & Society* 63.

39 J Campbell and M Oliver (eds), *Disability Politics: Understanding Our Past, Changing Our Future* (Psychology Press, 1996).

Reaching out to include the less-heard voices: spaces for cross-disability and broader community collaboration

The lacuna in representation and participation in deliberative processes presents a challenge to those organisations and individuals who are given a seat at the table – to make greater efforts to include people with disabilities in their delegations and provide space for them to give their own perspectives. That challenge extends to academia, as discussed in the previous chapter, to ensure that greater emphasis is placed on participatory action research, which includes people with disabilities as equal partners in the research process, and presents the findings of inclusive research to politicians and policy-makers who seek input on how law and policy affecting people with disabilities should be reformed.

Another key concern in deliberative processes on the rights of persons with disabilities is the risk that organisations of people with disabilities will be pitted against each other where their interests diverge, or will be forced to compete with each other and with other marginalised groups in society for scarce resources in terms of government funding. For example, in debates on legal capacity, organisations of people with intellectual and psycho-social disabilities may diverge on what the best approach is to secure equal respect for legal capacity (for example, people with psycho-social disabilities may want the introduction of legally binding advance directives,[40] whereas people with intellectual disabilities may prefer legally binding support agreements[41]).

Similarly, differences of opinion between people with cognitive disabilities and people with physical and sensory disabilities on legal capacity may emerge, as many people with physical or sensory disabilities may simply demand recognition of their legal capacity, and not support in order to exercise it. Where differences of opinion emerge, these can be used by government as a justification for not progressing with a reform process on the basis that there is no consensus among the groups as to what approach should be taken. Therefore, it is important to develop collaborative approaches among the organisations of people with disabilities, to reach consensus on the direction which reforms should take in a manner that will respect the rights of all persons with disabilities, as well as forming partnerships with other marginalised groups to strengthen the argument for reform. There are some good examples of collaborative approaches among disability organisations on core issues of disability rights, including the Irish civil society coalition for legal capacity reform, which brings together those with a broad disability focus and those with a specific focus on intellectual disability, mental health and older people's issues.[42] Further examples of collaboration between disability

---

40 See for example T Minkowitz, *No-Force Advocacy by Users and Survivors of Psychiatry* (Mental Health Commission, 2006).

41 See for example European Platform of Self Advocates, 'The Way Forward' (2011) *e-Include Journal of Inclusion Europe*, Article 895.

42 See for example Amnesty Ireland and Centre for Disability Law and Policy, *Essential Principles for Legal Capacity Reform* (2012), available at: <http://www.

organisations and other civil society groups can be found, including a partnership between disability activists and children's rights groups in South Africa to ensure that the rights of children with disabilities were adequately respected in the development of the Children's Act 2006.[43] These examples demonstrate the possibilities of collaboration both within the broader disability community and with other marginalised groups in society to create consensus-based advocacy for legislative reform.

Political Activism and Sustainable Change: Legislative Campaigns and the Role of Direct Action

Political activism is often the most effective means of achieving sustainable legal change – when compared with strategic litigation, which, while also an important mechanism for interpreting human rights and applying these to the disability context, has a number of weaknesses in terms of implementation and follow-up which may be mitigated by pursuing legislative reform. This is evident from the experience of disability activists in the United States, where the enactment of the Americans with Disabilities Act was seen as a major victory, albeit one which has perhaps subsequently been weakened in its effect and implementation by a number of court decisions which restrict its scope.[44] Similarly, in other areas of human rights activism, legislative reform has led to greater access to justice for marginalised groups than court decisions – for example, marriage equality has more often been secured through legislative reform than through strategic litigation – with recent examples of reform in the jurisdictions of Scotland, France and New Zealand leading the field.[45]

However, political activism does not always take the form of engagement in structured deliberative processes, such as the parliamentary fora for legislative development described in the previous section. In fact, since these processes are often compromised by lack of meaningful representation from people with disabilities themselves, many disabled people's organisations have used more confrontational approaches in their political activism. One prominent example of successful disability activism leading to legislative change to secure justice for people with disabilities was the nation-wide sit-ins in the United States during the early 1970s, held to ensure that regulations were passed to enforce section 504 of

---

nuigalway.ie/cdlp/documents/principles_web.pdf> (accessed 13 March 2013).

43 L Jamieson and P Proudlock, *From Sidelines to Centre Stage: The Inclusion of Children with Disabilities in the Children's Act* (Children's Institute Case Study Number 4, University of Cape Town, 2009).

44 See for example, M W Kelly, 'Weakening Title III of the Americans with Disabilities Act: The Buckhannon Decision and Other Developments Limiting Private Enforcement' (2002) 10 *Elder Law Journal* 361.

45 See for example, J S Schacter, 'Courts and the Politics of Backlash: Marriage Equality Litigation, Then and Now' (2008) 82 *S. Cal. L. Rev.* 1153.

the Rehabilitation Act 1973. This provision of the Act was the first federal attempt to prohibit discrimination against people with disabilities in federally funded programmes. Willig-Levy describes the protests as follows:

> With reason to fear that the 504 regulations were to be rescinded, [disabled activists] staged sit-ins in federal office buildings. In most cities, the demonstrations were over by day's end. In the nation's capital, officials would not allow food and drink into the building, starving the demonstrators out. But in San Francisco, [over 150] demonstrators stayed and stayed. They were not going to go away. After sleeping the first night on the hard floors, mattresses were delivered from the supplies of the State Health department. Food arrived from McDonald's, Delancy House's drug programs, the Black Panthers and Safeway. The Mayor himself scolded the federal officials for ignoring the needs of the uninvited guests and brought in shower attachments to be used in the tiled restrooms. On April 28, the demonstrators learned that Secretary Califano had signed the 504 regulations. They continued to occupy the building, however, until they had reviewed the final regulations and were satisfied with their content. On May 1st, the motley crew representing virtually every disability disbanded, knowing that this experience would unite them forever.[46]

Another example of this approach is the campaign of the Disabled People's Direct Action Network (DAN) in the UK – which was particularly active throughout the 1990s. Kitchin describes the DAN-led protests as being particularly cognisant of the power of space – as each demonstration site was chosen for its specific significance – often due to the physical location of power, such as the Houses of Parliament (where DAN protesters chained themselves to buses to highlight transport inaccessibility, timed to coincide with a legislative debate on the Disability Discrimination Act).[47] In more recent times, groups such as 'We Are Spartacus', 'Black Triangle' and 'Disabled People Against the Cuts' have led protests and collective action on issues such as the cuts to disability benefits, the changes in and outsourcing of the medical assessment for the disability living allowance, and in particular used the opportunity of the 2012 Paralympics, which were sponsored by a private company, ATOS, used by the Department of Work and Pensions to conduct work capability assessments, to critique the manner in which these assessments were conducted.[48]

---

46   C Willig Levy, *A People's History of the Independent Living Movement* (RTC/IL Monographs, 1998), 11–12.
47   R Kitchin, '"Out of Place", "Knowing One's Place": Space, Power and the Exclusion of Disabled People' (1998) 13(3) *Disability & Society* 343 at 353.
48   See for example, S Braye, T Gibbons and K Dixon, 'Disability "Rights" or "Wrongs"? The Claims of the International Paralympic Committee, the London 2012 Paralympics and Disability Rights in the UK' (2013) 18(3) *Sociological Research Online* 16.

The links between political engagement or activism and greater recognition of equality and access to justice, in the legislative and judicial arenas, have been demonstrated by many marginalised communities throughout history – including the campaigns for gender equality,[49] civil rights[50] and, more recently, environmental justice.[51] While a generation of disability activists did achieve significant legislative change, especially in terms of the prohibition of disability-based discrimination in various domestic jurisdictions throughout the 1990s, and the development of a global human rights standard for people with disabilities with the negotiation of the Convention on the Rights of Persons with Disabilities in 2006, it is vital that a new generation of disability activists is supported to emerge now – a movement which is fully inclusive of those more marginalised communities within disability – including people with cognitive disabilities and those who identify as disabled but also belong to other communities (LGBTQI, ethnic, cultural or linguistic minorities and older people with disabilities) to address the core justice concerns of the 21st century – including the continuing struggles to ensure equal recognition of legal capacity, and the right to live independently and be included in the community.

3. Individual Political Participation: Disability-Inclusive Electoral Processes

As discussed in section 1 above, where a broad understanding of the justice system includes the parliamentary and legislative processes, equal access to these fora must be ensured for persons with disabilities. The first step to formal political participation for most citizens is being given the opportunity to vote in electoral processes and referenda. Many people with disabilities over the age of majority continue to be explicitly denied this basic right, usually where they are under adult guardianship or some other form of substituted decision-making. A report from the Fundamental Rights Agency in 2010 found that a majority of EU Member States linked the right to vote to an individual's legal capacity, whereby 'the right to political participation [is denied] to all persons under a protective measure such as a partial and plenary guardianship, regardless of their actual and/or individual level of functional ability or whether they have an intellectual disability or a mental health problem'.[52] Even where the right to vote is linked to an individual's actual or perceived level of functioning (which the report notes occurs in France and Spain

---

49   See for example, M W McCann, *Rights at Work: Pay Equity Reform and the Politics of Legal Mobilization* (University of Chicago Press, 1994).

50   See for example, S F Lawson, 'Freedom Then, Freedom Now: The Historiography of the Civil Rights Movement' (1991) 96(2) *The American Historical Review* 456.

51   C Coglianese, 'Social Movements, Law, and Society: The Institutionalization of the Environmental Movement' (2001) 150(1) *University of Pennsylvania Law Review* 85.

52   Fundamental Rights Agency, *The Right to Political Participation of Persons with Mental Health Problems and Persons with Intellectual Disabilities* (FRA, 2010), 16.

for example),[53] this is still problematic, as it perpetuates a form of discrimination in the granting of the franchise, which if strictly applied, ought to exclude many more people from voting than simply those under adult guardianship or other forms of substituted decision-making. However, this report also pointed to some positive examples where the universal franchise was ensured for people with disabilities – e.g. in Austria, the Netherlands and Sweden.[54]

The Venice Commission within the Council of Europe considered this very issue in the development of its guidance to Member States on the right to vote of persons with disabilities. In an initial recommendation published in 2010, it suggested that 'no person with a disability can be excluded from the right to vote or to stand for election on the basis of her/his physical and/or mental disability unless the deprivation of the right to vote and to be elected is imposed by an individual decision of a court of law because of proven mental disability'.[55] Following significant challenges from NGOs and organisations of people with disabilities, as well as an intervention from the Council of Europe Commissioner for Human Rights,[56] the final text of the Venice Commission's guidance took a different stance, stating: 'Universal suffrage is a fundamental principle of the European Electoral Heritage. People with disabilities may not be discriminated against in this regard, in conformity with Article 29 of the Convention of the United Nations on the Rights of Persons with Disabilities and the caselaw of the European Court of Human Rights'.[57] Therefore, explicit exclusion from the ballot on the basis of actual or perceived deficits in an individual's decision-making skills is recognised as deeply problematic from a human rights perspective.

Implicit exclusion from the franchise also occurs in other ways, for example, where literature about elections is not made accessible to people with disabilities, polling stations and voting booths are physically inaccessible, or mechanisms to allow people with disabilities to vote by secret ballot are compromised by allowing a companion to support someone in casting a vote rather than making the process accessible so that a person can vote independently. Much analysis has been undertaken, in the United States in particular, on how electoral laws can directly or indirectly lead to the denial of votes to certain communities – including those with low literacy, prisoners, and those who lack the kind of formal identification which is required to be presented at polling stations (including homeless people

---

53 Ibid., 19.

54 Ibid., 22.

55 European Commission for Democracy Through Law, *Interpretative Declaration to the Code of Good Practice in Electoral Matters on the Participation of People with Disabilities in Elections* (Venice, 2010), para 2.

56 Council of Europe Commissioner for Human Rights, *Human Rights Comment: Persons with Disabilities Must Not Be Denied the Right to Vote* (Strasbourg, 2011).

57 European Commission for Democracy Through Law, *Revised Interpretative Declaration to the Code of Good Practice in Electoral Matters on the Participation of People with Disabilities in Elections* (Venice, 2011), para II.1.2.

and undocumented workers). Tokaji describes a number of historical examples of practices resulting in vote denial including 'literacy tests, poll taxes, all-white primaries, and English-only ballots'.[58] In more recent years he suggests that controversy surrounding 'felon disenfranchisement, voting machines, and voter ID laws' represent what he terms the 'new vote denial'.[59]

While some attempts to improve election accessibility for people with disabilities and other marginalised communities have been introduced, much more is needed in terms of reform to level the playing field for voters with disabilities. Efforts such as the imposition of minimum accessibility standards on polling stations and voting procedures have been introduced in many countries, including the Help America Vote Act 2002, accessibility amendments to the Canada Elections Act 1992, and other similar legislative reforms around the world, are an important first step, but the implementation and enforcement of these standards still leaves much to be desired.

Waterstone suggests that the key problems facing voters with disabilities are the accessibility of polling stations and the right to vote independently, while maintaining the secrecy of the ballot.[60] The solutions which are often used to address these problems, for example, the use of curb-side voting or absentee ballots are, he argues, not sufficient to ensure equality for people with disabilities in the electoral process.[61] He is similarly sceptical about the accessibility of various voting machines, paper ballots and electronic voting for persons with disabilities – especially people with visual impairments, for whom adaptations are often not made at all, and if an alternative is offered, it generally involves a third party entering the voter's choices, which does not sufficiently protect the secrecy of the ballot, or allow the individual to vote independently.[62]

Some innovative accommodations have been developed in various countries to ensure that people with disabilities can vote independently and by secret ballot. In the Second European Disability High Level Group Report on Implementation of the UN Convention on the Rights of Persons with Disabilities it was noted that in the UK each polling station now has a special 'tactile' voting device.[63] This report also notes that Austria provides a stencil for ballot papers that uses tactile paving to enable blind or visually impaired voters to vote independently.[64] Malta

---

58   D P Tokaji, 'The New Vote Denial: Where Election Reform Meets the Voting Rights Act' (2005) 57 *South Carolina Law Rev.* 689 at 691.

59   Ibid., at 692.

60   M Waterstone, 'Constitutional and Statutory Voting Rights for People with Disabilities' (2003) 14 *Stan. L. & Pol'y Rev.* 353.

61   Ibid., at 355.

62   Ibid., at 356.

63   European Union, *Second Disability High Level Group Report on Implementation of UN Convention on the Rights of Persons with Disabilities* (European Commission, 2009), 212.

64   Ibid., 13.

is also reported as an example of good practice, whereby a 'perforated template' is provided to voters with visual impairments.[65] In the initial State reports to the Committee on the Rights of Persons with Disabilities it was noted that the Australian Electoral Commission has a number of alternatives available to make voting more accessible including the use of telephone voting.[66] Telephone voting was used in Australia in the 2010 federal election to ensure blind or visually impaired voters could enjoy the right to vote by secret ballot.[67]

However, it is not simply developed countries which have innovated in this regard. In 2002, the International Foundation for Electoral Systems worked with the Ghana Association of the Blind and the Ghana Electoral Commission to design and test pilot a tactile ballot guide, to enable blind voters to vote independently and in secret.[68] Similarly, in 2010 it assisted the Association of Blind and Partially Sighted People in Kosovo to create tactile ballots for use by people with visual impairments and train voters to use the tactile ballot system.[69] These examples demonstrate that it is possible to develop more inclusive electoral systems which serve people with disabilities while preserving the secrecy of the ballot even in low-income countries. While recognising that there is no one-size-fits-all mechanism which can enable all people with disabilities equal access to the franchise, certain disabling barriers resulting in exclusion (including legal incapacity or physical inaccessibility) should certainly be removed to ensure more widespread access to the fundamental right to vote for people with disabilities.

Running for Election: The Inclusion of Candidates with Disabilities

D'Aubin and Stienstra comment extensively on the lack of knowledge about the participation of people with disabilities as candidates in Canadian elections:

> [T]here continues to be a significant under-representation of people with disabilities, particularly people with disabilities that require accommodations such as sign language interpreters, alternative media and other types of supports. There is no collected history or analysis of the presence or absence of people with disabilities in Canadian politics. As well, there are candidates and elected officials with disabilities who remain hidden, passing as non-disabled people.

---

65 Ibid., 141.

66 Committee on the Rights of Persons with Disabilities, *Initial Reports Submitted by States Parties under Article 35 of the Convention: Australia* (Geneva, 2012), para 179.

67 Part XVB, *Commonwealth Electoral Act 1918*.

68 International Foundation for Electoral Systems, *Ballot Guide Developed for Blind Voters in Ghana* (March 2002), available at: <http://www.ifes.org/Content/Publications/Press-Release/2002/Ballot-Guide-Developed-for-Blind-Voters-in-Ghana.aspx> (accessed 10 February 2014).

69 International Foundation for Electoral Systems, *IFES 2010 Annual Report* (2011), 17.

This under-representation stems in part from negative public attitudes about people with disabilities, lack of knowledge about the costs and potential contributions of disabled people, and lack of resources for candidates with disabilities, including appropriate disability supports, money, and access to political opportunities.[70]

As with the direct exclusion from the franchise, many countries explicitly prohibit certain people with disabilities from standing for election. For example, eligibility for election to the lower house of parliament is set out as follows in the Irish Constitution: 'Every citizen without distinction of sex who has reached the age of twenty-one years, and who is not placed under disability or incapacity by this Constitution or by law, shall be eligible for membership of Dáil Éireann'.[71] While the text of the Constitution itself does not suggest what such 'disability or incapacity' might be, the Electoral Act 1992 states that 'a person of unsound mind' is ineligible for election to the parliament.[72] This is thought to be a reference to the current legal procedure for depriving an individual of her legal capacity – known as the Ward of Court system in Ireland, which bases the deprivation of legal capacity on the person being of 'unsound mind' and 'incapable of governing himself or his property'.[73]

An international study by the UN Office of the High Commissioner on participation in political and public life by persons with disabilities has found the exclusion of people with disabilities from eligibility as election candidates is often connected to legal capacity, and that even where this has been relaxed to ensure the right to vote, as in France for example, where people under guardianship or curatorship can retain the right to vote, they do not retain the right to stand for election.[74] This study found only a few examples internationally where persons with disabilities were universally recognised as eligible to stand for election, including in the UK,[75] although a number of countries, including Mexico and Burkina Faso, were considering the introduction of quotas to incentivise political parties to be more inclusive of people with disabilities and to ensure greater representation of people with disabilities in parliament.[76]

---

70   A D'Aubin and D Stienstra, 'Access to Electoral Success: Challenges and Opportunities for Candidates with Disabilities in Canada' *Electoral Insight* (April 2004), available at: <http://www.elections.ca/res/eim/article_search/article.asp?id=16&lang=e&frmPageSize=> (accessed 10 February 2014).
71   Article 16.1.1°, Bunreacht na hÉireann, 1937.
72   Section 41(j), Electoral Act 1992.
73   Lunacy Regulation (Ireland) Act 1871.
74   UN Office of the High Commissioner for Human Rights, *Thematic Study on Participation in Political and Public Life by Persons with Disabilities* A/HRC/19/36 (UN, 2011), para 42.
75   Ibid., para 44.
76   Ibid., para 50.

Following the history of the hierarchies within the disability movement, it was often people with physical and sensory disabilities who first broke through the barriers to run for election. In his memoirs, Percy Wickman describes the barriers facing him as a physically disabled man running for election to a local city council in Canada in the 1970s:

> Then the whispers started. 'Why elect a disabled person, when there are so many healthy ones running?' 'If successful, he will only represent the handicapped'. Certainly some sympathy votes were picked up, particularly from those who sensed my determination and hunger for the job. But many, many votes were lost because of the unfounded fear that I could not do a proper job if elected.[77]

Similar bias was faced by a blind politician who described the public's reaction to him wearing sunglasses in his campaign literature:

> A fairly large number of people called in to ask who does this Ross Eadie guy think he is? My campaign manager (now a good friend) explained to those who called that I was blind. We will never know if this sunglass issue cost us votes ... A woman called into the office saying she was not going to vote for me if it was going to cost her more tax dollars ... Another fellow didn't even listen to me at the door. He just went in the house and came out with money for the blind guy. I told him I could use the money for the campaign, but I really wanted his vote.[78]

However, in more recent decades, people with physical and sensory disabilities have managed to overcome these discriminatory barriers in greater numbers to become elected representatives in parliaments around the world. Tammy Duckworth, the first disabled woman to be elected to the US House of Representatives, won her seat in the 2011 election, and was a vocal advocate in support of US ratification of the UN Convention on the Rights of Persons with Disabilities.[79] Her profile as an Iraq war veteran was a significant aspect of her campaign, following in the tradition of many other disabled veterans who have sought election to congress

---

77 P Wickman, *Wheels in the Fast Lane ... A Blessing in Disguise* (Triwicky Enterprises, 1987), 71.

78 Ross Eadie, 'A Politician Wanna Be' *The Canadian Blind Monitor* (Summer 2000), 27, available at: <www.nfbae.ca/publications/cbm_old/cbm_12.txt> (accessed 10 February 2014).

79 US Senate Foreign Relations Committee, 'Congresswoman Duckworth Testifies Before Senate Foreign Relations Committee on the Convention on the Rights of Persons with Disabilities' 5 November 2013, available at: <http://duckworth.house.gov/media-center/press-releases/congresswoman-duckworth-testifies-before-senate-foreign-relations> (accessed 11 February 2014).

and the senate and been stalwart advocates for disability rights – such as Bob Dole, John McCain and Daniel Inouye.[80]

The reduction in barriers for electoral candidates with intellectual and psycho-social disabilities has been a slower process, although some progress has been made on this issue in recent decades. For example, in 2004, the Liberal Party in Canada removed a question from its application form for party candidates which required potential electoral candidates to disclose whether or not they had a mental health condition, and the prime minister issued an apology to the Canadian Mental Health Association for the stigma this may have caused.[81] Similar progress was made in the UK last year when the House of Commons passed the Mental Health (Discrimination) Act 2013, repealing section 141 of the Mental Health Act 1983, which allowed for the removal of a member of parliament or members of devolved bodies (such as the Scottish, Welsh and Northern Ireland Assemblies) on the grounds of mental illness after a period of six months.[82] The 2013 Act also repealed any common law provisions which disqualified an individual from becoming a member of parliament due to mental illness.[83] Nevertheless, it is still incredibly rare for politicians and parliamentarians to self-identify as having a psycho-social disability. However, as Flinders describes, in an attempt to raise awareness about mental health stigma, a number of members of the British parliament did just that in June 2012:

> [A] number of MPs used a debate on mental health in the House of Commons to discuss their own psychological problems. Charles Walker MP described himself as a 'practising fruitcake' while outlining a battle he has been fighting with Obsessive Compulsive Disorder for more than three decades, Kevan Jones MP admitted to having suffered from bouts of depression, and two female MPs (Sarah Woolaston and Andrea Leadsom) also discussed their experience of post-natal depression. If we add Jack Straw and the Labour MP John Woodcock, who last December admitted to suffering from depression, this makes a grand total of six out of 650 MPs who have acknowledged their own mental health challenges when in reality the available data on mental health, in general, and stressful

---

80 L F Moore Jr., 'FDR Secret is Out: The Election of 2006 and Disabled Candidates' *Gibbs Magazine* (2007), available at: <http://www.gibbsmagazine.com/FDR%20Secret%20is%20Out.htm> (accessed 11 February 2014).

81 Jane Taber, 'Mercer puts Copps on the Spot' *The Globe and Mail*, 24 January 2004, A9, cited in A D'Aubin and D Stienstra, 'Access to Electoral Success: Challenges and Opportunities for Candidates with Disabilities in Canada' *Electoral Insight* (April 2004), available at: <http://www.elections.ca/res/eim/article_search/article.asp?id=16&lang=e&frmPageSize=> (accessed 10 February 2014).

82 Section 1(1), Mental Health (Discrimination) Act 2013.

83 Section 1(2), Mental Health (Discrimination) Act 2013.

occupations, in particular, would suggest that a far higher number of MPs will actually have experienced (or be experiencing) some form of mental disorder.[84]

These examples suggest that, since many people with psycho-social disabilities can 'pass' as non-disabled, parliamentarians and other politicians will choose not to self-identify as having a disability or mental health condition, due to the stigma that still surrounds these issues, and the questions this may lead to regarding their competency as legislators and policy-makers. The World Network of Users and Survivors of Psychiatry, in a submission to the UN Office of the High Commissioner for Human Rights, describes a number of scenarios where people with psycho-social disabilities experienced barriers due to their diagnosis when they sought to progress in their political careers – with one example of an MP in Uganda whose psycho-social disability was disclosed during the vetting process for a ministerial appointment and who subsequently lost the opportunity to represent her community as a minister.[85]

Another key concern for people with disabilities who wish to stand for election is that their campaign may be seen as 'tokenistic' by vested political interests. For example, a man with intellectual disability who ran for local elections in Ghent, Belgium, sparked political controversy as journalists and members of the public questioned whether his selection by the Flemish Christian Democrats Party was a positive statement of inclusion or merely a political stunt. The candidate, Didier Peleman, ran for election on a platform of accessibility and inclusion for citizens with disabilities, including a promise to develop more material about public services in 'easy read' formats for people with intellectual disabilities. However, in an article by the RT news service, members of the public expressed scepticism about his ability to fulfil his role as a public servant:

> 'If he's physically disabled it's not ridiculous, but he has mental disabilities so that's another question, he may have problems with reasoning,' one Ghent resident told RT.

> 'I think he's not capable of making decisions for other people. I do voluntary work myself with mentally disabled people. I've got a lot of respect for them, but they have to realize themselves that they are not able to do everything,' another shared.

---

84 M Flinders, 'Mad Politics: Politicians, Mental Health and the Pathology of Social Stigma' *University of Sheffield Politics Blog*, 11 February 2014, available at: <http://www.shef.ac.uk/politics/news/mad-politics-1.348849> (accessed 12 February 2014).

85 World Network of Users and Survivors of Psychiatry, *Submission to UN Office of High Commissioner for Human Rights for Thematic Study on Political Participation* (October 2011), 6.

'I know it's difficult when you criticize such a nice and good guy, but I don't want to criticize him as a person, I want to criticize his party for using him as a kind of political tool to get media attention at a time when we are close to the municipal election,' Ghent citizen Frederic Ranson argues.[86]

While Mr Peleman was not ultimately elected to the municipal council, his campaign certainly served to highlight accessibility issues and opened up a public discussion about greater inclusion in the electoral process. A similar debate arose in Ireland when a presidential candidate, Mary Davis, announced her intention, if elected, to appoint a person with an intellectual disability to the president's advisory body on Constitutional matters – known as the Council of State.[87] While efforts on the part of political authorities to promote inclusion of people with disabilities are in general to be welcomed, it is important to ensure there are sufficient supports in place to assist the individual in performing the political role in question, as otherwise, the appointment will certainly become simply tokenistic, regardless of the intention of the actors in question.

Crossing the Political Divide: From Activists to Elected Representatives

In moving from collective to individual political action, some prominent disability activists around the world have chosen to put themselves forward as elected representatives – running as members of parliament and for other forms of political office or executive appointment. This action inevitably invites questions about motives and mechanisms for achieving change. One prominent example of this is the journey of Jane Campbell – from disability activist and researcher to her appointment as a 'life peer' to the House of Lords, Britian's upper house of parliament. Campbell justifies her shift from activist and outsider to political decision-maker by arguing that a focus solely on politics of identity and recognition which she and others in the disability movement advocated for will not bring about the redistributive justice which people with disabilities seek.

Rather, she suggests that 'a politics of participation and consensus' is what is required – to acknowledge the identities and individual impairments which ground our experience, but to move past these to understand the experiences of others and to seek to share control and responsibility for political decisions based less on

---

86 RT News, 'Statement or Stunt? Ghent Voters Divided Over Mentally-Disabled Candidate' 7 August 2012, available at: <http://rt.com/news/belgium-elections-mental-peleman-029/> (accessed 12 February 2014).

87 See G Reilly, 'Davis Promises to Appoint Intellectually Disabled Person to Council of State' The Journal.ie, 17 October 2011, available at: <http://www.thejournal.ie/davis-promises-to-appoint-intellectually-disabled-person-to-council-of-state-256040-Oct2011/> (accessed 12 February 2014).

'separateness and difference' and more on 'interdependence and connection with others'.[88] She claims:

> Disabled people who are or have been associated with disability politics and have been active in the movement – and I include myself amongst them – must accept that what is ultimately important to the individual is their own and their loved ones' life chances; not those of the group one is considered to belong to. It is little comfort to an unemployed Bangladeshi woman with mental health problems – among the most disadvantaged of all people in Britain – to know that disabled people's employment rate has improved by 8 percentage points over the last decade. This is especially so when it is clear that neither the disability movement nor the social policy programmes aimed at improving disabled people's employment opportunity, have gone anywhere near recognising and responding to the complex barriers she is likely to face. Why should she feel part of a movement in which she is invisible?
>
> The politics of participation aims to ensure that the *genuine nature and causes* of discrimination and disadvantage that people face, are more likely to surface. It also seeks to engage those who might otherwise be or feel overlooked. It also aims to engage those who may see themselves as separate and uninvolved.[89]

From Campbell's statement it seems that she sees her mission as a parliamentarian as one to engage with the broader community of people with disabilities and to bring their concerns to the forefront in the development of new law and policy, and justifies her transition from activism to elected politics as one which can benefit more people with disabilities in concrete ways.

The participation of disabled people in the political system as elected representatives certainly can lead to greater representative diversity in our parliaments and legislatures. This links with the notion of 'symbolic justice' described by Bahdi[90] discussed in Chapter 1[91] – as it increases the potential for societies to be more inclusive of people with disabilities if these individuals hold valued roles and positions of power within the State, including in the political system, as part of the broader justice system. The desire to ensure greater diversity and inclusion of disabled people in parliaments necessarily raises the issue of positive action – and the effectiveness of quota systems in achieving greater

---

88   J Campbell, 'Fighting for a Slice, or for a Bigger Cake?' The 6th Annual Disability Lecture, University of Cambridge, St. John's College, 29 April 2008, 9.

89   Ibid., 10.

90   R Bahdi, *Background Paper on Women's Access to Justice in the MENA Region* (International Development Research Centre (IDRC), Women's Rights and Citizenship Program (WRC) and the Middle East Regional Office (MERO), Middle East and North African (MENA) Regional Consultation, 9–11 December 2007, Cairo, Egypt).

91   Ch 1, 16–17.

representation of minority groups, such as persons with disabilities, in political office, which I will discuss in the following section.

Representative Diversity in Parliamentary Processes: The Role of Quota Systems

There are some recent examples in the African context where quotas have been introduced as part of Constitutional reform processes to ensure greater representativeness in parliament as a whole for particularly excluded groups, such as women, young people and people with disabilities. For example, in Kenya the 2010 Constitution introduced the following system of representation in the National Assembly: 290 members, each elected by the registered voters of single-member constituencies; 47 women, each elected by the registered voters of the counties, each county constituting a single-member constituency; and 12 members nominated by parliamentary political parties according to their proportion of members of the National Assembly, to represent special interests including the youth, persons with disabilities and workers; and the Speaker, who is an ex officio member.[92]

Similarly, in the upper house of parliament in Kenya, the Senate, the Constitution provides that there shall be 47 members each elected by the registered voters of the counties, each county constituting a single-member constituency; 16 women members nominated by parliamentary political parties according to their proportion of members of the Senate; two members (one male and one female) to represent the youth; two members (one male and one female) to represent persons with disabilities and the Speaker, who is an ex officio member.[93] Interestingly, the Constitution also retains the disqualification of 'persons of unsound mind' from standing for election to either house of parliament.[94]

The disability caucus in the current Kenyan parliament held its first stakeholders meeting to discuss key political issues with the representative organisations of people with disabilities from civil society in June 2013.[95] Its members have already highlighted some key barriers to their full participation as individual parliamentarians since their election to parliament, including the physical accessibility of the chamber, access to the Speaker's office, the media centre, and toilet facilities, rules of procedure which prevented parliamentarians from covering their heads (even though one MP required a hat due to light-sensitivity), and the physical design of the chamber which meant MPs in wheelchairs were almost always seated at the back and found it difficult to raise points of order.[96]

---

92   Article 97, Constitution of Kenya, 2010.
93   Article 98, Constitution of Kenya, 2010.
94   Article 99(2)(e), Constitution of Kenya, 2010.
95   Parliament of Kenya, 'Kenya Disability Parliamentary (KEDIPA) Caucus Holds First Ever Stakeholders Meeting' (Mombasa, June 2013).
96   W Ndogna, 'Parliament Inhospitable to MPs with Disabilities' *Capital FM News*, 12 April 2013.

Much has been written about the effectiveness of parliamentary quotas in the context of gender equality which can provide some useful insight to those seeking to operate similar systems to facilitate greater representation of parliamentarians with disabilities. For example, Tamale writes from the experience of a similar system in Uganda's parliament (which, like Kenya, combines a gender quota with a smaller number of reserved seats for representatives of people with disabilities), that while the use of quotas has at one level increased the numbers of women in parliament, the system has many flaws.[97] She notes that the implementation of the quota system and the identification of suitable women candidates was accomplished in a male-dominated environment, and the policy was seen as a 'top-down' decision, made in the absence of any grassroots mobilisation of the women's movement in Uganda.[98] Therefore, she argues that: 'The patriarchal structures and institutions within which politicians operate have themselves not altered one bit. So, basically what we have are women in power without power!'[99] This critique resonates deeply with the concerns of the Kenyan parliamentarians with disabilities discussed above.

Therefore, Campbell's call for a participatory and consensus-based politics[100] retains its validity, as it seems that while representation among elected politicians may be an important step in the campaign for law and policy reform, in itself, mere representation will not necessarily accomplish these goals, unless the political structures and institutions themselves are open to reform.

From Local to Global and Back Again: The Role of International Law-Makers

The participation of people with disabilities in exercises of political authority at international level is also significant, as it helps to keep governments accountable to their commitments to improve the rights of persons with disabilities at the domestic level. In this context, the members of the UN Committee on the Rights of Persons with Disabilities – the treaty monitoring body for the UN Convention on the Rights of Persons with Disabilities – play a significant role. Each member is nominated by a State Party to the Convention, but once appointed, is required to be independent in the performance of her functions. To this end, no Committee member is permitted to participate in the examination of his State Party by the Committee – and therefore, does not attend the dialogue held between State Party representatives and the other members of the Committee as part of the examination

---

97 S Tamale, 'Introducing Quotas: Discourse and Legal Reform in Uganda' in J Billingdon (ed), *The Implementation of Quotas: African Experiences* (International Institute for Democracy and Electoral Assistance, 2004), 38.

98 Ibid., 40.

99 Ibid.

100 J Campbell, 'Fighting for a Slice, or for a Bigger Cake?' The 6th Annual Disability Lecture, University of Cambridge, St. John's College, 29 April 2008.

process, or contribute to the development of the Concluding Observations for that State.[101]

As interpreter of international human rights norms, the Committee also plays a crucial role, in applying the principles (inevitably the product of international compromise and diplomacy) agreed by the drafters to concrete situations, and providing comprehensive guidance to States on the implementation of core rights. Its proactive stance in initial interpretations of the Convention provided through Concluding Observations and the General Comments on Articles 9 and 12 to date indicate a positive trajectory, broadly consistent with the views advocated by the civil society representatives of persons with disabilities, and requiring a high standard of commitment from States Parties to achieve full implementation.

The Committee has been noted for its vocal and adversarial stance with states on key issues of importance to the disability community, including legal capacity, independent living and inclusive education.[102] The fact that 17 of its 18 members at the time of writing are themselves persons with various kinds of disabilities, is also important in achieving this task, from the perspective of symbolic justice (in terms of recognition and representation) and also provides the Committee with legitimacy in its interactions with States Parties on questions of implementing and upholding the rights of persons with disabilities around the globe.

4. Conclusion: Barriers and Proposed Solutions in Creating a More Representative and Inclusive Democracy

Throughout this chapter, many of the barriers which prevent people with disabilities from playing an active role in public and political life have been identified. For example, people with disabilities are often deliberately or inadvertently excluded from the franchise, or may feel disenfranchised due to a perceived lack of voting power. Apart from the obvious need to remedy explicit exclusions of people with disabilities from the electorate, there is also a requirement to engage in consciousness-raising to ensure that people with disabilities as a collective can exercise voting power and make disability equality a campaign issue during elections.

Another issue which emerges from the history of disenfranchisement is the low numbers of people with disabilities in our parliaments, which raises broader questions about the representativeness and inclusiveness of parliaments in general. Much has been learned from the experience of enhancing gender equality and diversity in parliaments – both from the positive and negative experiences in the

---

101 United Nations Committee on the Rights of Persons with Disabilities, *Rules of Procedure* CRPD/C/4/2/Rev.1 (Geneva, 2013), 16.

102 R McCallum, 'The United Nations Convention on the Rights of Persons with Disabilities in 2011 and Beyond: A View from its Treaty Body' paper presented at the Nordic Network for Disability Research conference, Reyjavik, 27 May 2011.

use of quota systems, to the more practical supports and accommodations that are required to make participation in political life a realistic option for people with disabilities. The generation of campaign funding specifically for disabled candidates, similar to initiatives such as Emily's List[103] for women candidates, is one example of how the inclusion of people with disabilities in our parliaments could be achieved. Another practical support would be the provision of accessibility allowances to meet the disability-related expenses which disabled politicians may legitimately incur (for example, needing to take taxis due to inaccessible public transport) – and thus to enable them to play a more active role in political life. Similarly, the adaptation of the physical structures, and deliberative procedures used in our parliaments, to ensure accessibility and ease of use by all people with disabilities, is another important step towards achieving greater diversity in the political system.

In running for election, people with disabilities face a number of barriers and have to confront stigma and disablist prejudices head-on, as described above. There is the risk of people with disabilities running for election being seen as 'single-issue' candidates, only interested in disability equality, or welfare reform, in the way perhaps that women parliamentarians may have been viewed in the past – and these perceptions can only be challenged by increasing the number of disabled people in politics and the diversity of issues they campaign on. Once elected, further barriers have to be overcome to ensure that people with disabilities can play an active role in political life – and this will require both general accessibility measures and more individualised reasonable accommodation.

Beyond the individual nature of political participation by people with disabilities as voters and elected representatives, securing justice for people with disabilities in the political sphere also requires a reform of the deliberative processes used by parliaments and other forms of political decision-making which seeks to involve the broader community as partners in law and policy-making. Consciousness-raising is required in the disability community to ensure that individuals and groups are aware of these processes and equipped to effectively participate, and similarly, those in positions of political power need to deliberately involve the disability community in these deliberative exercises. As demonstrated above, it is particularly important that the legitimate voices of people with disabilities themselves are heard, and that politicians seek out these representatives rather than simply assuming that family organisations, disability service providers and academics will provide the same perspective as disabled people themselves.

However, it is also important to acknowledge that these processes have their limits, as described in the illustrative examples above, and part of the disability community's evolution as a social movement has involved developing the political acumen to know when to work within these structures and when to work

---

103   J L Lawless, *It Takes a Candidate: Why Women Don't Run for Office* (Cambridge University Press, 2005).

around or outside them.[104] Alternative approaches can involve the use of collective direct action, protest and activist strategies to highlight issues of grave political concern, reaching executive decision-makers (Cabinet ministers and so on) who may be political allies and bringing the attention of the public to these issues via print, broadcast and new media in a more direct way where deliberation has failed. A combination of approaches is often required – with some individuals and groups maintaining their involvement in deliberative processes or negotiating with political leaders, while others, through strategic collaboration, use more confrontational tactics to highlight disability rights issues or justice claims. This combination of approaches is, I suggest, necessary to stimulate both individual and collective involvement of people with disabilities at all levels of public and political life – and to ensure effective access to justice, at both a symbolic and a substantive level.

---

104 R Kitchin, '"Out of Place", "Knowing One's Place": Space, Power and the Exclusion of Disabled People' (1998) 13(3) *Disability & Society* 343.

Conclusion and Recommendations for Reform

Throughout my consideration of the core areas of access to justice in Chapters 3–6 a number of global themes have emerged, which can provide guidance as to how effective access to justice for people with disabilities can be secured around the globe. I propose to address each of these themes in turn, with recommendations for how these concepts can lead to substantive reform across concrete areas of law, policy and practice in the field of disability and access to justice.

1. Recognition: Understanding and Accommodating Difference

As I have consistently demonstrated throughout this book, people with disabilities are a unique but not homogeneous group, who have experienced distinct barriers in accessing justice due to a combination of stigma, discriminatory laws and policies, and a failure of the non-disabled world to accept and respond to their claims for justice. In keeping with Fraser's argument[1] – people with disabilities, along with others, seek 'recognition' of their difference, as well as the fair redistribution of society's social and economic capital to facilitate their full inclusion and participation. The kind of 'recognition' which would be necessary in the context of access to justice would include recognition of the equality of people with disabilities, and a prohibition on discrimination, which can be applied to all elements of the justice system, broadly defined, to include all aspects of the legislative, judicial and executive branches of the State. It would be remiss of me not to argue for the extension of the prohibition of discrimination into the private sphere, as this is where the potential for most exploitation occurs – and in order to facilitate true access to justice, the State must have an obligation to ensure that both public and private actors recognise the equality of persons with disabilities before the law.

This prohibition on discrimination should also include the recognition that, for people with disabilities, a denial of reasonable accommodation is in fact discrimination.[2] Similarly, in keeping with the concept of intersectionality, it is

---

1 N Fraser, 'From Redistribution to Recognition? Dilemmas of Justice in a "Post-Socialist" Age' (1995) *New Left Review* 68.
2 This is acknowledged in the definition of 'discrimination' used in the UN CRPD, Article 2.

important that legal prohibitions on discrimination against persons with disabilities recognise the diversity of the disability community, and the multiple identities we as individuals hold, which may in turn compound or substantially alter the experience of discrimination. Legal frameworks which prohibit intersectional discrimination should acknowledge that discrimination can occur in the space 'between' prohibited grounds, and not merely require the individual to prove discrimination on several grounds separately, or indeed limit the number of grounds upon which an individual can base a claim of discrimination.[3]

In the move beyond traditional anti-discrimination statutes, regard should be had to incorporating the valuable perspective of Article 12 CRPD which includes the right to enjoyment of legal capacity on an equal basis with others in all aspects of life as a component of the right to equal recognition before the law.[4] Recognition of legal capacity is particularly significant for persons with disabilities in securing effective access to justice, as it is the baseline for so many entry points into the broad justice system – including the right to bring a claim to court and instruct a lawyer,[5] the right to vote and stand for election,[6] and the right to give evidence and be heard in court,[7] as addressed in Chapters 3, 4 and 6 respectively. Therefore, the broad recognition of this right, and the subsequent right of people with disabilities to support, where desired, for the exercise of legal capacity, should be enshrined in domestic legal frameworks in order to facilitate meaningful access to justice for disabled people. However, true 'recognition' requires much more than mere law reform, and will entail societal acceptance and understanding of the lived experience of people with disabilities. This theme will be addressed further in the following section.

2. Inclusive Spaces and Legitimate Voices: Acknowledging the Lived Experience

A constant theme throughout this text has been the historical exclusion of people with disabilities from the spaces and places in which questions of justice are addressed – including the parliamentary process as well as litigation in court. In order to accommodate and include people with disabilities in the broad justice system, these processes must explicitly reach out and seek their active involvement – both as contributors (e.g. civil society activists) and direct participants (e.g. elected

---

3 T Degener, 'Disadvantage at the Intersection of Race and Disability: Key Challenges for EU Non-Discrimination Law' in D Schiek and A Lawson (eds), *European Union Non-Discrimination Law and Intersectionality: Investigating the Triangle of Racial, Gender and Disability Discrimination* (Ashgate, 2011).
4 Article 12(2), CRPD.
5 Ch 3, section 4.
6 Ch 6, section 3.
7 Ch 4, sections 3 and 5.

representatives). This requires, as discussed in Chapter 6, a system which is open and receptive to the views of people with disabilities (while acknowledging that these views will not be homogeneous, and may even conflict with each other or with those of other citizens), at all levels of State interaction with citizens. These spaces include the formal political and judicial systems, addressed in Chapters 3–6; as well as some aspects of those systems not addressed in this book, such as the role of law enforcement and the prison system.

In order to be receptive to people with disabilities, these aspects of our broad justice system must first be accessible to people with disabilities – and the challenge of improving accessibility should not be underestimated. True accessibility requires much more than ensuring that people with disabilities can access the physical infrastructure of the justice system, as discussed in Chapter 4,[8] but also requires procedural and substantive change to ensure that people with disabilities can effectively communicate – in all their diverse and unconventional methods – their lived experience, to those who make determinations about how justice will be done in law, policy and practice. It is important to consider how the legitimate voices of people with disabilities can be brought to the forefront in these processes – rather than assuming that family organisations, disability service providers and academics will provide the same perspective as people with disabilities themselves. However, this also will involve contestation – whereby different lived experiences of disability may clash with each other – but rather than viewing such conflict as something to be avoided, it should be regarded as an honest expression of the intersectional and diverse experiences of the disability community.

There are so many examples, in both legislation and case law, of how people with disabilities are portrayed, and how their concerns are articulated and adjudicated by those who have never met the individuals or communities to whom these legal frameworks apply, and do not fully understand the impact that such laws will have on the daily lives of people with disabilities, their families and their broader communities. In order to redress this imbalance – whereby people with disabilities have often had little or no involvement in shaping the law which affects them – the CRPD asks explicitly for their active participation in processes to develop law, policy and programmes which will affect them.[9]

3. Consciousness-Raising: Educating and Informing the Next Generation

Finally, given that the justice system is inevitably situated within a broader political, social, economic and cultural context, it is important to look outside its narrow confines to understand how society can be shaped to continue to adapt its systems and processes in a way that facilitates the active engagement and inclusion

---

8   Ch 4, section 2.
9   Article 4(3), CRPD.

of people with disabilities. To achieve this, I suggest a return to consciousness-raising as defined in feminist scholarship,[10] as an approach which has also been validated in the disability context by Phillips et al., who argue that the definition of awareness-raising in Article 8 CRPD is closely aligned to the feminist concept of consciousness-raising.[11] While consciousness-raising is clearly needed in the existing formal aspects of the justice system, such as the legislative and judicial processes, it also needs to begin with the individual actors who will go on to shape the future development of law and policy reform concerning people with disabilities. This includes educating the next generation of lawyers and policy-makers about the justice claims of people with disabilities, as well as ensuring that people with disabilities themselves have access to these high profile positions within our justice system, as discussed in Chapter 5.

In conclusion, I hope that these three themes present a starting point for further deliberation on how we can reconfigure our laws, policies and practice at the local and global levels, to ensure more effective access to justice for people with disabilities.

---

[10] See for example C Keating, 'Building Coalitional Consciousness' (2005) 17(2) *NWSA Journal* 86–103.

[11] B Phillips, N Emmenegger, B Trezzini and M Keogh, 'Raising Awareness about Awareness: Insights from the Feminist Movement on Interpreting Article 8 of the UN Convention on the Rights of Persons with Disabilities' in C O'Mahony and G Quinn (eds), *The UN Convention on the Rights of Persons with Disabilities: Comparative, Regional and Thematic Perspectives* (Intersentia, 2014).

Index

AAC (Alternative and Augmented Communication), court system 92–95
access to justice
   active participation 14–15
   antecedents in human rights law 21–48
   defining 5, 11–13
   inclusion in parliamentary process 145–46, 172–73
   participatory 2, 18–19, 26, 39–40, 46, 173
      individual political participation 155–67, 167–68, 172–73
         right to vote 155–58, 167, 172
         running for election 158–67, 167–68, 172
      involvement in international law 166–67
      lobbying for legislative change 141–55, 169
      quota systems 165–66
   political activism 153–55, 169
   procedural 13, 15–16, 173
   regional treaty provisions 29–31
   substantive 13–15, 173
   symbolic 13, 16–17, 142, 164
   women's 13
   see also CRPD, Article 13
accessibility
   adaptations to rules of evidence and procedure 108–12, 115–16, 117
   communicating with the court 90–111, 115–16, 172–73
      alternative and augmented communication (AAC) 92–95
      amicus briefs 105–6, 129
      facilitated communication 92–95
      guardian ad litem 99–102
      independent advocates 95–104
      interpreters 91–92

      'McKenzie friend' 102–3
      'next friend' 99–102
      self-represented litigants 102–3
   courtroom design 88–90, 115, 173
   disability bias in courtroom 1–2, 106–8
      fitness to plead or competence to testify 111
   easy to read documents 56–58
   and reasonable accommodation 53–55, 171–73
   specialised legal aid services 59–60, 131
   see also court system; disability; legal education
advocacy, communicating with the court 95–104
affirmation solutions 10–11
African Charter of Human and People's Rights 29–31
Alston, P. 126
American Convention on Human Rights 29–31
Americans with Disabilities Act (1990) 85, 86, 102, 113, 120, 133, 142
amicus briefs, communicating with the court 105–6, 129
Anderson, Val 145
ARCH Disability Law Centre (Canada) 59
Arstein-Kerslake, Anna 1, 61–62
assessment approaches, mental capacity 61–62, 105
Assisted Decision-Making (Capacity) Bill 143
'court friend' 103–4

Bagenstos, S. 143
Baggs, A.M. 94–95
Bahdi, Reem 6, 11, 85–86, 89–90, 164
   procedural access to justice 13, 15–16

substantive access to justice 13–15
symbolic access to justice 13, 16–17, 142, 164
Balfe, J.M. 141
Bartlett, P. 37–38, 70, 73–74
Basser-Marks, Lee Ann 17
Berubé, M. 127
Bleyer, K. 114

Campbell, J. 144–45, 149–50
Campbell, Jane 163–64
Cappelletti, Mauro 11–12
Care Quality Commission (UK) 52n8
Colker, R. 102
Committee on Economic, Social and Cultural Rights 23
Community Care (Direct Payments) Act (1996; England and Wales) 144
complaints mechanisms, human rights 49, 75–80
Convention Against Torture (CAT) 21, 26–27, 29
Convention on the Elimination of All Forms of Discrimination Against Women (CEDAW) 21, 28, 42–43
Convention on the Elimination of All Forms of Racial Discrimination (CERD) 21, 27–28
Convention on the Protection of All Persons from Forced Disappearance 21, 29
Convention on the Protection of the Rights of All Migrant Workers 21, 28
Convention on the Rights of the Child (CRC) 21, 28
Convention on the Rights of Persons with Disabilities (CRPD) 2, 6–7, 13, 14, 18, 21, 31
  Article 5 35–36
  Article 8 39
  Article 9 38, 40–41, 46, 56, 60
  Article 12 37, 40–41, 46–47, 62–67, 100, 104–6, 111, 172
  Article 13 18–19, 22, 32–45, 47–48, 67
  Article 16 39
  Article 19 51–52, 105
  Article 21 38
  Article 29 39, 142, 156
  dialogues with individual States Parties 41–45
Cottrell, J. 50
court system
  evidentiary access 83
  jury selection and service 92, 112–15
  physical access 83, 84–90, 115, 173
  physical and procedural adaptations 84, 88–90, 115–16, 173
  procedural access 83–84, 115–16
  role of third parties 83–84
Crenshaw, K. 2, 8, 14, 19
  identity politics 9
  theory of intersectionality 2, 5, 171

D'Aubin, A. 158–59
Davis, Mary 163
de Bhailís, C. 70–71
Dhanda, A. 1
disability
  access to legal advice and representation 2, 3, 49, 58–60, 80–81, 117
  access to legal information 49–58, 117
  accessibility of information 55–58, 80–81
  reasonable accommodation obligations 54–55n15, 171, 172
  application of Fraser's conception of recognition and redistribution 8–9, 171–72
  attempts to define legally 6–7
  awareness raising obligations 39, 51, 53, 173–74
  cross-disability collaboration 152–53
  disabled persons' organisations (DPOs) 145–49
  experiences mirrored by other minority groups 1, 50
  intersectionality of disability and other minority politics 1, 2, 9–10, 50, 171–72
  litigation capacity 38, 49, 53, 60–72, 80
  making a complaint about a rights-violation 49, 75–80

right to self-identify 150
specialised legal aid services 59–60
training 35, 40–41, 72–73
see also accessibility
disability bias in courtroom, accessibility 1–2, 106–8
Disability Discrimination Legal Service (Australia) 59
Disability Law Service (UK) 5
disability training 35, 40–41, 72–73
Disabled People's Direct Action Network (DAN; UK) 154
disabled persons' organisations (DPOs) 145–49
Dole, Bob 160–61
D'Sa, R.M. 30
Duckworth, Tammy 160–61

Eadie, Ross 160
effective remedy, the right to an 22–23, 32–34, 40
Emmenegger, N. 173–74
Equality Act (2010; England and Wales) 125
Equality and Human Rights Commission (England and Wales) 76
Eth, Dr Spencer 133
European Convention on Human Rights (ECHR) 29–31
evidentiary access, court system 83

facilitated communication, communicating with the court 92–95
fair hearing, the right to 23–25, 40, 114
Familant, B.M. 135–36
Flinders, M. 161–62
Flowers, N. 141
Forum of People with Disabilities 151n36
Francis, L.P. 85–86
Frank, Jerome 128, 129
Fraser, N. 5, 6, 8, 9–11, 14, 20
recognition and redistribution 2, 8–9, 171–72
French, P. 18, 37
functional approach, mental capacity 61–62, 63–64n42, 67

Garth, B. 11–12

Garvey, S.P. 107
Genn, H. 16, 18–19
Ghai, A. 150–51
Ghai, Y. 50
Gibbons, B.N. 107
Gibbons, F.X. 107
Gibson, Frances 75
Goodley, D. 149–50
Goodman, R. 126
Gould, K. 86, 87
guardian ad litem, communicating with the court 99–102
guardianship 73–74, 139, 142
of people with disabilities 52–53n9, 67–68
Guernsey, K.N. 141

Hamraie, A. 89–90
Harkin, Senator Tom 143
Health Information and Quality Authority (HIQA) 52n8
Hennessy, Joe 147
Herr, Stanley 73, 74, 133
Heyns, C. 30
Heywood, S.S. 132–33
Hill, Millie 147
human rights
antecedents to development of access to justice 21–48
complaints mechanisms 49, 75–80
the right to an effective remedy 22–23, 32–34, 40
the right to a fair hearing 23–25, 40, 114
Human Rights Committee (HRC) 24–25
human rights law, antecedents 21–48
Humphrey, J.C. 150
Hurst, Rachel 146

impairment, attempts to define disability legally 6–7
independent living movement 51–53
Independent Mental Capacity Advocate (ICMA; England and Wales) 96, 97–98
Inouye, Daniel 160–61
institutionalisation 105

as barrier to accessing legal information 51–53
International Covenant on Civil and Political Rights (ICCPR) 23–25, 30, 31, 74
International Covenant on Economic, Social and Cultural Rights (ICESC) 25
interpreters, communicating with the court 91–92
Investigation and Testimony Procedural Act (2005; Israel) 108–9
Irish Law Reform Commission 113–14

Jolly-Ryan, J. 123–24
Jones, Beverly 85
Jones, Melinda 17
Juries Act (1976; Ireland) 112–13
jury selection and service, court system 92, 112–15

Karr, V.L. 141
Kaul, Dr Sudha 148
Kayess, R. 18, 37
Keogh, M. 173–74
Kitchin, R. 154

Lane, George 85
Lawson, Anna 1, 31–32, 54, 119, 125, 126, 131
lawyer-client relationships 72–74
legal capacity 61–72
    the right to legal capacity in Article 12 62–67, 100–102, 104–6, 111, 172
    right to vote 142, 155–56, 172
legal education 3, 117–40
    adaptation of law school curricula 121–24
    admission to practice 132–35
    alternative 'access' to university 120–21n9
    anti-discrimination legislation 119–20
    clinical legal education 118, 128–31
    disability issues in course content 126–28
    educators with disabilities 118, 124–26
    ongoing training and CPD for legal professionals 139–40
    professional legal training 2, 137–39
    students with disabilities 118, 119–24
    training of legal professionals on disability issues 118, 131–32
Lewis, O. 37–38, 70, 73–74
Linton, S. 127
Lipskar, L.B. 137
litigation capacity 38, 49, 53, 60–72
Llewellyn, G. 107
Lord, J. 12–13, 141

McCain, John 160–61
McCarty, K.S. 114
McChesney, A. 138–39
McConnell, D. 107
Maher, Chrissie 56–57
Massey, P.A. 130
mental capacity 61–72
    assessment approaches 61–62, 105
    functional approach 61–62, 63–64n42, 67
    outcome approach 61
    status approach 61n36
    'best interests' and 'expressed wishes' 68–69, 100–101, 104, 144
    Mental Capacity Act (2005; England and Wales) 62, 96, 97
Mental Capacity Act (2005; England and Wales) 62, 96, 97
Mental Health Commission (UK) 52n8
Mental Health Services Inspectorate 52n8
Morris, Jenny 9
Mulcahy, L. 88, 89
Muller, Esthe 84

National Advocacy Service (NAS) 96–97n50, 104
National Disability Rights Network (US) 59
National Disability Strategy Implementation Group 147–48
Norah Fry Research Centre 58–59
Nussbaum, Martha 5, 8

Oliver, Michael 6, 7, 149–50
Ortoleva, S. 84, 119

participatory
   access to justice 2, 18–19, 26, 39–40, 46, 173
   individual political participation 155–67, 167–68, 172–73
   right to vote 155–58, 167, 172
   running for election 158–67, 167–68, 172
   involvement in international law 166–67
   lobbying for legislative change 141–55, 169
   quota systems 165–66
Peleman, Didier 162–63
People with Disabilities in Ireland 151n36
Perlin, Michael 74, 107, 136–37
Phillips, B. 173–74
Plain English Campaign 56–57
political activism 153–55, 169
Priestley, M. 131
procedural, access to justice 13, 15–16, 173
Provost, R. 23

Quigley, F. 129–30

Rae, Anna 147
Rawls, John 8
   A Theory of Justice 5
reasonable accommodation 36, 86, 119, 171, 172
   and universal accessibility 53–55, 87
Rehman, J. 127
Roht-Arriaza, N. 22
Rosenbaum, S.A. 130
Rothstein, L.F. 136
Ruegger, M. 100–101

Sawin, L.L.C. 107
Schwartz, M. 91

self-identification 150
self-represented litigants, communicating with the court 102–3
Sen, Amartya 5, 8
Series, L. 68, 71, 98, 99–100, 104
Silvers, Anita 7–8, 85
Smith, K.H. 120, 123
Solum, L.B. 18–19
specialised legal aid services, disability 59–60
Steiner, H.J. 126
Stienstra, D. 158–59
Stone, E. 131
symbolic access to justice 13, 16–17, 142, 164

terminology 3, 6–7, 54n15
Thorold, O. 37–38, 70, 73–74
Tokaji, D.P. 157
transformation solutions 10–11
Trezzini, B. 173–74

universal accessibility, and reasonable accommodation 53–55, 87
Universal Declaration of Human Rights (UDHR) 21, 23, 30, 31

Waddington, L. 54
Waterstone, M. 157
Weicker, L.P. Jr 143
Weisman, L.K. 90
Wickman, Percy 160
Willig-Levy, C. 154
Wood, E. 114

Young, Iris Marion 141

Ziv, N. 109